Evoking Scripture

Evoking Scripture

*Seeing the Old Testament
in the New*

by

Steve Moyise

t&t clark

Published by T&T Clark
A Continuum imprint
The Tower Building, 11 York Road, London SE1 7NX
80 Maiden Lane, Suite 704, New York, NY 10038

www.continuumbooks.com

British Library Cataloguing-in-Publication Data
A catalogue record for this book is available from the British Library

Typeset by Free Range Book Design & Production
Printed on acid-free paper in Great Britain by Cromwell Press Ltd, Trowbridge, Wiltshire

ISBN 13 (Hardback): 9780567033246
ISBN: 0567033244
ISBN 13 (Paperback): 9780567033253
ISBN: 0567033252

Contents

~

Abbreviations

AB	Anchor Bible
AUSS	*Andrews University Seminary Studies*
BECNT	Baker Exegetical Commentary on the New Testament
BNTC	Black's New Testament Commentary
BR	*Biblical Research*
ConBNT	Coniectanea Biblica, New Testament
ExpT	*Expository Times*
FRLANT	Forschungen zur Religion und Literatur des Alten und Neuen Testaments
ICC	International Critical Commentary
JSNT	*Journal for the Study of the New Testament*
JSNTSup	*Journal for the Study of the New Testament*, Supplement Series
JSOTSup	*Journal for the Study of the Old Testament*, Supplement Series
LNTS	Library of New Testament Studies
LXX	Septuagint
MT	Masoretic Text
NIGTC	The New International Greek Testament Commentary
OTL	Old Testament Library
PIBA	*Proceedings of the Irish Biblical Association*
SBL	Society of Biblical Literature
SBLDS	Society of Biblical Literature, Dissertation Series
TDOT	*Theological Dictionary of the Old Testament* (eds G.J. Botterwick and H. Ringgren)
TSAJ	Texte und Studien zum Antiken Judentum
WBC	Word Biblical Commentary
WUNT	Wissenschaftliche Untersuchungen zum Neuen Testament
ZNW	*Zeitschrift für die neutestamentliche Wissenschaft*

1

~

Introduction

The study of how the New Testament authors read and interpreted Scripture is experiencing something of a revival at the present time. This is being fuelled by a renewed interest in at least three areas, the first of which is the Septuagint (LXX). It is a tribute to the quality of scholarship behind the Göttingen series that several decades of relative inactivity followed. But this is no longer the case. Major translation projects in English (NETS), French (La Bible d'Alexandra) and German (Septuaginta-deutsch) have raised fundamental questions about the nature of the LXX. In particular, would the New Testament authors have understood the text known to them primarily as a translation or as an authoritative text in its own right? And what of their recipients? Would they have taken the quoted text at face value or would they have known that it sometimes differs from other LXX manuscripts and from the Hebrew text being read in the synagogues? Indeed, what were once explained as deliberate changes by the various New Testament authors, are now more likely to be taken as evidence for early revisions of the LXX.[1]

Secondly, there has been a growing interest in using literary theory to understand the role or function of Scripture in the New Testament. This was given a major impetus in 1989 with Richard Hays's use of intertextuality for understanding Paul's use of Scripture. Instead of seeing quotations and allusions as subsidiary to Paul's main arguments, Hays sees letters like Romans, Galatians and Corinthians as an ongoing conversation with Scripture.[2] The approach was soon extended to other New Testament writings and subject to a number of refinements (and challenges).

---

[1] See W. Kraus and R.G. Wooden (eds), *Septuagint Research. Issues and Challenges in the Study of the Greek Jewish Scriptures* (Atlanta: SBL, 2006).

[2] R.B. Hays, *Echoes of Scripture in the Letters of Paul* (New Haven: Yale University Press, 1989).

More recently, Tom Hatina[3] has explicitly drawn on narrative theory to understand the function of Scripture in Mark's Gospel, while others have drawn on ancient and modern rhetoric, relevance theory and speech-act theory. Scriptural quotations and allusions are now seen as a literary as well as a theological phenomenon in the New Testament.

Thirdly, there has been a renewed interest in biblical theology and the development of theological or canonical interpretation (particularly associated with Baker Books and Paternoster Press, but also Intervarsity and others). Scriptural quotations and allusions, it is argued, should not be studied in isolation but are part of the broader question of the relationship between the two Testaments. Historical approaches have tended to treat the Bible as a more or less random collection of writings but this does not do justice to the religious claim that the Bible is Scripture. It is only by attending to this that the study of scriptural material in the New Testament receives it proper orientation.[4]

As a result of these three areas,[5] studies of Scripture in the New Testament are often conducted from quite specific theological or literary standpoints. For example, some scholars take the unity of Scripture as a basic presupposition for their work. There is no question of the New Testament authors taking texts out of context or giving them new meaning, for the One who promised in the Old Testament is the one who fulfils in the New Testament. Apparent differences of meaning are explained as 'organic' developments of the original rather than changes of meaning. On the other hand, other scholars think that the coming of Christ and the birth of the Church gave the New Testament authors a vantage point that was unavailable to the ancient authors (sometimes quoting 2 Cor. 3.14). Since meaning is related to context, it is to be expected that the New Testament authors found new meaning in the ancient texts. For such scholars, the task is to show how the new situation led to the new meaning.

There is a similar dichotomy in the interpretation of the New Testament texts themselves. Some scholars take a diachronic view that the meaning of words, and hence sentences and paragraphs, is dependent on previous usage. Thus in order to

---

[3] T. Hatina, *In Search of a Context: The Function of Scripture in Mark's Narrative* (JSNTSup, 232; Sheffield: Sheffield Academic Press, 2002).

[4] This is most clearly seen in the differences between Jewish interpretation, which accepts only the Hebrew books as Scripture, and Christian interpretation, which also accepts the 27 books of the New Testament (and in some traditions, the additional books of the LXX via the Vulgate). Referring to the 'Old Testament' and the 'New Testament' already represents a particular interpretative framework. For this reason, many scholars prefer to speak more neutrally of 'Hebrew Bible', but this is not altogether satisfactory for our subject, since it is the 'Greek Bible' that has primarily influenced the New Testament authors. We will thus continue to speak of 'Old Testament' as those Scriptures that are prior to what came to be known as the 'New Testament', while acknowledging that the relationship between these collections is a matter of dispute.

[5] A fourth would of course be Qumran, though this is not so much a 'renewed interest' but a continuous influence over the last decades.

understand a quotation, it is necessary to understand its original context (and subsequent contexts). On this view, a quotation is not just someone else's words but a vehicle for transferring meaning from one context to another. Other scholars take a synchronic view that the meaning of words is determined by current usage, not etymology. The meaning of a quotation derives from the role or function the words have in the new work, not what they once meant to someone else. To describe someone as 'gay' in the twenty-first century is to say something about their sexuality. To add that they are 'happy and cheery' because that is what the word meant in the first half of the twentieth century is a misunderstanding of how language works.

This raises a further question of whether the focus of our study should be on the New Testament author's intention to cite or the reader's ability to perceive. In the example just quoted, an older reader might know that the word 'gay' used to mean 'happy and cheery' and so could plausibly ask whether the author is intending the new meaning or the old meaning. If it was known that the author 'had a way with words', it might even be possible to suggest that she or he was intending to evoke both meanings. On the other hand, a younger reader (unless well-read) would probably be unaware that the word ever had a different meaning and so this possibility is ruled out. The significance of this for our topic is this: does it makes any sense to describe the meaning of a quotation in terms of its original context if that context is unknown to the readers? Some would say, Yes, for it could have been intended by the author, even if the congregations were too dim to perceive it. Others would say, No, as the conditions for the quotation to work in that way are absent.

Mention of author and reader leads into literary debates about the locus of textual meaning. Some believe that the meaning of a text is only to be identified with what the original author intended, and this should be distinguished from all later interpretations. Others regard this as too narrow. Texts are vehicles of communication and one cannot talk of communication without speaking of both author and reader. In particular, since the work of the three masters of suspicion (Marx, Freud and Nietzsche), it is doubtful that anyone is fully aware of the author's intentions or that a text can ever be a perfect reproduction of them. To return to our previous example, if an author disclosed at a press conference that he or she detested the corruption of the English language (even making 'wicked' something desirable!), and had purposely used the word 'gay' in its older sense, would that then be the meaning of the text? Put another way, would readers who took the word 'gay' to be a reference to sexuality be guilty of *misreading* the text because the author claims that was not her or his intention? Or have such readers given the true meaning of the text (in their twenty-first century context), and the author is guilty of not saying what she or he meant?

The studies that follow all take a particular quotation or allusion (or in some cases, a group of them) and ask, What is it that is being evoked? As this question receives different answers depending on the particular theological and literary standpoint of the scholar, several perspectives are presented before an analysis is offered. The first two studies focus on Mark's Gospel. In the first (Mk 1.2-3), the thesis that

Mark intends his opening quotation to provide a scriptural framework for understanding Jesus is examined. It is based on the location of the quotation at the
beginning of the work, parallels between the quoted texts and Mark's prologue, and
the repetition of such themes elsewhere in the Gospel. This is contrasted with a
narrative approach, which sees the role of the quotation as introducing the key
characters in the story (John, Jesus, followers) and outlining its plot (proclamation
of the kingdom of God). Such an approach regards the scriptural-framework view
as an imposition on the text.

The second study focuses on a number of Mark's references to the law (Mk 2.27;
7.15-19; 10.2-9; 12.33). Some scholars think that Mark included these references to
show his Gentile readers that Jesus undermined the ritual ('Thus he declared all foods
clean' – 7.19) and sacrificial ('this is much more important than all whole burnt
offerings and sacrifices' – 12.33) aspects of the law. Others think the opposite, noting
that the man suffering from leprosy is commanded to go and make the prescribed
sacrifices (Mk 1.41) and that the young man seeking eternal life is directed to the
commandments (Mk 10.19). In this study, we explore how the answer to this question
affects one's understanding of Mark's use of Scripture.

Three studies on Paul's use of Scripture follow. In the first (Rom. 2.24), there
is an interesting contrast to Mk 1.2-3 in that the Isaiah quotation (Isa. 52.5) does not
come at the beginning of the work and appears to be taken out of context. However,
when the reader reaches Romans 9–11, she or he will discover that (Deutero-) Isaiah
is very important to Paul and he even includes a quotation from the same passage
(Isa. 52.7). For some, this invites a retrospective reading, demanding a sophisticated
understanding of the function of Isa. 52.5 in Rom. 2.24. Others point out that Paul's
readers would be very unlikely to know that the text, 'How beautiful are the feet of
those who bring good news', comes two verses after the text, 'The name of God is
blasphemed among the Gentiles because of you', and so would not have made such
connections.

If the position of the quotation of Isa. 52.5 (in Rom. 2.24) makes it difficult to
assign it a pivotal role in the interpretation of Romans, the same cannot be said for
the quotation of Hab. 2.4 in Rom. 1.17. Here we have the interesting phenomenon
of a text that is clearly important to Paul (he quotes it again in Gal. 3.11) but shows
no interest in any other verse from the book (at least, according to the margins of
Nestle-Aland 27). Is he using it as a convenient summary of his gospel message
('The one who is righteous will live by faith') or has this text been influential in the
formulation of his gospel?

The third study focuses on Gal. 3.10-14, where we have two interesting
phenomena. First, we have two quotations (Deut. 27.26; Lev. 18.5) that indicate the
absolute importance of keeping every aspect of the law; yet Paul is using them to show
that Gentile Christians need not, indeed, should not be attempting to keep it.
Secondly, the exegesis turns on a bold assertion that 'the law does not rest on faith'
(Gal. 3.12). Some take this as Paul's fundamental standpoint and believe he is

challenging the law's claim to give life. Others see his categorical denial in Gal. 3.21, that the law is in any way opposed to God's promises, as the standpoint for understanding his exegesis. The scholar's overall view of 'Paul and the law' is decisive for understanding the role of Scripture in Romans and Galatians.

Our study of 1 Pet. 1.10-12 gives us an opportunity to explore some of the claims of biblical theology. Some have taken this so-called 'prophecy theory' as meaning that the prophets were fully cognizant of the christological implications of their utterances. Others have taken it to mean that they said more than they knew (*sensus plenior*). Scholars who adopt the first position see the 'prophecy theory' as a hermeneutical guide for understanding the author's use of Scripture (and in some cases, the whole of the New Testament). Those who hold the second position allow the author's actual uses of Scripture to determine the meaning of the 'prophecy theory'. This chapter makes a contribution to the debate by correlating the author's actual uses of Isaiah with the 'prophecy theory' of 1 Pet. 1.10-12.

Our final two studies are from the book of Revelation. It is well known that 'lamb' is the key christological title of the book but when it is first introduced (Rev. 5.5-6), it is juxtaposed with the expression 'the lion of the tribe of Judah'. Given that the lamb is associated with a considerable amount of violence in the book, the question arises as to whether the lion imagery has been added in order to further this end, or whether it itself is being reinterpreted or replaced by the lamb. Our second study looks like a classic case of misdirection. Rev. 15.3 introduces the song sung by the heavenly choir as, 'the song of Moses, the servant of God, and of the Lamb'. However, the song that follows bears no relationship to the song of Moses recorded in Exodus 15 and very little to Deuteronomy 32. Why then does the author evoke this important song only to quote something else?

The final chapter offers some theological and literary reflections on our studies. The gap between the meaning of scriptural texts in their original context and the meaning assigned to them in the New Testament has been explained in a variety of ways. Some look to expand the definition of authorial intention by speaking of 'communicative acts' or 'transhistorical intentions'. Others focus on the intentions of readers, who are not trying to stand in the author's shoes (Schleiermacher) but discern the meaning of texts for their contemporaries. These contrasting literary theories are related to contrasting theological positions. Some take the unity of Scripture as a presupposition and so regard the relationship between the two Testaments as one of continuity. Others see a considerable amount of discontinuity between the covenant of law (restricted to Jews) and the covenant of grace (open to all) and thus see the relationship between the Testaments as more complex. Our conclusion is that while some of these options can be shown to be more or less probable than others, their positive insights requires a multi-faceted approach to the subject. Only then can the activity of 'evoking Scripture' be seen in all its richness and complexity.[6]

---

[6] Biblical quotations are taken from the New Revised Standard Version unless otherwise stated.

2

~

Evoking a scriptural framework for understanding Jesus?*

Mk 1.2-3

Introduction

~

All four Gospels include a quotation of Isa. 40.3 (Mk 1.3; Mt. 3.3; Lk. 3.4; Jn 1.23) but only Mark combines this with words taken from Exod. 23.20 and Mal. 3.1. There can be little doubt that the composite quotation is important for Mark since: (1) it is located at the beginning of the Gospel, even before John and Jesus have been introduced; (2) this is the only editorial quotation from Mark – all the other quotations (about 20) appear on the lips of Jesus or other characters in the story;[1] (3) the composite quotation of Exod. 23.20/Mal. 3.1 ('See, I am sending my messenger ahead of you, who will prepare your way'), which appears as words of Jesus in Mt. 11.10/Lk. 7.27, is included before the citation of Isa. 40.3, even though it clashes with the introductory formula ('As it is written in the prophet Isaiah'). An extremely literal translation of the relevant texts is as follows:[2]

---

* A revised and expanded version of my chapter, 'The Wilderness Quotation in Mark 1:2-3' can be found in R.S. Sugirtharajah (ed.), *Wilderness: Essays in Honour of Frances Young* (London & New York: T&T Clark, 2005), pp. 78–87.

[1] Pharisees (10.4); crowd (11.9-10); Sadducees (12.19); scribe (12.32-3).
[2] Adapted from J. Marcus, *The Way of the Lord. Christological Exegesis of the Old Testament in the Gospel of Mark* (Edinburgh: T&T Clark, 1992), p. 14.

Mk 1.2	*Mt. 11.10=Lk. 7.27*	*Exod. 23.20*	*Mal. 3.1*
behold I send	behold I send	behold I send	behold I send out
(*apostellō*)	(*apostellō*)	(*apostellō*)	(*exapostellō*)
my messenger	my messenger	my messenger	my messenger
before your face	before your face	before your face	
who will prepare	who will prepare	to guard	and he will clear/survey
(*kataskeuasei*)	(*kataskeuasei*)	(*phulaxē*)	(*pnh/epiblepsetai*)
your way	your way	you on the way	a way
	before you		before your face

Mk 1.3=Mt=Lk.	*Jn 1.23*	*Isa. 40.3 MT*	*Isa. 40.3 LXX*
the voice of one	I am the voice of one	the voice of one	the voice of one
crying in the	crying in the	crying in the	crying in the
wilderness	wilderness	wilderness	wilderness
prepare	straighten	clear	prepare
(*hetoimasate*)	(*euthunate*)	(*pnh*)	(*hetoimasate*)
the way of the Lord	the way of the Lord	the way of the Lord	the way of the Lord
straight make		straighten	straight make
(*eutheias poieite*)		in the desert	(*eutheias poieite*)
his paths		a highway for our God	the paths of our God

On the hypothesis of Markan priority, it would seem that Matthew and Luke have dismantled the composite quotation, so that only words from Isaiah follow the ascription to Isaiah.[3] However, given the fact that Matthew and Luke both include the Malachi/Exodus material later in their Gospels, that it occurs in an almost identically worded pericope about John the Baptist,[4] and that both include the additional phrase 'before you', most scholars have concluded that it was present in Q.[5] If this is so, then Q or its source is responsible for introducing the word *kataskeuasei* ('prepare') as a rendering of Malachi's *pnh*, for it can hardly be a rendering of the verb 'guard' found in Exod. 23.20. This is sufficiently unusual[6] to suggest that either Mark knew this Q tradition or both are dependent on an earlier source. Either way, it is

---

[3] Scribes had a different solution, changing the ascription in Mk 1.2 from 'Isaiah' to 'the prophets'. 'Isaiah' is read by ℵ B L Δ 33 565 892 1241 2427 al sy[p.hmg] co; Or[pt].

[4] The two passages (Mt. 11.9-10; Lk. 7.26-7) agree in 30 out of 31 words (Matthew includes the personal pronoun *egō* before the verb, as in the LXX).

[5] Or for those who do not accept the Q hypothesis, Matthew knew it from another source and Luke followed Matthew. Either way, the composite quotation existed in another source.

[6] The LXX uses over 30 verbs to render *pnh* but never *kataskeuazō* .

unlikely that Mark himself is responsible for the *kataskeuasei* but found it in an existing (Greek) source. In other words, Mark is not the originator of this part of the composite quotation (Exodus/Malachi), and indeed we cannot be sure whether he would have recognized it as composite.

On the other hand, it would appear that Mark is responsible for introducing the composite quotation directly before his quotation of Isa. 40.3 (thus producing his own composite quotation!). The link between the two texts is clearly the idea of 'preparing the way', even though the Greek texts use different words for 'prepare'. Joel Marcus thinks that Mark would have known that the Hebrew text of Mal. 3.1 uses *pnh* for 'prepare', just as Isa. 40.3 does, and that this explains why the two texts have been brought together.[7] This is possible but we should not imagine that texts can only be brought together if they contain identical wording. Mark knew two texts (one composite, though he may not have realized it) which he understood as prophesying a messenger who would 'prepare the way'. His Isaiah quotation is undoubtedly drawn from the LXX (or a source that has used the LXX), as can be seen by its periphrastic rendering of 'make straight' (*eutheias poieite*), the plural 'paths' (*tribous*) for the singular 'highway' and the omission of the final 'in the desert' clause. There is little evidence to suggest that Mark knew the Hebrew text of this verse, especially as its parallelism (in the wilderness/in the desert) implies that the actual 'preparation' rather than just the 'voice' are to be located there. It would appear that Mark knew two Greek texts that he understood as predictions of a messenger who would prepare the way of Jesus and he largely quoted them in the form that he knew them.[8]

The role of the Old Testament background(s) in determining Mark's meaning

⌒

Isaiah

In an article entitled, 'Streams of Tradition Emerging from Isaiah 40:1-5 and their Adaptation in the New Testament', Klyne Snodgrass first demonstrates the influence of this text in other Old Testament books (Mal. 3.1), Qumran (1QS 8.12-16; 9.17-20), the Pseudepigrapha (*1 Bar.* 5.5-7), Apocrypha (*Ass. Mos.* 10.1-5) and the rabbis (*Pes. R.* 29-33). He then turns to the Gospels, where he thinks that Luke has been influenced by this text in 1.17, 76-9; 2.30-31 and 9.52, as well as the extended

---

[7] Marcus, *The Way of the Lord*, pp. 12–17.

[8] Such conservatism is indicated by the fact that Mark did not conform the *kataskeuazō* of the composite quotation (a word he never uses again) to the *hetoimazō* of the Isaiah quotation (which he uses on four other occasions). This could indicate that the change from 'the paths of our God' to 'his paths' might already have been present in Mark's source, especially as this is found in Luke, even though Luke extends the quotation to include Isa. 40.4-5.

quotation in Lk. 3.4-6. As for Mark, its pivotal position at the beginning of the Gospel suggests that the author has 'adopted a stream of tradition which will summarize immediately what his gospel is about'.[9] He notes particularly the way that *hodos* ('way') is later used for the 'way of God' (Mk 12.14) and the 'way of discipleship' (Mk 10.52), and so 'the composite quotation not only provides a link with the Old Testament, but also establishes a theme that is integral in Mark's explanation of discipleship'.[10] He concludes the article with the statement that the 'formative role that these verses have particularly in Mark and Luke can be appreciated only in light of previous usage'.[11]

Joel Marcus begins his study of Mk 1.2-3 by offering five arguments in favour of the view that Mark is responsible for inserting the Exod. 23.20/Mal. 3.1 material into his Isaiah quotation and placing it *before* John the Baptist is introduced.[12] He then draws on Robert Guelich's study[13] that *kathōs gegraptai* ('as it is written') always plays a transitional role in the New Testament, acting as a bridge between a previously mentioned fact or event and the Old Testament quotation.[14] That being the case, the primary role of the quotation is not the location of John in the wilderness or even John as the forerunner of Jesus, both of which follow the quotation, but its link with the opening verse. According to Marcus, Mark begins his Gospel with the assertion that the 'good news of Jesus Christ' is 'written in the prophet Isaiah'.

Marcus is aware of the dangers of assuming that Old Testament quotations always evoke their wider context[15] but in this case, he thinks it is justified. He cites a number of studies that have already suggested that Isaiah 40 is the most likely background for understanding Mark's use of *evangelion* ('good news/gospel').[16] He also notes common themes, such as the revelation of God's kingly power (Isa. 40.9-10/Mk 1.9-11) and the requirement to proclaim the good news (Isa. 40.9/Mk 1.15). Citing Snodgrass's article concerning streams of tradition from Isa. 40.1-5, Marcus asserts that:

---

[9] K.R. Snodgrass, 'Streams of Tradition Emerging from Isaiah 40:1-5 and their Adaptation in the New Testament', *JSNT* 8 (1980), p. 36.

[10] Snodgrass, 'Streams of Tradition', p. 36.

[11] Snodgrass, 'Streams of Tradition', p. 40.

[12] (1) The technique of beginning a work with references to Scripture is common in the New Testament (Matthew, John, Romans, Hebrews); (2) Conflation is part of Mark's style (1.11; 11.9-10; 11.17; 13.24-26; 14.62); (3) It explains the reference to 'Isaiah'; (4) By eliminating the words 'before you', Mark has improved the parallelism between v. 2 and v. 3; (5) By so doing, he has accented the parallelism between 'your way' and 'the way of the Lord' which coheres with the importance of this theme later in the Gospel. See Marcus, *The Way of the Lord*, pp. 15–16.

[13] R.A. Guelich, '"The Beginning of the Gospel": Mark 1:1-15', *BR* 27 (1982), pp. 5–15.

[14] He argues that the four possible counter-examples (Lk. 11.30; 17.26; Jn 3.14; 1 Cor. 2.9) are not true parallels to Mk 1.2 and so Guelich's conclusion is correct.

[15] A view often associated with C.H. Dodd, *According to the Scriptures: The Sub-structure of New Testament Theology* (London: Nisbet, 1952).

[16] P. Stuhlmacher, *Die paulinische Evangelium*, vol 1, *Vorgeschichte* (FRLANT, 95; Göttingen: Vandenhoeck & Ruprecht, 1968).

John the Baptist and Jesus are set firmly within the context of Jewish apocalyptic eschatology by the citation of Isa. 40:3 in Mark 1:3. Their appearance on the scene fulfills the
prophecies of old because it heralds eschatological events, because it is the preparation
for and the beginning of the fulfillment of that end so eagerly yearned for since Old
Testament times: the triumphant march of the holy warrior, Yahweh, leading his people
through the wilderness to their true homeland in a mighty demonstration of saving
power.[17]

This 'way' through the wilderness links with Mark 8–10, which has often been
characterized as 'following Jesus on the way' because of the occurrence of *en tē hodō*
in Mk 8.27 and 10.52.[18] The reader, says Marcus, would connect this 'way to Jerusalem'
with the promised 'way' quoted in Mk 1.2-3 and so deduce that 'the fearful trek of
the befuddled, bedraggled little band of disciples *is* the return of Israel to Zion, and Jesus'
suffering and death there *are* the prophesied apocalyptic victory of the divine warrior.'[19]
Of course, it would be difficult to argue that this is what the prophet had in mind when
he spoke of a triumphant march through the wilderness. In a graphic description of
Mark's hermeneutics, he says that 'Mark takes the raw ore of Jewish apocalyptic concep-
tions and subjects them to a Christological neutron bombardment, thereby producing
a powerful, disturbing, unpredictable new form of apocalyptic eschatology.'[20] Mark is
not simply reproducing the thought of Isaiah 40, he is offering a 'radical, cross-*centred
adaptation* of it'.[21]

Richard Schneck builds on this by asserting that a significant quotation or
allusion to Isaiah can be found in each of Mark's first eight chapters. He begins by
asserting that the prologue to Mark's Gospel, which he considers to be Mk 1.1-15,
has a number of similarities to the prologue of Deutero-Isaiah (Isa. 40.1-11). These
are: (1) reference to a 'voice in the wilderness'; (2) the role both texts play as
'prologues' to larger works; (3) the use of *evangelion* or *evangelizomenos* for God's
joyful intervention; (4) stress on the power of the one who is to come; (5) focus on
the rule or reign of God, especially in the Targumic reading of Isa. 40.9 ('The
kingdom of your God is revealed'); (6) the need for the word of God to be jubilantly
proclaimed; and (7) a concern for the forgiveness of sins (Isa. 40.2; Mk 1.4). Schneck
concludes from this that 'the whole unit of Isa 40:1-11 was intended by Mark to be
taken into account for a full and proper understanding of the Markan prologue'.[22]

He then seeks to show that there is a significant quotation or allusion to Isaiah
in chapters 2–8 of Mark. In Mark 4 and 7, there is an explicit quotation (Isa. 6.9-10;

---

[17] Marcus, *The Way of the Lord*, p. 29.
[18] And five occurrences of *hodos* between 8.17 and 10.52. See E. Best, *Following Jesus: Discipleship in the
Gospel of Mark* (JSNTSup, 4; Sheffield: JSOT Press, 1981), p. 5.
[19] Marcus, *The Way of the Lord*, p. 36.
[20] Marcus, *The Way of the Lord*, p. 41.
[21] Marcus, *The Way of the Lord*, p. 36.
[22] R. Schneck, *Isaiah in the Gospel of Mark, I-VIII* (Berkeley: BIBAL Press, 1994), p. 42.

29.13). He suggests in Mk 2.16-20, that Isa. 58.2-7 lies behind the discourse on fasting ('you fast only to quarrel and to fight ... Is not this the fast that I choose: to loose the bonds of injustice ...?'). On the surface, he notes that Mark 3 seems devoid of allusions to Isaiah but this is mistaken, for Isa. 49.24-25 ('Can the prey be taken from the mighty?') is the background for Mk 3.27 ('But no one can enter a strong man's house and plunder his property without first tying up the strong man'). On the basis of this allusion, Schneck finds other connections between Isaiah 49 and Mark 3 and concludes that 'the surrounding context in Isaiah 49 was intended as a help for the catechist in order to explain the mission of Jesus as the servant of God portrayed in Deutero-Isaiah'.[23]

For Mark 5, he thinks the story of the demoniac is clothed in imagery borrowed from Isa. 65:1-7 (pigs, demons, tombs, pagan territory). Mark 6 probably contains allusions to Isa. 55.1-3 (Mk 6.34-44) and Isa. 25.6 (Mk 6.39-40) but the strongest evidence is the reappearance of Isa. 6.9-10 in Mk 6.52. Lastly, Mk 8.17 also contains an allusion back to Isa. 6.9-10 and Mk 8.25 probably alludes to Isa. 42.6-7. Schneck concludes from this that Isaiah was Mark's most important scriptural source and that by quotation and allusion, Mark intends to evoke this important salvation-history background for understanding the story of Jesus.

Isaiah and Malachi
Rikk Watts agrees with this but also wishes to do justice to the fact that the quotation is composite and includes a reference to Exod. 23.20/Mal. 3.1. The first reference belongs to the Exodus tradition and preparations for the conquest of Canaan. The coincidence of language suggests that Mal. 3.1 is an ironic reworking of this tradition,[24] since it is now the wicked of Israel who are threatened with destruction.[25] Thus Mark's aim is to signal not only the salvation background of Isaiah but also the judgement theme of Malachi:

> Mark's opening composite citation is intended to evoke two different but closely related schemata. First, the appeal to Isaiah 40 evinces Israel's great hope of Yahweh's coming to initiate her restorational NE [New Exodus]. Second, the allusion to Malachi not only recalls the delay of this NE but also sounds an ominous note of warning in that the nation must be prepared or else face purging judgement ... These twin themes of the fulfilment of the delayed INE [Isaian New Exodus] promise and possible judgement due to lack of preparedness are fused in Mark's opening citation and together seem to establish the basic thematic contours for his presentation of Jesus.[26]

[23] Schneck, *Isaiah in the Gospel of Mark*, p. 100.
[24] The texts are later combined in *Exod. R.* 32.9 and Mann thinks they were linked in an ancient synagogue lectionary. See J. Mann, *The Bible as Read and Preached in the Old Synagogue* (New York: KTAV, 1971).
[25] R.E. Watts, *Isaiah's New Exodus and Mark* (WUNT, 2.88; Tübingen: Mohr Siebeck, 1997), p. 72.
[26] Watts, *Isaiah's New Exodus*, p. 370.

Watts supports this by showing how the Malachi theme is picked up elsewhere in Mark's narrative. For example, the discussion in Mk 9.9-13 as to why Elijah must come first is a reference to the final words of Malachi ('Lo, I will send you the prophet Elijah before the great and terrible day of the LORD comes'). The cleansing of the temple, cursing of the fig tree and the rent curtain can all plausibly be understood in the light of 'the Lord whom you seek will suddenly come to his temple' (Mal. 3.1b), while the rejection of Jesus by the religious leaders could be seen as evidence of their unpreparedness, which would then offer a rationale for why judgement will inevitably follow. Watts believes that the composite quotation evokes not only the Isaian new exodus background but also the Elijah/judgement theme from the book of Malachi. He summarizes the function of the combined citation with five propositions:

1. It is not so much the Exodus text that is important to Mark but its eschatological reinterpretation by Malachi;
2. The Malachi background suggests that more emphasis should be placed on the 'judgment' aspect of John's mission, especially against Israel's leaders and the temple;
3. As a *locus classicus* for Israel's eschatological hope, the citation of Isa. 40.3 is almost certainly an announcement of the beginning of the Isaian New Exodus;
4. In keeping with the history of interpretation and the original contexts, the focus of the citation is on what the herald announces, not the herald himself;
5. The application of these texts to Jesus suggests that he is in someway being identified with the 'Lord' and 'messenger of the covenant' of Malachi and in terms of Isa. 40.3, the presence of Yahweh himself.[27]

Isaiah and Exodus
Larry Perkins notes that Exodus material plays a prominent role in Mark.[28] There are direct quotations in Mk 7.10 (honour parents – Exod. 20.12/21.17), Mk 10.19 (second table of the law – Exod. 20.12-16) and Mk 12.26 (burning bush and God's self-revelation – Exod. 3.6,15). There are specific allusions in Mk 2.27 (purpose of the Sabbath – Exod. 20.8-10), Mk 14.12-13 (meaning of Passover – Exod. 12.6,14-20) and Mk 14.24 (establishing covenant in blood – Exod. 24.8) and there are also a number of common themes: journey, wilderness, temptation, plagues/miracles, self-revelation of God, tabernacle/temple and hardness of heart. In the light of these parallels, Perkins says of Mark:

---

[27] Watts, *Isaiah's New Exodus*, pp. 86–87 (my summary).
[28] L. Perkins, 'Kingdom, Messianic Authority and the Re-constituting of God's People – Tracing the Function of Exodus Material in Mark's Narrative' in T.R. Hatina (ed.), *Biblical Interpretation in Early Christian Gospels Volume 1: The Gospel of Mark* (LNTS, 304; London and New York: T&T Clark, 2006), pp. 100–15.

It seems that he desires his readers to set the mission of Jesus within the larger story of Israel's formation as told in the Exodus narrative, but also to show that Jesus' mission is a separate, though connected, stage in God's plans for Israel. Jesus will affirm God's word as revealed to Moses. He will offer a revised interpretation and understanding of God's covenantal intent for Israel. The deliberate conflation of the Exodus text with the Isaiah quotation probably indicates that the author wanted his readers to see the new exodus of Isaiah as a revised exodus paradigm.[29]

Reviewing the textual data, he notes that Mal. 3.1 is probably a conscious re-working of Exod. 23.20 but the use of *apostellō* rather than *exapostellō* and the position of the phrase 'before your face' indicate that Exod. 23.20 is the 'primary referent'. He notes how the presence of the composite quotation in Luke and Matthew 'might suggest that the Markan author did not create something new here, but rather was dependent upon a tradition'[30] but does not see this as an obstacle to affirming that Mark 'begins *his* story by comparing God's action in providing a divine messenger to lead and protect Israel on its journey to Canaan, with God's action in sending John the Baptist as a messenger to prepare the way for Jesus Messiah and his new vision for God's people'.[31] As a result, the presence of the composite quotation at the beginning of Mark's Gospel 'invites the reader to set the entire story of Jesus that will unfold, in the referential context of the original Exodus narrative, but also in terms of its prophesied renewal in Isaiah'.[32]

The influence of the new narrative context on the meaning of the Old Testament quotations

Despite the apparent fruitfulness of this 'maximal' approach, a number of scholars have begun to question its basic assumptions. Thomas Hatina, for example, complains that instead of focusing on key themes of Mark's narrative, such as charac-terization and plot, the 'source-orientated practitioner subverts this process by assuming that the hermeneutical key is to be found in Mark's exegesis of Scripture'.[33] For Hatina, the meaning of a scriptural quotation derives primarily from its narrative function in the Gospel, not from something outside of it. Drawing a parallel with lexicography, where the meaning of a word depends on current usage rather than

[29] Perkins, 'Kingdom', p. 104.
[30] Perkins, 'Kingdom', p. 104.
[31] Perkins, 'Kingdom', p. 108.
[32] Perkins, 'Kingdom', p. 104.
[33] T.R. Hatina, *In Search of a Context: The Function of Scripture in Mark's Narrative* (JSNTSup, 232; Sheffield: Sheffield Academic Press, 2002), p. 46.

etymology, he insists that priority should be given to the role and function of the words in their new context. In this case, it is clear that Mark is not envisaging construction work in the wilderness and is therefore using the words in quite a different sense to Isaiah. It is therefore methodologically unsound to use Isaiah as the controlling principle for understanding Mark. Priority must be given to the new context so as to establish how Mark understands the words and how he wishes them to function in his narrative.

The case for regarding Malachi as a controlling narrative is even shakier, for there is little indication in the prologue (Mk 1.1-15) that this is what Mark intended. The prologue begins with the statement, 'The beginning of the good news of Jesus Christ, the Son of God' (1.1) and ends with Jesus' programmatic words, 'The time is fulfilled, and the kingdom of God has come near; repent, and believe in the good news' (1.15). There is nothing in these key statements to suggest that they should be understood in the light of Malachi rather than ordinary Christian usage (good news, kingdom of God, repent, believe). It is true that Mal. 3.1b ('the LORD whom you seek will suddenly come to his temple') is poignant given what happens later, but this text is not quoted here or indeed anywhere else in the Gospel. The quoted words (a fusion of Exod. 23.20 and Mal. 3.1) refer to a messenger who will prepare the way and it is clear from what follows that this is fulfilled in John.[34]

Hatina also considers the 'maximal' approach to be flawed and self-contradictory. For example, it claims to situate the author within early Jewish exegesis but analysis of the relevant literature (Apocrypha, Pseudepigrapha, Qumran) hardly supports the view that first-century exegesis was always historically and contextually sensitive.[35] Though the use of Isa. 40.3 in such texts as the *Community Rule*, *Baruch* and *Assumption of Moses* is interesting, it does not in itself support the view that Mark must have been a contextually sensitive exegete. Furthermore, since scholars then proceed to show how Mark's Christian presuppositions led him to very different conclusions (the return from exile is not fulfilled in construction work in the wilderness or study of Torah), the argument about placing Mark within his first-century environment evaporates.[36]

Secondly, he thinks the assumption that quotations evoke their surrounding contexts is flawed. For example, Mal. 3.3 says, 'he will purify the descendants of Levi

---

[34] Hatina, *In Search of a Context*, pp. 147–48.

[35] Many cite D. Instone Brewer, *Techniques and Assumptions in Jewish Exegesis before 70 CE* (TSAJ, 30; Tübingen: Mohr Siebeck, 1992) to support the view that early Jewish interpretation was interested in original context. He is able to show that such exegesis is not as 'arbitrary' as is often claimed and that one can often discover a rationale behind the exegesis. However, this is still a far cry from the sort of historically aware contextual exegesis that is being suggested for Mark.

[36] 'Marcus's antagonism toward the view that Mark exegeted Scripture atomistically results in forcing too much of the context of the scriptural passage into the Markan context. Further, one wonders, given Marcus's acquaintance with the relevant Jewish primary literature, why he has not allowed for atomistic exegesis since this was the norm in early Jewish interpretation.' (Hatina, *In Search of Context*, p. 42).

and refine them like gold and silver, until they present offerings to the LORD in right-eousness'. Does Watts wish to suggest that Jesus' mission is to purify the descendants of Levi so that they may once again offer the prescribed sacrifices? Of course not. Watts knows the Gospel story and selects what he wants from Malachi to construct the so-called 'original context' of Mal. 3.1. Themes that do not cohere with this, despite their proximity to Mal. 3.1, are simply ignored.

Thirdly, Hatina challenges the weight being put on certain linguistic arguments. For example, there are good grounds for suggesting that the introductory formula in 1 Cor. 2.9 (*kathōs gegraptai*) does begin a new sentence (as in NRSV) and refers to what follows rather than what has gone before. Thus taking Mk 1.2 with what follows is not an anomaly and in fact allows Mk 1.1 to be taken as a title, as the use of *archē* ('beginning') suggests. He also points out that the connection between Isa. 40.9 and Jesus' proclamation of the kingdom depends on the Targum rather than the Hebrew or Septuagint.[37] The connection between the noun *evangelion* and the participle *evangelizomenos* is not as secure as Marcus assumes and the fact that *hodos* ('way') has a variety of functions in the Gospel[38] makes it unlikely that Mark is intending it as a technical term. Hatina acknowledges that the task of determining influence is difficult but suggests that the following questions should be borne in mind:

(1) Does the assessment of the quotation presuppose ancient quotation techniques or contemporary Western ideals? (2) Does the quotation have a range of possible rhetorical functions within the context in which it is now embedded? (3) Does the original context of the quotation cohere with the prior assessment of Mark's narrative? In other words, is the narrative made to conform to the quotation or the reverse? And (4) are the dictional and thematic links, such as 'gospel' and forgiveness respectively, necessarily from a single source like Isaiah? Since Mark uses quotations from other books of Scripture, such as the Psalms, Daniel, Zechariah and the Pentateuch, how does one confirm that it is only Isaiah which is intended in the prologue?[39]

[37] It has of course been argued that Jesus knew and used an Isaiah Targum, even though evidence for its written form is much later. It is much less clear, however, whether the same can be said of Mark. See B. Chilton, *A Galilean Rabbi and His Bible: Jesus' Own Interpretation of Isaiah* (London: SPCK, 1984); C.A. Evans, *To See and Not Perceive: Isaiah 6.9-10 in Early Jewish and Christian Interpretation* (JSOTSup, 64; Sheffield: Sheffield Academic Press, 1989).

[38] 'When all 16 uses of *hodos* in Mark are examined, a variety of nuances emerge. Some refer to a road (4.4, 15; 10.46; 11.8), some to journeys whose destinations are other than Jerusalem (Caesarea Philippi in 8.27; Capernaum in 9.33, 34), some to journeys which exclude Jesus (disciples in 6.8; the 4000 in 8.3), one refers to God's teaching (12.14), and one simply refers to movement (2.23) ... The use of *hodos* in 1.2-3 hardly coheres semantically or theologically with each use in the central section, let alone with every other use in the Gospel.' (Hatina, *In Search of a Context*, p. 168).

[39] Hatina, *In Search of a Context*, p. 159.

How then does Hatina understand the role and function of the composite quotation? First, he notes that the quotation is part of a prologue (Mk 1.1-15) which introduces the main theme of the Gospel, namely, the coming of Jesus to usher in the kingdom of God (1.14-15). In preparation for that, Mark introduces us to the role of the forerunner, mentioning his location ('wilderness'), actions ('baptizing'), diet ('locusts and wild honey'), clothes ('camel hair') and message ('one who is more powerful than I is coming'). According to Hatina, the quoted material can be adequately understood in the light of this. Thus God announces that he will send a messenger (John) to prepare the way (the whole of John's ministry) for Jesus. In turn, John announces to the people that they are to prepare the way of the Lord by repenting of their sins and undergoing baptism 'as a public demonstration of their purification before the coming of the "Mighty One" who will baptize in the Holy Spirit'.[40] The original meaning of 'clearing a path' through the wilderness is discarded in favour of identifying John as the messenger or forerunner of Jesus.

What does Mark envisage when he has John the Baptist say, 'Prepare the way of the Lord, make his paths straight'? Marcus and Watts think that readers would immediately connect the 'highway' that signals the end of the exile with Jesus' 'way' to the cross, but the fact that Mark (or his source) follows the LXX use of *hetoimazō* ('prepare') and *tribous* ('paths') blunts the connection with a singular 'highway' and thus points to a more ethical interpretation, as at Qumran. John is 'preparing the people to travel along a road that the "Mightier One" will ask them to travel. By coming to baptism, the people metaphorically prepare for ethical (and even religious) transformation'.[41]

Analysis

∽

It is clear that one of the major differences between these different interpretations of Mk 1.2-3 is methodological, indeed ideological. Marcus, Schneck, Watts and Perkins employ forms of historical criticism which assume the importance of diachronic analysis, that is, the ongoing influence of prior texts and contexts for understanding the meaning of a new work. Hatina, though not wishing to deny such influence altogether, is more impressed with the sort of synchronic analysis offered by narrative critics, whereby meaning derives primarily (some would say solely) from the role or function of the words in the new context. We will not debate the validity of these two approaches at this point but focus on a number of issues where both sides are appealing to similar arguments.

[40] Hatina, *In Search of a Context*, p. 182.
[41] Hatina, *In Search of a Context*, p. 181.

First, we should note that adopting an historical approach does not necessarily lead to a 'maximal' interpretation. Some highly educated authors would no doubt know the original context of many of their quotations but many would not. Is Mark to be situated with the former or the latter? As we have seen, appeal is often made to the hermeneutical complexity of the Dead Sea Scrolls or the rabbis but again, is this where Mark is to be situated? Should we understand Mark's use of Scripture in the light of trained scribes, who have spent a lifetime copying and commenting on ancient manuscripts? Furthermore, even if we were to locate Mark among the scribes, it is by no means clear that faithfulness to original context was a prime concern for early Jewish exegesis. Hatina puts it too strongly when he claims that atomistic exegesis was the 'norm' for early Jewish interpretation but it would be difficult to maintain the opposite. Citing the Dead Sea Scrolls or the rabbis as parallels does not, in itself, further the case that Mark was a contextually aware interpreter of Scripture. Such a conclusion will have to be supported on other grounds.

Secondly, one cannot base an argument solely on the principle that quoted texts evoke their surrounding contexts. On what hermeneutical theory would a quotation of Mal. 3.1 evoke the content of Mal. 4.5 ('Lo, I will send you the prophet Elijah') but not the content of Mal. 3.3? It cannot be a general principle that quoted texts evoke their surrounding contexts, since Mal. 3.3 is far closer to Mal. 3.1 than Mal. 4.5.[42] Despite the lack of *any* verbal agreement[43] between Mk 3.27 ('But no one can enter a strong man's house') and Isa. 49.24-25 ('Can the prey be taken from the mighty?'), Schneck moves back to the servant passage (Isa. 49.6) and suggests parallels with Mk 3.4-5 (restore the survivors of Israel/restore the withered hand), Mk 3.14 (raise up tribes of Israel/appointment of the twelve) and forward to Isa. 50.1 (mother Zion estranged from her husband) and Mk 3.31-32 (Jesus' mother is outside). He concludes:

> Some of these contacts between Mark 3 and Isaiah 49 do not seem too significant in themselves. However, the number of both major and minor coincidences between these two sections supports the hypothesis that when Isa 49:24-25 is indirectly cited in Mark, the surrounding context in Isaiah 49 was intended as a help for the catechist in order to explain the mission of Jesus as the servant of God portrayed in Deutero-Isaiah.[44]

However, without the presumption that texts always evoke their surrounding contexts, a different assessment is possible: Mk 3.27/Isa. 49.24-25 represent a *minor*

---

[42] The quotation of Hos. 11.1 in Mt. 2.15 offers a more dramatic example. Scholars may debate the exact reason for associating Jesus with the 'son' who leaves Egypt in Hos. 11.1, but none think that Matthew also wants to associate Jesus with the following verse ('The more I called them, the more they went from me; they kept sacrificing to the Baals, and offering incense to idols').

[43] In fact, he says the LXX of Isa. 49.24-25 is corrupt and so Mk 3.27 reflects the MT.

[44] Schneck, *Isaiah in the Gospel of Mark*, p. 100.

agreement and the rest of the cited parallels are non-existent (they are absent from the margins of NA[27]). It would not then warrant the conclusion that Mark is intending to portray Jesus as the servant of Deutero-Isaiah in Mark 3.

In fact, what Marcus, Schneck, Watts and Perkins are actually doing is assuming that complex texts like Exodus, Deutero-Isaiah and Malachi had already given rise to certain well-known 'stories' or 'narratives', with themes like 'exodus', 'new exodus', and 'suffering servant'. Such stories do not integrate every verse of the book into a coherent whole (cf. the Jewish Passover ritual) but offer a synthesis, usually as a vehicle for a particular theology/ideology. Since these were well known (so it is claimed), the slightest allusion is sufficient to activate the whole story (e.g. a reference to blood on the doorposts would evoke the whole Passover story – but not every verse of Exodus 12). Hatina accuses Watts of knowing the Gospel story, selecting verses from Malachi that cohere with it, and then magically presenting this as the surrounding context of Mal. 3.1. But a different interpretation is possible. Watts thinks that Malachi had already given rise to a 'story' whose theme is 'judgement due to lack of preparedness' and this is what is being invoked in the opening quotation. Perkins thinks the combined references to the messenger of Exod. 23.20 and the voice of Isa. 40.3 would evoke 'the Exodus story in the light of its re-visioning in Isaiah 40'.[45] Whether such 'stories' were well known in the first century is an historical question which, in principle, is answerable, though one would have to define criteria for what constitutes 'well known'. It would also be important to establish whether it is important that both author and readers were aware of it.

Thirdly, the existence of a variety of historical reconstructions inevitably raises a question mark against the importance being placed upon any one of them. It is not that quotations must evoke a single context and therefore somebody has to be wrong. Indeed, it is quite plausible that a richly textured quotation like that found in Mk 1.2-3 might well evoke ideas and themes from Exodus, Malachi and Isaiah. The problem is that the resulting complexity is then artificially reduced so as to make one particular proposal more convincing than the others. Thus although the messenger of Exod. 23.20, who guards Israel on their way to the promised land, is conceptually the most distant (of the cited texts) from the actual role of John the Baptist, Perkins nevertheless claims that Mark begins his Gospel by 'comparing God's action in providing a divine messenger to lead and protect Israel on its journey to Canaan, with God's action in sending John the Baptist'.[46]

---

[45] Perkins, 'Kingdom', p. 115.

[46] Writing on the possible sources of the words at Jesus' baptism (Mark 1.11), Hatina writes: 'When two or more options are available and fit into the narrative, the historical-critical scholar attempts all the more to verify a single influence. The approach is not only myopic, but undermines the entire process. By trying to demonstrate the weaknesses of competing options, the historical-critic indirectly succeeds in showing the instability of his own position' – T.R. Hatina, 'Embedded Scripture Texts and the Plurality of Meaning: The Announcement of the "Voice from Heaven" in Mark 1.11 as a Case Study' in Hatina (ed.), *Biblical Interpretation in Early Christian Gospels*, p. 98. I would add that the same is true of narrative critics, who often write as if they have definitively established *the* plot or *the* characterization of a Gospel.

Fourthly, despite the methodological/ideological need to emphasize *either* the importance of the Old Testament background *or* the new narrative context, it would appear that we must reckon with *some* influence from both. Thus Marcus maintains that Mark utilized the Deutero-Isaian framework and exposed it to what he graphically calls a 'christological neutron bombardment'.[47] He thinks that we must therefore account for both continuity and discontinuity with the tradition, concluding that 'Mark has certainly learned much of what he knows about Jesus Christ from the scriptures. He would never have learned it, however, if he had not already known that Jesus Christ is the key to the scriptures.'[48] Perkins notes many parallels between Exodus and Mark but also makes it clear that Mark's narrative is not 'bound by them'. The readers are invited to read the Gospel in the light of what the 'Exodus quotations, allusions and motifs contribute to the Jesus Story', but this is done by 'reflecting upon Israel's Exodus experience and Isaiah's prophecies of a new exodus in the light of Jesus' words and deeds'.[49]

Hatina argues that discontinuity with the Old Testament background (Mark does not envisage construction work in the wilderness) shows that Isaiah 40 is not being used as a controlling paradigm. Having made that point, however, he does admit that: 'Since the quotation appears in the prologue, and at the beginning of the narrative, the importance of its function should not be minimized.'[50] Thus while it is 'not used as a reference to Yahweh leading his people out of exile', it does provide a 'basis for the Baptist's presence and activity in the Judean desert'.[51] It is significant that Hatina calls this section of his chapter, 'Towards a Narrative-Historical Reading', rather than simply a 'Narrative Reading'. Evidently what is needed is a method which can analyse the interaction between influences coming from previous contexts as well as the new narrative context.

Lastly, it is clear that the linguistic competence of Mark and the availability of texts is a key task in any such investigation. Marcus thinks that Mark 'had a rather good knowledge of the Hebrew or Aramaic text of the Old Testament' and supports it by referring to the large number of Aramaic words in the Gospel.[52] As we have seen, this allows him to offer an explanation for why Mark combined the Exod. 23.20/Mal. 3.1 material with Isa. 40.3. On the other hand, knowing the meaning of a few Aramaic words like *Boanerges* (3.17), *Talitha cum* (5.41), *Corban* (7.11), *Ephphatha* (7.34), *Golgotha* (15.22) and *Eloi, Eloi, lema sabachtani* (15.34) hardly makes him a

---

[47] Marcus, *The Way of the Lord*, p. 41.

[48] Marcus, *The Way of the Lord*, p. 203. Watts asserts a greater level of continuity in that he sees the composite quotation as evoking both a salvation (Isaiah) and judgement (Malachi) background. He can thus argue that 'surprising' interpretations of Isaiah are a product of this dual background. We will have more to say about this in future chapters.

[49] Perkins, 'Kingdom', p. 115.

[50] Hatina, *In Search of a Context*, p. 163.

[51] Hatina, *In Search of a Context*, p. 163.

[52] Drawing on M. Hengel, *Studies in the Gospel of Mark* (Philadelphia: Fortress Press, 1985).

biblical scholar, and some of the quotations (including Isa. 40.3) show dependence on the LXX. Since it is likely that Mark took the composite Exod. 23.20/Mal. 3.1 material and Isa. 40.3 from existing Greek texts, it is quite possible that he combined them because of their common theme and not because the underlying Hebrew texts share a common word.

Conclusion

Unless it can be demonstrated that either a synchronic or diachronic approach is invalid, it would appear that the meaning of an Old Testament quotation in the New Testament must take into account both approaches. For words to mean anything, a hearer or reader must have some experience of having heard or seen them before, and so it is to be expected that *some* connotations or associations will carry over from previous contexts. If this were not the case, then the concept of quotation would be 'sense-less'. On the other hand, Hatina has demonstrated that we should not move from this commonsense observation to much larger claims that a quotation necessarily evokes all of its surrounding context. As in lexicography, the meaning of words is determined by actual usage not etymology. Indeed, the same argument that would suggest that a quotation must be understood in the light of its original (or subsequent) context(s) can be used to show that a quotation must be understood in the light of its new context. How these different influences (previous context, new context) relate to one another will be a constant feature of the chapters that follow.

3

Evoking a legal framework in order to undermine it?
Mk 2.25-8; 7.15-19; 10.2-9; 12.33

Introduction

Although opinions vary as to the nature and significance of the texts evoked in Mark's opening quotation, there is general agreement that they are being evoked for positive reasons. They contribute to Mark's story and may even evoke a scriptural framework that is necessary to understand it. There is no such agreement concerning Mark's relationship to the law, however. In particular, four texts have been used to support the view that Mark evokes the law in order to undermine it. In the controversy story over plucking corn on the sabbath, Mark has Jesus give an illustration of how David broke the law (2.25) and concludes that, 'The sabbath was made for humankind, and not humankind for the sabbath; so the Son of Man is lord even of the sabbath' (Mk 2.27-8). Following the aphorism that 'there is nothing outside a person that by going in can defile' (Mk 7.15), Mark makes the deduction, 'Thus he declared all foods clean' (Mk 7.19). In the controversy concerning divorce, Jesus appears to contrast God's will, as shown in the creation accounts ('and the two shall become one flesh'), with the requirement to provide a bill of divorce in Deuteronomy 24, which Moses gave as a concession to human weakness (Mk 10.5). And in a dialogue concerning the greatest commandment, Mark has Jesus give approval to the scribe's remark that loving God and neighbour 'is much more important than all whole burnt offerings and sacrifices' (Mk 12.33). On the basis of these four texts, a case can be made that Mark deliberately evokes a Jewish legal framework in order to undermine it. As William Loader says, 'for Mark Jesus has a new teaching with authority which dispenses with laws concerning unclean foods and ritual purity related to externals ... Mark sets this in its wider context by seeing Jesus' teaching as removing the barriers for accepting Gentiles on equal terms'.[1]

---

[1] W.R.G. Loader, *Jesus' Attitude to the Law* (WUNT, 2.97; Tübingen: Mohr Siebeck, 1997), pp. 72–9.

On the other hand, there are an equal number of texts that could be used to support the view that Mark upholds the traditional role of the law. For example, when Jesus heals a man suffering from leprosy, he tells him to 'go, show yourself to the priest, and offer for your cleansing what Moses commanded' (Mk 1.44). In the hand-washing controversy, Jesus challenges his opponents' use of the Corban tradition because it undermines the commandment to honour mother and father. In successive verses, Mark has Jesus make the following accusations: 'You abandon the commandment of God and hold to human tradition' (Mk 7.8); 'You have a fine way of rejecting the commandment of God in order to keep your tradition!' (Mk 7.9). And when the rich young man asks what he must do to inherit eternal life, Jesus refers him to the commandments (Mk 10.19), even if he has more to learn about giving up his many possessions. If explicit quotations of Isaiah dominate the first half of the Gospel (Mk 1.3; 4.12; 7.7), it is quotations from the law that dominate the middle section (Mk 7.10; 10.4, 6, 7, 19; 12.19, 26, 29, 31). Is this evidence for the importance of the law for Mark or is it being evoked in order to be undermined?

The case for Mark undermining the importance of the law[2]
∽

Mk 2.25-28 and the sabbath
As is well known, Mk 2.1–3.6 consists of a series of controversy stories where Jesus' actions provoke hostility because he pronounces forgiveness on a paralytic (Mk 2.1-12), eats with tax-collectors and sinners (Mk 2.13-17), fails to observe times of fasting (Mk 2.18-22), allows his disciples to pluck corn on the sabbath (Mk 2.23-8) and heals a man with a withered hand on the sabbath (Mk 3.1-6). If the latter is understood as an emergency, Jewish tradition would agree that 'saving life overrules the sabbath' (*b. Yoma* 85b) but that could hardly be argued for the plucking of corn by the disciples, where there is no mention of hunger, let alone starvation.[3] Jesus' response to the accusation is three-fold: (1) there is precedent for such an action since David and his companions transgressed the law by eating the shewbread in time of need (1 Samuel 21); (2) 'the sabbath was made (*egeneto*) for humankind and not humankind for the sabbath'; and (3) 'the Son of Man is lord even of the Sabbath'.

None of these responses is straightforward. The story of David eating the forbidden shewbread is an odd parallel to the disciples plucking corn on the Sabbath. Indeed, 1 Samuel 21 does not specifically say that David was in need or that he gave

---

[2] The following draws on my 'Deuteronomy in Mark's Gospel' in M.J.J. Menken and S. Moyise (eds), *Deuteronomy in the New Testament* (LNTS, 358; London and New York: T&T Clark, 2007), pp. 27–41.

[3] It is not literally true even for the man with the withered hand, since his life was unlikely to have been in danger had Jesus waited until the sabbath was over.

the bread to his companions or that the incident happened on a sabbath. In fact, David defends his right to eat the bread because both he and his companions (who are not with him at this point) have kept themselves from women and maintained the purity of their vessels (1 Sam. 21.5).[4] The second response would naturally evoke the principal passages concerning the sabbath (Exod. 20.8-10; Deut. 5.12-15) but the use of *egeneto* ('came into being', 'created') suggests that the creation story is also in mind. Is this then an argument from priority, that because humankind was created *before* the sabbath, it was never intended to be subservient to it? The third response is seen by most commentators as the key to the passage: Jesus is Lord of the sabbath. However, this could also have a variety of meanings: Jesus is free to break the sabbath; Jesus can determine what constitutes a legitimate suspension of the sabbath; Jesus can determine that his disciples' activity does not break the sabbath.

Mk 7.15-19 and the food laws

Mk 7.1-23 is a complex controversy-narrative in three sections. The first section (Mk 7.1-8) begins with the 'Pharisees and the scribes' asking why Jesus' disciples do not 'live according to the tradition of the elders, but eat with defiled hands' (Mk 7.5). Jesus responds by calling them hypocrites and quoting a text from Isaiah to the effect that they care more about their traditions than honouring God. The second section (Mk 7.8-13) gives an illustration of this by reference to the tradition of Corban, that is, devoting property or goods to God. Mark appears to imply that the Pharisees and scribes regard such oaths as binding ('you no longer permit doing anything for a father or mother'), even if this leads to hardship for one's parents. The issue is directly addressed in the Mishnah (*m. Ned.* 9.1), which agrees with Jesus that in cases of conflict, priority should be given to the commandment to honour parents. It would therefore appear that Mark has either misrepresented the views of contemporary Pharisees (whether deliberately or in ignorance) or this harsher view was subsequently softened by the second-century rabbis.[5]

---

[4] The latter is obscure. The NRSV renders the Hebrew: 'the vessels of the young men are holy even when it is a common journey' but the LXX says, 'even though it is a common journey, today will be made holy because of my *skeuē* (vessels, goods, weapons?)'.

[5] Marcus (*Mark 1-8*, p. 445) adopts the latter but France notes that there is some ambiguity in the Mishnah for *m. Ned.* 5.6 tells this story: 'a man who had excluded his father under such a vow from any enjoyment of his property now wished to evade the force of his oath so as to enable the father to join in his grandson's wedding feast; he therefore made a gift of his courtyard and the feast to a friend, so that his father could be admitted (to what was now the friend's property), but the friend in turn made a similar vow with regard to his newly acquired property, thus frustrating the donor's intention! This case illustrates two points relevant to our passage: (i) the original *qorbān* vow was regarded as unalterable, even though the son himself now wished to repeal it; (ii) the property so "dedicated" remained still at the son's disposal, even though out of his father's reach. It is such a situation which is apparently presupposed by Jesus' comments here.' See R.T. France, *The Gospel of Mark* (NIGTC; Grand Rapids: Eerdmans/Carlisle: Paternoster, 2002), p. 287.

The third section (Mk 7.14-23) could be a continuation of what has gone before or the beginning of a new subject ('Then he called the crowd again'). It begins with Jesus quoting an aphorism that 'there is nothing outside a person that by going in can defile, but the things that come out are what defile' (Mk 7.16). Lest the disciples take this too literally (eating and excreting), Jesus clarifies that it is not food going into the stomach (or coming out) that defiles but the evil that is within. Mark then draws the conclusion that Jesus 'declared all foods clean' (*katharizōn panta ta brōmata*), seemingly annulling the scriptural distinction between clean and unclean food. Loader says:

> The approach is consistent with the image we found of Jesus in 2:1–3:6: Jesus is the ultimate authority beside and beyond Torah. Yet here, for the first time, we see the ultimate implications of this claim to authority: it may include permanently setting aside specific Torah provisions and demeaning them as worthless![6]

Discussion of this verse has largely focused on whether Mark has misrepresented Jesus[7] or whether it is a correct deduction from the aphorism.[8] Few scholars have doubted that Mark was intending to annul the food laws for the sake of his Gentile readers.[9]

Mk 10.2-9 and divorce

This pericope on marriage and divorce begins with a question from the Pharisees ('Is it lawful for a man to divorce his wife?'), which Mark tells us was a test. Jesus responds by asking them a question: 'What did Moses *command* you?' Predictably, they answer by citing words from Deut. 24.1-4, the only passage in the law to speak about divorce, and conclude that, 'Moses *allowed* a man to write a certificate of dismissal and to divorce her' (Mk 10.4). Jesus then responds by stating that Moses wrote this *commandment* 'because (*pros*) of your hardness of heart' but God's will is expressed in the creation stories, where 'God made them male and female' (Gen. 1.27) and 'For this reason a man shall leave his father and mother and be joined to his wife,[10] and the two shall become one flesh' (Gen. 2.24). Though divorce is not

---

[6] Loader, *Jesus' Attitude to the Law*, p. 78.

[7] 'there is no indication that Jesus and his disciples did not eat kosher food, although the importance of Mark's comment for churches which included Gentiles is obvious', E.P. Sanders, *Jesus and Judaism* (London: SCM, 1985), p. 266.

[8] 'The aphorism – it's not what goes in but what comes out that defiles – is a categorical challenge to the laws governing pollution and purity'. R.W. Funk *et al.*, *The Five Gospels. The Search for the Authentic Words of Jesus* (New York: Polebridge Press, 1993), p. 69.

[9] Notable exceptions are: J. Svartik, *Mark and Mission: Mark 7.1-23 in its Narrative and Historical Contexts* (ConBNT, 32; Stockholm: Almqvist & Wiksell, 2000); J.G. Crossley, *The Date of Mark's Gospel. Insight from the Law in Earliest Christianity* (JSNTSup, 266; London and New York: T&T Clark, 2004).

[10] The words 'and be joined to his wife' are omitted by ℵ B Ψ 892* 2427 sy^s but favoured by most modern commentators.

mentioned in these texts, Jesus deduces that 'one flesh' implies the impossibility of separation, and so concludes that the one who 'divorces his wife and marries another commits adultery' (10.11), as is also true for a wife divorcing her husband.[11]

What is striking about the way Mark presents this debate is that Jesus contrasts a *command* of Moses with the *will of God* expressed in the creation stories. Two arguments support this. First, Jesus claims that the command was given '*pros* your hardness of heart'. Most commentators take the preposition *pros* to mean 'with regard to' or 'because of' and the 'your' to refer to humanity in general or perhaps the Jewish race.[12] In other words, the commandment of Deut. 24.1-4 does not express the will of God but was a *concession* to human weakness. Secondly, the creation stories take priority because they state what was so 'from the beginning of creation'. Emerson Powery draws a wide-ranging conclusion from this:

> By the use of this wider narrative or script, Jesus levels the Mosaic law to a post-creation period for 'hardened' humanity. That is, it is not the ideal. Jesus' scriptural choice serves as a *corrective*. This interpretative tension (script against scripture) sets up elements in a hermeneutical (preferential) system: (1) God's act over Moses' commands; (2) the creation period as the ideal; and (3) historical narrative balances law.[13]

Mk 12.28-34 and the greatest commandment

Following a debate with the Sadducees concerning resurrection, a scribe asks Jesus, 'Which commandment is the first of all?' (Mk 12.28). Jesus replies by citing the opening words of the *Shema* (Deut. 6.4-5): 'Hear, O Israel: the LORD our God, the LORD is one; you shall love the Lord your God with all your heart, and with all your soul, and with all your mind, and with all your strength.' He adds a second from Lev. 19.18, 'You shall love your neighbour as yourself', and concludes that 'There is no other commandment greater than these'. Rather strangely, Mark then has the scribe

---

[11] Marriage and divorce were keenly debated in the second Temple period, and in rabbinic literature an entire tractate is devoted to it (*Gittin*). Much of the debate focused on the meaning of the phrase 'something objectionable' in Deut. 24.1. Shammai took the rigorous view that divorce should only be permitted for some shameful act, whereas Hillel took the more liberal view that it could be for a variety of faults, even as trivial as spoiling the dinner (*M. Git.* 9.10). Josephus took the liberal view: 'He who desires to be divorced from the wife who is living with him for whatsoever cause – and with mortals many such may arise – must certify in writing that he will have no further intercourse with her' (*Ant* 5.253). At Qumran, divorce is accepted without comment in CD 13.17 and 11QT 54.4-5 but CD 4.20-5.2 accuses the 'builders of the wall' of unchastity because 'they take two wives in their lives, while the foundation of creation is male and female he created them'.

[12] R.H. Gundry (*Mark: A Commentary on His Apology for the Cross* [Grand Rapids: Eerdmans, 1993], p. 538) insists that the 'your' relates only to the Pharisees and thus cannot be the reason Moses gave such a command. He thus takes *pros* in a telic sense and oddly concludes that Moses gave the command in order to 'incite the Pharisees to divorce their wives against God's ordinance'.

[13] E.B. Powery, *Jesus Reads Scripture. The Function of Jesus' Use of Scripture in the Synoptic Gospels* (Leiden: Brill, 2003), p. 52.

repeat Jesus' answer in a different form. He repeats the phrase 'he is one' and then adds words from Deut. 4.35 ('and besides him there is no other').[14] He then abbreviates the four faculties to three by omitting 'soul' and substituting 'understanding' for 'mind', deducing that 'this is much more important than all whole burnt offerings and sacrifices' (absent from Matthew and Luke), which Mark regards as a wise answer (Mk 12.34). Loader concludes that Mark is deliberately establishing a contrast between 'heart religion' and 'cultic activity', just as he has done with the sabbath and the food laws.[15]

The Case for Mark upholding the law
∽

Mark 1.44 and the man with leprosy

Following the call of the fishermen (Mk 1.16-20), Jesus and his disciples went to Capernaum and 'when the Sabbath came, he entered the synagogue and taught' (Mk 1.21). During the service, 'a man with an unclean spirit' started crying out, causing Jesus to rebuke the spirit with the words: 'Be silent, and come out of him' (Mk 1.25). The spirit obeyed, causing astonishment but apparently no objection to doing such a thing on the Sabbath. Some time later, a man suffering from leprosy came to him saying, 'If you choose, you can make me clean' (Mk 1.40). Jesus stretched out his hand, touched him and said, 'Be clean'. The man is healed and told to 'go, show yourself to the priest, and offer for your cleansing what Moses commanded, as a testimony to them' (Mk 1.44). It is difficult to see how anyone reading the first chapter of Mark would conclude that Jesus is not a law-abiding Jew and it could be argued (as is done for Mk 1.2-3) that this should set the framework for understanding the rest of the Gospel stories.

For example, while there is nothing to suggest that 'extreme hunger' lies behind Jesus' permission for the disciples to pluck corn on the Sabbath, they have left everything to follow him and so could probably be described as poor. If that is the case, then they might have thought that the permission granted in Lev. 19.9-10, for the poor to pluck from the edges of the field, applied to them. Though the law does not specifically say that this could be done on the Sabbath, neither does it forbid it. Thus the saying that Jesus has authority over the Sabbath could be taken to mean that Jesus is the one who decides what does and does not constitute a breaking of the Sabbath. In this instance, his ruling is that plucking from the edges of the field by the impoverished disciples does not break the Sabbath laws.

---

[14] Similar phrases occur elsewhere, e.g. 2 Sam. 7.22; 1 Kgs 8.60; 2 Kgs 19.19; Isa. 37.20.
[15] Loader, *Jesus Attitude Towards the Law*, p. 101.

Mk 7.1-23 and the contrast between God's word and human tradition

Most scholars agree that in the first two sections of Mk 7.1-23, Jesus is rebuking the Pharisees and scribes for regarding their traditions as more important than God's law. This is emphasized in the initial question ('Why do your disciples not live according to the tradition of the elders …?'), the quotation of Isa. 29.13 ('in vain do they worship me, teaching human precepts as doctrines') and the double accusation in Mk 7.8-9 that contrasts the commandment of God with 'human tradition'/'your traditions'. The question then is whether it is feasible to believe that in the third section (Mk 7.14-23), Mark wishes to present Jesus as setting aside the commandment of God with respect to the food laws, on the strength of a non-scriptural human aphorism? Robert Gundry thinks that 'Mark's point is exactly this: Jesus has authority to change the commandments because he is divine and the elders are not'[16] but James Crossley finds this incredible. First, it is highly unlikely that Mark would present Jesus using a (human) aphorism to undermine the food laws when he has just berated the Pharisees for 'making void the word of God through your tradition'. Secondly, we are explicitly told in Mk 7.2, 5 that the controversy is about handwashing rituals, not clean and unclean food. Whatever the pre-history of the material, Mark's placement of it here suggests that he sees it as a continuation of that debate. Thirdly, there exist *halacha* traditions that argue that impurity can pass from hand to food to eater via contact with liquid.[17] Jesus states that food is not made unclean in this way and so Mark draws the conclusion that all foods are clean, referring of course to those foods that the law prescribes as clean. Foods that the law prescribes as unclean play no part in the discussion.[18]

Mk 10.17-22 and the commandments

Mark follows the discussion on marriage and divorce (Mk 10.2-9) with the blessing of the children (Mk 10.13-16), followed by a dialogue with a rich young man (Luke calls him a ruler). The man addresses Jesus with the unusual epithet, 'Good Teacher', followed by a question, 'what must I do to inherit eternal life?' (Mk 10.17). After a puzzling counter-question ('Why do you call me good? No one is good but God alone'), Jesus responds by quoting from the second table of the Ten Commandments (Exod. 20.16-20/Deut. 5.16-20), along with a command not to defraud.[19] The man responds that he has kept these since his youth, which, judging by Jesus' response ('Jesus, looking at him, loved him'), is to be taken as sincere. Jesus then adds: 'You lack one thing; go, sell what you own, and give the money to the poor…; then come, follow

---

[16] R.H. Gundry, *Mark: A Commentary on his Apology for the Cross* (Grand Rapids: Eerdmans, 1993), p. 356.

[17] b.*Pesah.* 115a-b; m.*Berakot* 8.2; *Ber.* 52a.

[18] Crossley, *The Date of Mark's Gospel*, pp. 228–31.

[19] Gundry (*Mark*, p. 553) suggests this is in place of the command not to covet because (a) it is more visible and thus allows the man to claim that he has kept the commandments since youth, and (b) the rich have less need to covet but might well have gained their riches by defrauding.

me' (Mk 10.21). While it is true that the man's eyes need to be opened to the true depth of God's commandments, this exchange can hardly be taken as implying their annulment.

Mk 12.18-27 and proof of the resurrection

Confronted with a concocted story of seven brothers all marrying the same woman in order to ridicule belief in the resurrection, Mark presents Jesus as justifying this belief by quoting from Exod. 3.6 ('I am the God of Abraham, the God of Isaac, and the God of Jacob') and stating that God is a God of the living, not the dead. John Meier suggests the logic of the scriptural proof is as follows:

1. *Major Premise*: According to God's self-chosen definition, the very being of God involves being the God of Abraham, Isaac, and Jacob. This is his permanent self-definition.
2. *Minor Premise*: But, as the whole of the OT proclaims, God is God only of the living, not the defiling, unclean dead, with whom he has no relation.
3. *Unspoken Conclusion*: Therefore, if God's being is truly defined by his permanent relationship to the three patriarchs, the three patriarchs must be (now or in the future) living and in living relationship to God.[20]

Though this is not a dispute about the law, it is significant that Mark has Jesus upholding the doctrine of resurrection with a text from the law.[21] He also takes the opportunity of accusing the Sadducees of knowing 'neither the scriptures nor the power of God' (Mk 12.24). It is apparently not enough to cite individual texts. Knowing Scripture means knowing how different texts relate to one another. Powery thinks this is a critical passage for understanding Mark's hermeneutics. Scriptural interpretation, according to Mark, requires a proper theology of God. It is not a literal or historical interpretation but one that stems from a specific theological conviction, in this case, 'He is God not of the dead, but of the living'.[22]

---

[20] J.P. Meier, *A Marginal Jew: Companions and Competitors Vol 3* (New York: Doubleday, 2001), pp. 429–30.

[21] As most commentators point out, a proof based on the Prophets or Writings would not have carried any weight for the Sadducees.

[22] Powery, *Jesus Reads Scripture*, p. 69. Schüssler Fiorenza makes a different point. The Sadducees not only have a faulty theology of resurrection, but they also have a faulty patriarchal understanding of marriage ('whose wife will she be?'). Jesus challenges this with his view of the afterlife, where 'they neither marry nor are given in marriage'. See E. Schüssler Fiorenza, *In Memory of Her: A Feminist Theological Reconstruction of Christian Origins* (rev. edn; London: SCM Press, 1994), pp. 143–5.

Mk 12.28-34 and the greatest commandment

As we have seen, Mark has a scribe ask Jesus about the greatest commandment, and Jesus responds by quoting the opening of the *Shema* and the command to love one's neighbour. Combining the commandments to love God and neighbour has partial parallels in *T.Iss.* 5.2 ('love the LORD and your neighbour') and *T.Dan* 5.3 ('love the LORD and one another with a true heart') but citing the actual commandments in this way appears to be original. It might have been prompted by the fact that the Hebrew texts both use a relatively rare form for 'you shall love' (translated *agapēseis*)[23] or simply as a convenient summary of the second table of the Ten Commandments (already quoted in Mk 10.19). Mark then has Jesus declare, 'There is no other commandment greater than these' (Mk 12.31). Although approval is then given to the scribe's own formulation ('this is much more important than all whole burnt offerings and sacrifices'), this does not go beyond what many of Israel's prophets had declared.[24] As Powery observes, 'Neither Jesus' final statement, "there are no greater laws than these," nor the scribes' final statement, "it is much more than sacrifices," suggests annulling these practices!'[25] It is simply a question of priorities.

Analysis

∼

As in our previous chapter, it is apparent that scholarly conclusions are strongly influenced by the chosen starting point. For some, the command to 'offer for your cleansing what Moses commanded' (Mk 1.44), the double accusation that the Pharisees are guilty of abandoning the word of God (Mk 7.8-9) and the multiple citation of the commandments (Mk 7.10; 10.19, 12.30) is sufficient to demonstrate that Mark's Jesus clearly upholds the law. More ambiguous passages are then interpreted in the light of this. For example, both the 'eating corn' controversy and the debate concerning divorce can be understood in terms of Jesus expounding the true intent of the law, rather than undermining it. Indeed, this is quite explicit in the divorce controversy and also offers a plausible understanding for Jesus' attack on 'human traditions'. For scholars who opt for this starting point, Mark does not present Jesus as undermining the law but having the authority to discern its true intention, especially against later *halacha* traditions.

On the other hand, other scholars regard the parenthesis in Mk 7.19 ('Thus he declared all foods clean') as unequivocal and consistent both with Mark's belittling of Jewish tradition ('and there are also many other traditions that they observe' – Mk

---

[23] Gundry, *Mark*, p. 711.

[24] One such text is Hos. 6.6 ('I desire mercy, not sacrifice'), which Matthew has Jesus quote on two occasions (9.13; 12.7).

[25] Powery, *Jesus Reads Scripture*, p. 73 n.210. See also France, *The Gospel of Mark*, p. 481.

7.5) and Jesus' challenges to sabbath and divorce laws. Mark even has Jesus adding to the Ten Commandments ('do not defraud') and assigning meanings to texts that they could not possibly have had in their original setting ('I am the God of Abraham' as proof of resurrection). It is true that Jesus does sometimes cite the commandments but only when it suits his argument; he never cites commandments to uphold the sabbath or food laws. In the light of this, it could be argued that the instruction to the leper should not be taken as indicating Jesus' conformity to the law but simply as a testimony. When the people see the man offering sacrifices again, they will know that the priest has declared him free from leprosy and that a miracle has taken place.[26]

Though arriving at opposite conclusions, these interpretations have two presuppositions in common: (1) they both assume that Mark offers a single coherent view of Jesus' attitude to the law; and (2) they both assume that this view can be described in terms of a single principle. But are these safe assumptions? The first has been necessary for redaction criticism, for it is only by assuming a coherent purpose that one can make judgements about an author's shaping of sources. In short, it is assumed that had Mark not agreed with the emphasis of a particular story, he would either have changed it or excluded it. But this does not allow for the possibility that Mark might have had a particular reason for including a story that has little to do with the current interests of modern redaction critics. For example, Mark might have included the healing of the man with leprosy because he knew people who suffered from the disease; he may not have realized that it could be used to support a view of the law that was contrary to his own.[27] This is not to accuse Mark of stupidity. It is simply to acknowledge that he might not have aimed at consistency in all the matters that now interest redaction critics. As Clifton Black has demonstrated, the quest for establishing a consistent purpose for Mark is fraught with difficulties and certainly cannot be assumed from the outset.[28]

Literary approaches work to a different agenda. The problem of using textual evidence to determine the 'intention' of authors was brought to the attention of New Testament scholars by the work of David Rhoads and David Michie on Mark (1982)[29]

---

[26] It is denied by Gundry (*Mark*, p. 103), who says: 'though a portrayal of Jesus as respectful of the Law might shield him in advance from criticisms lodged by the scribes and Pharisees in 2:1–3:6, the emphasis in 2:23–3:6 on his lordship over the Law and in 7.19 (in an editorial phrase) on his reversing the Law does not sit easily on this interpretation of Mark's present point'.

[27] One does not have to agree with all that Wrede wrote to acknowledge that Mark is an opaque Gospel. Whether it is large questions like, 'Did Jesus want to be recognized as Messiah or not?' or smaller questions like, 'Why did he curse a fig tree for not producing figs out of season?', Mark is hardly known for his clarity.

[28] C.C. Black, *The Disciples according to Mark: Markan Redaction in Current Debate* (JSNTSup, 27; Sheffield: Sheffield Academic Press, 1989).

[29] D. Rhoads and D. Michie, *Mark As Story: An Introduction to the Narrative of a Gospel* (Philadelphia: Fortress Press, 1982).

and Alan Culpepper on John (1983).[30] Scholars have access to texts, not the minds of the people who wrote them. Thus language such as 'Mark intends' is misleading for it actually refers to a particular construction or configuration of the text that we call Mark's Gospel.[31] Literary approaches, therefore, speak of the 'implied' author or reader rather than any actual author(s) or reader(s) and speak about the text's 'point of view' rather than the author's 'intention'. Nevertheless, it is also a presupposition rather than a conclusion that a text offers a coherent 'point of view', though in order to describe it, it might well be necessary to use complex forms of discourse.

This appears to be the case for the present question of whether Mark (now understood as the Gospel rather than its author) evokes the law in order to undermine it. If we assume a coherent 'point of view' but cannot accept that the evidence points exclusively to a 'Yes' or 'No' answer, then we must consider a more complex description. All sides accept that Jesus is presented as the one who has authority to interpret the law. It would seem that we must also accept that this was not only manifested by authoritative quotation, but also by prioritizing one text over another and by determining what does and does not constitute a 'suspension' or a 'breaking' of it. The second of these is particularly interesting in that Mark 10 has Jesus prioritizing Gen. 1.27/2.24 over Deut. 24.1-3, while Mark 12 has him pronouncing that there is no commandment greater than Deut. 6.4-5 and Lev. 18.5. Thus Powery's statement that 'Jesus levels the Mosaic law to a post-creation period for "hardened" humanity' should not be generalized beyond the divorce pericope. According to Mark's Jesus, the two greatest commandments come from Deuteronomy and Leviticus, not the creation stories. Thus we must reckon with a complex hermeneutic where different principles come to the fore depending on the context.

Can we go behind the principle that Jesus is presented as an authoritative interpreter of the law? A christological approach might suggest that Jesus is presented as the unique son of God (Mk 1.1, 11; 13.32; 15.39) and it is this relationship that enables him to discern (or know) the true intent of the law. This is probably correct but we should be cautious about drawing too many conclusions from it. After all, we would probably not have expected Mark to portray the unique son of God as ignorant of the time of the end (Mk 13.32) or ending his life by asking God why he has been forsaken (Mk 15.34). Jesus' unique relationship with God might well be the single principle behind Mark's portrayal of Jesus but as most scholars acknowledge, it has resulted in a Gospel with many ambiguities and difficulties.[32] This appears to be true also of Mark's portrayal of Jesus' relationship with the law.

[30] A. Culpepper, *Anatomy of the Fourth Gospel: A Study in Literary Design* (Philadelphia: Fortress Press, 1983).

[31] More precisely, the text as reconstructed by NA[27], with or without any 'corrections' favoured by the individual scholar.

[32] Gundry is a notable exception, who begins his commentary with a series of denials and a statement: 'The Gospel of Mark contains no ciphers, no hidden meanings, no sleight of hand: No messianic secret ... No Christology of irony that means the reverse of what it says ... Mark's meaning lies on the surface. He writes a straightforward apology for the Cross' (Gundry, *Mark*, p. 1). However, it is difficult to reconcile this statement with some of Gundry's more unusual interpretations, such as Jesus' exhalation on the cross as responsible for

Conclusion

In our previous chapter, the main methodological decision was whether to adopt a diachronic or synchronic approach in order to determine the meaning of an Old Testament quotation. One might say that this is primarily an ideological decision, though it clearly has theological implications. Here, it would appear that theological considerations are the more significant. The question of whether Jesus upheld the law or was a major critic of it is clearly important for theological reconstructions. Some scholars think the weight of evidence points to one side or the other and that more ambiguous texts should be interpreted in that light. This of course involves a further assumption, namely, that Mark has a unified coherent understanding of Jesus' relationship with the law. This can either be an historical judgement about the author of the Gospel or a narrative assumption about Mark's Gospel. But given the fact that we have no other works by the author of the Gospel to enable comparisons, they probably amount to the same thing.

Without this assumption, other scholars are prepared to acknowledge that there is evidence on both sides of the debate, either implying that Mark is self-contradictory (on this issue) or that any account of Mark's view will be complex, perhaps holding a number of principles (dialogically) in tension. Given that the New Testament authors wish to uphold the authority of Scripture *and* what has been revealed in the Christ-event, this should not be surprising. Unless one is persuaded that what has been revealed in the Christ-event is identical *at every point* to what has gone before, some sort of dialogical tension is inevitable. As H. Davidson says of that most allusive of texts, 'The Waste Land' (T.S. Eliot): 'The work's meaning is in the tension between its previous contextual definition and its present context'.[33] Tension should not be regarded as a fault or criticism of a work; it is the inevitable product of engaging more than one context.

Edwin Broadhead prefers the term 'reciprocity' to 'dialogical'. In his study of the traditions behind the 'son of man' material in Mark, he concludes that: 'The Gospel of Mark invokes a variety of traditions and texts in its portrayal of Jesus. These previously existing texts have been appropriated under a guiding hermeneutic whose effect is not correction, but reciprocity'.[34] The challenge is to find appropriate ways, whether literary, theological or philosophical, to analyse such 'reciprocal' or 'dialogical' tensions between texts and traditions.

---

tearing the temple curtain (*Mark*, p. 950) or, as already noted, his view that Moses gave the command to divorce in order to 'incite the Pharisees to divorce their wives against God's ordinance' (*Mark*, p. 538).

[33] H. Davidson, *T.S. Eliot and Hermeneutics: Absence and Presence in the Waste Land* (Baton Rouge: Louisiana State University Press, 1985), p. 117.

[34] E.K. Broadhead, 'Reconfiguring Jesus: The Son of Man in Markan Perspective' in T.R. Hatina (ed.), *Biblical Interpretation in Early Christian Gospels*, p. 30.

4

~

Evoking an Isaiah framework for understanding Romans?*
Rom. 2.24

Introduction
~

A s with Mark's Gospel, Paul's letter to the Romans begins with the claim that his message ('the gospel of God') was 'promised beforehand through the prophets in the holy scriptures' (Rom. 1.2). However, unlike Mark, he does not cite a particular passage of Scripture at this point. His first explicit quotation comes in Rom. 1.17, where he cites Hab. 2.4 ('The one who is righteous will live by faith'). The next quotation is from Isa. 52.5 and appears in Rom. 2.24 ('The name of God is blasphemed among the Gentiles because of you'). Psalm quotations[1] take centre-stage in Romans 3 and much of Romans 4 is an exposition of Gen. 15.6.[2] There are only a few quotations in Romans 5–8[3] and 12–14[4] but in Romans 9–11 and 15, they appear with great frequency. Romans 9–11 contains half of the letter's sixty or so quotations,[5] a frequency of one quotation every three verses. Romans 15 contains six

---

* A slightly modified version of my article, 'Paul and Scripture in Dispute: Romans 2:24 as Test-case', *PIBA* (forthcoming).

[1] 3.4 (Ps. 51.4); 3.10-12 (Ps. 14.1-3); 3.13 (Ps. 5.9/140.3); 3.14 (Ps. 10.7); 3.15-17 (Isa. 59.7-8); 3.18 (Ps. 36.1).

[2] 4.3 (Gen. 15.6); 4.7-8 (Ps. 32.1-2); 4.9 (Gen. 15.6); 4.17 (Gen. 17.5); 4.18 (Gen. 17.5/15.5); 4.22 (Gen. 15.6).

[3] 7.7 (Exod. 20.17/Deut. 5.21); 8.36 (Ps. 44.22).

[4] 12.19 (Deut. 32.35); 12.20 (Prov. 25.21-2); 13.9 (Exod. 20.13-15/Lev. 19.18); 14.11 (Isa. 49.18/45.23).

[5] 9.7 (Gen. 21.12); 9.9 (Gen. 18.10,14); 9.12 (Gen. 25.23); 9.13 (Mal. 1.2-3); 9.15 (Exod. 33.19); 9.17 (Exod. 9.16); 9.25 (Hos. 2.23); 9.26 (Hos. 1.10); 9.27-8 (Isa. 10.22-3); 9.29 (Isa. 1.9); 9.33 (Isa. 8.14/28.16); 10.5 (Lev. 18.5); 10.6 (Deut. 9.4); 10.6-8 (Deut. 30.12-14); 10.11 (Isa. 28.16); 10.13 (Joel 2.32); 10.15 (Isa.

quotations,[6] a frequency of one quotation every six verses. It would appear that Paul is capable of constructing detailed arguments with extensive scriptural support (Romans 3–4, 9–11, 15) and without it (Romans 1–2, 5–8, 12–14). Given this variation,[7] how should a reader approach Paul's first quotation of Isaiah in Rom. 2.24?

Rom. 2.17-24

∼

> But if you call yourself a Jew and rely on the law and boast of your relation to God and know his will and determine what is best because you are instructed in the law, and if you are sure that you are a guide to the blind, a light to those who are in darkness, a corrector of the foolish, a teacher of children, having in the law the embodiment of knowledge and truth, you, then, that teach others, will you not teach yourself? While you preach against stealing, do you steal? You that forbid adultery, do you commit adultery? You that abhor idols, do you rob temples? You that boast in the law, do you dishonour God by breaking the law? For, as it is written, 'The name of God is blasphemed among the Gentiles because of you.'

In Rom. 2.17-24, it would appear that Paul is seeking to expose the hypocrisy of Jews who teach against stealing, adultery, desecration and law-breaking while guilty of the very same offences. If this is the case, it is hardly a controversial point and the majority of Jews would no doubt answer Paul's rhetorical questions[8] ('do you steal?'/'do you commit adultery?') with a resounding No! Furthermore, they would no doubt agree with Paul that such hypocritical behaviour, especially by those who call themselves teachers, should indeed be censured. What is controversial about this passage is that Paul's hypothetical addressee in v. 17 ('But if you call yourself a Jew') and the quotation from Isa. 52.5 ('The name of God is blasphemed among the Gentiles because of you [plural])', appears to indict Jews *in general* rather than just a few hypocritical teachers.[9] Charles H. Dodd famously argued that there is 'evidence

52.7); 10.16 (Isa. 53.1); 10.18 (Ps. 19.4); 10.19 (Deut. 32.21); 10.20 (Isa. 65.1); 10.21 (Isa. 65.2); 11.3 (1 Kgs 19.10,14); 11.4 (1 Kgs 19.18); 11.8 (Deut. 29.4/Isa. 29.10); 11.9-10 (Ps. 69.22-3); 11.26-7 (Isa. 59.20-21/27.9); 11.34 (Isa. 40.13); 11.35 (Job 41.11).

6 15.3 (Ps. 69.9); 15.9 (Ps. 18.49); 15.10 (Deut. 32.43); 15.11 (Ps. 117.1); 15.12 (Isa. 11.10); 15.21 (Isa. 52.15).

7 Even more pronounced if we consider the whole Pauline corpus, where scriptural quotations are concentrated in 1 and 2 Corinthians, Galatians and Romans, with comparatively few or none in the other books.

8 Lack of original punctuation means that they could be assertions but the majority of Bible translations and commentators take them as rhetorical questions.

9 Stowers denies this. He thinks that Paul's target is restricted to the 'pretentious teacher', who thinks Gentiles can be made acceptable to God by teaching them the commandments: '2.17-29 criticizes not Jews

enough of the terrible degradation of Jewish morals in the period preceding the Destruction of the Temple'[10] but few have found this convincing. As Charles K. Barrett notes, 'it is simply not true that the average Jewish missionary acted in this way. It was the purity of Jewish ethics ... which ... made the deepest impression on the Gentile world.'[11] Paul's accusations and the supporting quotation thus require some explanation.

Perhaps the most popular is what we might call the 'Sermon on the Mount' explanation, where the commandments are deepened to include thoughts and motivations.[12] Thus while it is true that only a few Jews are literally guilty of adultery and theft, no one can claim to be free from lust or envy. As Paul says at the end of the chapter, 'a person is a Jew who is one inwardly, and real circumcision is a matter of the heart' (2.29). This explains how Paul can conclude that 'all, both Jews and Greeks, are under the power of sin' (3.9), and support it by this string of quotations:

> There is no one who is righteous, not even one; there is no one who has understanding, there is no one who reeks God. All have turned aside, together they have become worthless; there is no one who shows kindness, there is not even one. Their throats are opened graves; they use their tongues to deceive. The venom of vipers is under their lips. Their mouths are full of cursing and bitterness. Their feet are swift to shed blood; ruin and misery are in their paths, and the way of peace they have not known. There is no fear of God before their eyes. (Rom. 3.10-18)[13]

The weakness of this position, however, is the emphasis placed on 'deeds' throughout Romans 2. The person who will receive eternal life is the one who is 'patiently doing good' (2.7), 'who does good' (2.10), who is not just a 'hearer' of the law but a 'doer' of it (2.13). The principle is stated in 2.6: 'For he will repay according to each one's deeds'. It would therefore seem more logical to interpret Rom. 2.29 ('a person is a Jew

---

or Judaism as such but teachers who in Paul's view stand in antithesis to his own gospel concerning the justification of the gentile peoples through the faithfulness of Jesus Christ' (p. 153). See S.K. Stowers, *A Rereading of Romans* (New Haven: Yale University Press, 1994).

[10] C.H. Dodd, *The Epistle to the Romans* (London: Fontana Books, 1959), p. 64. It is also the view of M. Black, *Romans* (London: Oliphants, 1973), who says 'the Jews abhorred idolatry, but were not above removing from pagan shrines their gold or silver idols for their own private use and profit' (pp. 59–60); S.J. Gathercole, *Where is Boasting? Early Jewish Soteriology and Paul's response in Romans 1-5* (Grand Rapids: Eerdmans, 2002), p. 212: 'Just as the gentiles are defiled with immorality and idolatry in 1:18-32, so Israel as a nation is subject to the same defilement because of these three transgressions: stealing, adultery, and robbery of pagan temples. The charge that Paul has made against the nation that his interlocutor represents is grounded in empirical evidence.'

[11] C.K. Barrett, *The Epistle to the Romans* (London: A. & C. Black, 1957), p. 56.

[12] So Barrett, *The Epistle to the Romans*, p. 56; C.E.B. Cranfield, *A Critical and Exegetical Commentary on the Epistle to the Romans* (ICC; Edinburgh: T&T Clark), I. p. 169.

[13] This string of quotations is not without its problems, since the majority of references come from Psalms which draw a distinction between the wicked (to whom the phrases are aimed) and the righteous. See S. Moyise, 'The Catena of Rom. 3.10-18', *ExpT* 106 (1995), 367–70.

who is one inwardly') in the light of this emphasis, rather than reinterpret all these references to 'deeds' as really meaning 'thoughts' or 'motivations'. Thus the true Jew, the one whose heart has been circumcised, is the one who not only hears the law but also obeys it (2.25).

A second explanation relies on the idea of corporate solidarity. Thus James D. G. Dunn thinks that Paul is contrasting 'the national pride of the typical Jew in the law, over against instances of transgression of the law by Jews'.[14] In other words, possession of the law is evidently not sufficient to keep the nation from transgression. Paul is not saying that every Jew is guilty of theft and adultery (literally or in thought) but that these sins are found among Jews as well as Gentiles: 'The argument is that the transgression of any individual Jew is enough to call in question the Jewish assumption that as a Jew he stands in a position of privilege and superiority before God as compared with the Gentile'.[15]

Support for such a view could come from the rhetorical questions in Rom. 3.1 ('Then what advantage has the Jew?') and Rom. 3.3 ('What if some were unfaithful?'). On the other hand, if Dunn is correct, one might have expected Paul's answers to these questions to be 'No advantage' to the first and 'Israel has forfeited her advantage' to the second. Instead, Paul answers: 'Much, in every way' to the first, and to the second, he denies the implication that the faithlessness of some nullifies the faithfulness of God. This is not fatal to Dunn's position, for the assertion of God's faithfulness has never implied Israel's exemption from judgement. But it does introduce a complexity to Paul's argument. The unfaithfulness of some Jews does not change the faithfulness of God but it does call into question any notion of 'privilege and superiority before God as compared with the Gentile'.

A third explanation draws on the fact that Israel's own prophets made precisely the same accusations against the people of Israel. Thus Timothy Berkley argues that Paul is drawing his accusations from Jer. 7.9-11; 9.23-4; Ezek. 36.16-27 and it is thus the authoritative verdict of Scripture. Just as Jeremiah looked forward to a new covenant and Ezekiel a new heart, Paul could assume that the present Israel was under the power of sin (Rom. 3.9) and therefore in need of salvation (Rom. 3.24-5). It is not 'contemporary examples of law-breaking that makes Paul's case … Paul concludes that Jews of his day remain guilty precisely because their guilt has already been established in the prophetic statements of scripture'.[16] If this is the case, it is strange that Paul does not make his dependence on Jeremiah and Ezekiel more explicit but as we shall see later, Berkley has an answer for this.

Turning now to the explicit quotation that is used to substantiate Paul's accusations, it is generally agreed that it is taken from Isa. 52.5, but since the Hebrew text lacks the phrases 'among the Gentiles' and 'because of you', it would appear that Paul

---

[14] J.D.G. Dunn, *Romans 1–8* (WBC, 38A; Dallas: Word Books 1988), p. 116.

[15] Dunn, *Romans 1–8*, p. 116.

[16] T.W. Berkley, *From a Broken Covenant to Circumcision of the Heart. Pauline Intertextual Exegesis in Romans 2.17-29* (SBLDS, 175; Atlanta: SBL, 2000), p. 139.

has the LXX in mind. Paul differs from the text printed by Rahlfs and Ziegler by omitting the phrase *dia pantos* ('continually') and changing the first person speech ('my name') to 'the name of God'. However, it is not these textual differences that have evoked discussion but the context of the passage in Isaiah:

> You were sold for nothing, and you shall be redeemed without money. For thus says the Lord GOD. Long ago, my people went down into Egypt to reside there as aliens; the Assyrian, too, has oppressed them without cause. Now therefore what am I doing here, says the LORD, seeing that my people are taken away without cause? Their rulers howl, says the LORD, *and continually, all day long, my name is despised.* Therefore my people shall know my name; therefore in that day they shall know that it is I who speak; here am I. (Isa. 52.3-6)

The despising (Hebrew) or blaspheming (Greek) of God's name is not because of the sinfulness of Israel but her piteous state ('reside there as aliens'/'oppressed them without cause'/'taken away without cause'). According to the translation above (NRSV), this piteous state is compounded by the 'howl' of her rulers, as Israel is forced into exile. An alternative reading is that it refers to the 'howl' of the Babylonian rulers as they celebrate their victory (NJB: 'their masters howl in triumph'). The LXX does not refer to 'rulers' at all but has taken the consonants (*msl*) as a verb and rendered it with *thaumazete* ('you marvel'). Byrne says: 'According to both the Hebrew original and the LXX it was Israel's *misfortune* that led to the reviling of God's name by the nations. Paul, however, interprets the LXX phrase "on account of you" as "because of your fault," thereby converting what was originally an oracle of compassion towards Israel into one of judgment.'[17] If Byrne is correct, then Paul appears to have taken a text out of context in order to support a rather dubious set of accusations. Is a more positive assessment possible?

Richard Hays

Richard Hays begins his chapter on 'Intertextual Echo in Romans' by first noting that Paul's opening sentence claims that the 'gospel of God' was 'promised beforehand through his prophets in the holy scriptures' (Rom. 1.1-2).[18] Hays takes this as a statement of intent and thus challenges the work of historical-critical scholars who interpret the text 'through hypotheses about the historical circumstances surrounding the letter's composition or about the social composition of the community to which it is addressed'.[19] For Hays, the most fruitful way of reading Romans is as an 'intertextual conversation between Paul and the voice of Scripture, that powerful ancestral

---

[17] B. Byrne, *Romans* (Collegeville: Liturgical Press, 1996), p. 101.

[18] R.B. Hays, *Echoes of Scripture in the Letters of Paul* (New Haven: Yale University Press, 1989), p. 34.

[19] Hays, *Echoes of Scripture*, p. 35.

presence with which Paul grapples'.[20] He thus assumes a high level of scriptural interaction throughout Romans and not just in those chapters where there are a large number of explicit quotations.

When he comes to the quotation in Rom. 2.24, he freely admits that from the standpoint of critical exegesis, it is a 'stunning misreading' of Isa. 52.5. The original context is clearly 'part of Yahweh's reassurance of Israel in exile' and it is 'precisely because Israel's oppressed condition allows the nations to despise the power of Israel's God, the people can trust more surely that God will reveal himself and act to vindicate his own name'. Paul has indeed 'transformed Isaiah's oracle of promise into a word of reproach'.[21] However, that is not the end of the matter, for Paul quotes Isa. 52.7 ('How beautiful are the feet of those who bring good news!') in Rom. 10.15, demonstrating that he knows this is an oracle of salvation. It is thus nonsense to assume that Paul was either unaware or had no interest in the context of Isa. 52.5. How then should we understand Paul's quotation in Rom. 2.24?

Though Hays calls it a 'provocative misreading', he insists that this is only provisional: 'If he reads Isa. 52:5 as a reproach, it is a reproach only in the same way that the historical event to which it refers was a reproach'.[22] As the argument of Romans unfolds, it becomes clear that Paul does not think that this reproach is final. By the time we get to Romans 11, we discover that the hardening of Israel is temporary and that in the end, 'all Israel will be saved' (11.26). At this point, the reader will understand that Paul's 'misreading' of Isa. 52.5 was temporary and that its message of hope is ultimately Paul's message also. In short, the meaning of Isa. 52.5 in Rom. 2.24 can be understood only from multiple readings of the text:

> The letter's rhetorical structure lures the reader into expecting Israel's final condemnation, but the later chapters undercut such an expectation, requiring the reader in subsequent encounters with the text to understand the Isaiah quotation more deeply in relation to its original prophetic context.[23]

Ross Wagner

Building on the work of Hays, J. Ross Wagner offers an impressive monograph on *Isaiah and Paul 'In Concert' in the Letter of Romans*. In his introduction, he states that 'to confine one's interpretive interests to what listeners might have picked up on the first hearing of Romans is to seriously underestimate the actual impact of this letter on a community that took its message seriously'.[24] He departs from Hays's sequential approach and focuses on Romans 9–11 and 15, occasionally stepping back to show

---

[20] Hays, *Echoes of Scripture*, pp. 34–5.

[21] Hays, *Echoes of Scripture*, p. 45.

[22] Hays, *Echoes of Scripture*, p. 45.

[23] Hays, *Echoes of Scripture*, p. 46.

[24] J. Ross Wagner, *Heralds of the Good News. Isaiah and Paul 'In Concert' in the Letter to the Romans* (Leiden: Brill, 2002), p. 39.

how Paul's arguments were anticipated earlier in the letter. This is not to assume that every argument develops in a linear or straightforward manner. Like Hays, Wagner acknowledges that the 'concert' of voices are sometimes in tension with one another. But they are heading toward a goal:

> By adopting as his own the stories Isaiah and his fellow scriptural witnesses tell about God's unquenchable love for his people, Paul is able to maintain confidently that the God who is now embracing Gentiles as his own will be faithful to redeem and restore his covenant people Israel as well, so that Jew and Gentile can with one voice laud the incomparable mercy of their God.[25]

Wagner comments on Paul's use of Isa. 52.5 in an excursus following his discussion of the use of Isa. 52.7 in Rom. 10.15. He acknowledges that, 'On the surface, Paul appears to be harsh and vindictive, completely oblivious to the original setting of Isaiah 52:5'.[26] However, the conclusion of his exposition so far (Rom. 9.1–10.15) leads him to assert that 'such an impression is mistaken' and this for two reasons. First, contrary to Hays and most commentators, Wagner thinks the context of Isa. 52.1-10 LXX *does* blame Israel for her piteous state in exile. It is the LXX, not Paul, which has added 'because of you' and 'among the Gentiles' and turned the statement about rulers howling into a complaint by Israel ('Because my people were taken away for nothing, you marvel and you cry aloud'). If anything, Paul has softened the blow by omitting the phrase 'continually'. Thus Wagner denies that Paul has taken Isa. 52.5 out of context.

Secondly, like Hays, Wagner uses Rom. 10.15 as evidence that Paul clearly knows the context of Isa. 52.5. The reason he did not quote from the following verses immediately is part of Paul's rhetorical strategy:

> Paul quotes Isaiah 52:5 in Romans 2:24 precisely because he believes that without the gospel, Israel is, figuratively speaking, still in exile, still in bondage to the power of sin like the rest of humanity (Rom 3:9). But just as the word of judgment in Isaiah 52:5 precedes the herald's announcement of the return from exile in Isaiah 52:7-10, so also Romans 2:24 precedes Paul's exposition of the gospel (the righteousness of God *for the Jew first* and also for the Greek [1:16]), in Romans 3:21ff.[27]

Wagner thus concludes that Paul has used both passages (Isa. 52.5 and 52.7) with their original setting in mind, a conclusion that coheres with the whole of his study:

---

[25] Wagner, *Heralds of the Good News*, p. 41.
[26] Wagner, *Heralds of the Good News*, p. 176.
[27] Wagner, *Heralds of the Good News*, p. 178.

Paul's citations and allusions to Isaiah are not plunder from random raids on Israel's sacred texts. Rather, they are the product of sustained and careful attention to the rhythms and cadences of individual passages as well as to larger themes and motifs that run throughout the prophet's oracles.[28]

Timothy Berkley

Timothy Berkley also draws on Hays's work but moves in a different direction. Hays frequently argues that allusions and echoes can be just as important for understanding Paul's thought as his explicit quotations. Berkley agrees but wishes to establish another category, which he calls 'reference texts'. These are the texts which have engaged Paul in serious reflection and exegesis and form the foundation of his arguments. However, they are largely hidden from view and have to be 'detected' (like allusions and echoes) by the application of various criteria. This has two important consequences: (1) Berkley does not think the explicit quotations are generally 'reference texts', that is, sites of exegesis; they are usually proof-texts to crown an argument reached on other grounds; (2) Even though 'reference texts' lie below the surface and therefore have to be 'detected', they do not lead to a variety of literary effects, as has been argued for allusion and echo. Berkley thinks they are in fact our clearest guide to Paul's intended meaning.

Applied to our passage, Berkley explains Paul's accusations by referring to Jer. 7.9-11; 9.23-4 and Ezek. 36.16-27. The first passage explains how Paul can accuse those who think their relationship to God will protect them from judgement. Not only does Paul derive the sins of theft, adultery and temple robbery from this passage, he also derives the accusation that such things are a slur on God's name:

> Will you *steal*, murder, commit *adultery*, swear falsely, make offerings to Baal, and go after other gods that you have not known, and then come and stand before me in this house, which is called by *my name*, and say, 'We are safe!' – only to go on doing all these abominations? Has this house, which is called by *my name*, become a den of *robbers* in your sight? (Jer. 7.9-11)

Secondly, the accusation about misplaced 'boasting' (Rom. 2.17, 23) derives from Jer. 9.23-4, where the word occurs no fewer than five times. Berkley argues that this text meets his conditions for a 'reference text' by common vocabulary, Paul's use of it elsewhere (1 Cor. 1.31; 2 Cor. 10.17) and the fact that both Paul and Jeremiah go on to contrast physical circumcision with circumcision of the heart (Jer. 9.25-6/Rom. 2.25-9):

> Thus says the LORD: Do not let the wise *boast* in their wisdom, do not let the mighty *boast* in their might, do not let the wealthy *boast* in their wealth; but let those who *boast boast* in

---

[28] Wagner, *Heralds of the Good News*, p. 356.

this, that they understand and know me, that I am the LORD … days are surely coming, says the LORD, when I will attend to all those who are *circumcised* only in the foreskin … For all these nations are uncircumcised, and all the house of Israel is *uncircumcised in heart.* (Jer. 9.23-26)

Thirdly, the accusation that God's name is 'profaned among the nations' comes from Ezek. 36.21-3, where the phrase occurs three times. This text qualifies as a 'reference text' by common vocabulary, Paul's use elsewhere (2 Cor. 3.3), links with the Jeremiah passages and the fact that both Ezekiel and Paul go on to contrast flesh and heart:

> But I had concern for *my holy name*, which the house of Israel had *profaned among the nations* to which they came. Therefore say to the house of Israel, Thus says the Lord GOD: It is not for your sake, O house of Israel, that I am about to act, but for the sake of *my holy name*, which you have *profaned among the nations* to which you came. I will sanctify my great name, which has been *profaned among the nations*, and which you have *profaned among them*; and the nations shall know that I am the LORD, says the Lord GOD, when through you I display my holiness before their eyes … *A new heart I will give you, and a new spirit I will put within you*; and I will remove from your body the heart of stone and give you a heart of flesh. (Ezek. 36.21-3, 26)

By establishing these 'reference texts', Berkley concludes that Paul can indict Israel of such sins because it stands written in Scripture. What then is the function of Isa. 52.5? Contrary to Hays and Wagner, Berkley does not think that Paul has seriously studied this verse for it does not meet his criteria as a 'reference text'. In his view, 'Isa 52.5 provides the concise declarative statement Paul needs in order for the quotation to conform to the form of his indictment, but it does not make Paul's point.'[29] It is Paul's exegesis of the 'reference texts' that establishes his point and since Isa. 52.5 shares common language with Ezek. 36.17-23, Paul's Jewish background would allow him to assume that Isa. 52.5 can be interpreted in the light of Ezek. 36.17-23.

A challenge from a reader-reception perspective
∽

Christopher Stanley challenges such 'maximal' interpretations of Paul's use of Scripture by appealing to the relatively low levels of literacy present in the first century and thus likely to be present in Paul's congregations. He states his objections in the form of nine assumptions made by such scholars as Hays and Wagner (he does not mention Berkley), most of which he regards as dubious. We can group them under three headings:

---

[29] Berkley, *From a Broken Covenant*, pp. 139–40.

1. Paul and his churches had ready access to the LXX

Stanley accuses scholars of referring to the LXX as if it were a single book that one could take down off the shelf and use at will. The reality in the first century was that there was no such collection. There were individual scrolls but these were expensive to produce and very few of Paul's congregations would have been able to read them anyway. Citing the work of Harris[30] and Gamble,[31] Stanley concludes that 'not more than a few individuals in Paul's churches, those recruited from the educated elite, would have been capable of reading and studying the Scriptures for themselves.'[32] This makes it highly unlikely that the majority of Christians would 'hear' the allusions and echoes that scholars such as Hays and Wagner propose. Indeed, with the possible exception of a few well-known sections of Scripture (Decalogue, exploits of Abraham, Moses and David), it would be almost impossible for the congregation to know the surrounding context of Paul's references, even if they were marked by a quotation formula.

2. It is necessary to know the 'original context' of a quotation to discern its present meaning

Scholars routinely explain Paul's quotations by reference to their original context and thus make the effectiveness of Paul's rhetoric dependent on the audience's ability to know the surrounding verses. This is precarious for a number of reasons. First, Paul takes his quotations from Greek translations rather than Hebrew scrolls and so talk of 'original context' is somewhat misleading. It might even be that Paul 'takes' his quotations from notebooks or collections since he hardly travelled around with dozens of scrolls. Secondly, given the fact that the so-called 'original meaning' of Paul's quotations continues to be a matter of debate, one can only assume that the majority of Paul's arguments were misunderstood (in some cases, until the publication of a particular scholar's monograph!). Thirdly, as a consequence of this, one would have to seriously question Paul's abilities as a communicator, as he clearly misjudged the capabilities of the majority of his audience.[33]

---

[30] W. Harris, *Ancient Literacy* (Cambridge, MA: Harvard University Press, 1989).

[31] H.Y. Gamble, *Books and Readers in the Early Church. A History of Early Christian Texts* (New Haven: Yale University Press, 1995).

[32] C.D. Stanley, *Arguing with Scripture. The Rhetoric of Quotations in the Letters of Paul* (New York and London: T&T Clark, 2004), p. 45.

[33] In a footnote, Stanley (p. 56 n.46) says: 'Ross Wagner rightly calls attention to Paul's "radical rereading" of Scripture (*Heralds*, 25, 82, 154, 271) that includes numerous "misreadings" of Scripture that Wagner labels "shocking" (82), "tendentious" (185, 212), "stunning" (205), and "brazen" (211), along with at least one passage where Paul "brazenly contradicts the scriptures, certainly as they were read by most of his contemporaries" (159). These observations pose serious problems for Wagner's presumption (*Heralds*, 36–37) that Paul expected the literate members of his congregation to retrace, approve, and explain the intricacies of his biblical argumentation to the majority who had little or no formal education and little free time to devote to the task. If this was Paul's intention, his decision to include so many "brazen misreadings of Scripture" in his letters must be judged a major rhetorical miscalculation.'

3. The meaning of a quotation is to be equated with the author's intention

According to Stanley, one of the 'central canons of contemporary literary criticism is that the "meaning" of a text resides not in the mind or intentions of the author, but in the dynamic interplay among author, text, and audience'.[34] Paul's letters are real communication between an author and a set of recipients. One cannot therefore discuss the 'meaning' of Paul's quotations without considering how the recipients would have understood them.

Stanley thus proposes a method whereby he will gauge how three different types of recipient would most likely have understood Paul's quotations. He defines them as follows:

- *An informed audience* – those who would know the original context of every one of Paul's quotations and be willing to engage in critical dialogue with him.
- *A competent audience* – those who know the broad outline of the scriptures but would not know the precise location of Paul's quotations.
- *A minimal audience* – those with little knowledge of the scriptures but would perhaps appreciate/admire those like Paul who appear to be skilled in them.[35]

When applied to Rom. 2.24, Stanley thinks the *informed audience* would have considered the original context of Isa. 52.5 and 'found themselves more confused than helped'.[36] They would immediately notice that the emphasis of the passage is deliverance not judgement and thus runs counter to the direction in which Paul is going. They would see what most commentators have seen – that God's name is blasphemed because of the piteous state of Israel, not her sin, leading them to 'question the entire premise of Paul's argument'.[37] The suggestion that Paul is reading Isa. 52.5 through the lens of Ezek. 36.20 is dismissed with the words: 'How could Paul have expected the Romans to know this in the absence of any explicit reference?'[38] For Stanley, not even an *informed audience* could rise to this level of sophistication.

The *competent audience* would have been saved from these problems as they would not have known the original context of the quotation. They would assume, as no doubt the majority of Christians do today, that it means what Paul says it means. Hypocritical Jews, like those denounced in Rom. 2.21-3, give God a bad name, as Scripture declares. Thus although the quotation does not support Paul's eventual conclusion that 'Jews as a class stand alongside Gentiles as the objects of God's

---

[34] Stanley, *Arguing with Scripture*, p. 59. The pioneer essay on this is usually taken to be W.K. Wimsatt and M.C. Beardsley, 'The Intentional Fallacy' in *idem, The Verbal Icon. Studies in the Meaning of Poetry* (Lexington: University of Kentucky Press, 1954), pp. 1–18.

[35] Stanley, *Arguing with Scripture*, pp. 68–9 (my summary).

[36] Stanley, *Arguing with Scripture*, p. 147.

[37] Stanley, *Arguing with Scripture*, p. 148.

[38] Stanley, *Arguing with Scripture*, p. 148 n.30. He refers to the earlier work of H. Schlier, *Der Römerbrief* (Freiberg: Herder, 1977), p. 87, rather than Berkley.

threatened Judgment', it does offer strong support for the 'more limited indictment in 2.17-23 of Jews who hypocritically neglect their covenantal obligations'.[39]

The *minimal audience* would be much the same. They would have no way of knowing the context of Isa. 52.5 or even where the quotation comes from. They would be impressed by Paul's ability to find quotations that support his argument, especially as it lays the foundation for his discussion of 'true' and 'false' Jews in the next section. Stanley suggests that since Paul could not rely on his apostolic authority to a church he has never visited, his mastery of the Scriptures would enhance his stature among the Romans and increase their openness to his argument.

Analysis

∽

As in our study of Mk 1.2-3, a great deal hinges on the question of whether quotations (or allusions) are thought to evoke larger frameworks of meaning. For Mk 1.2-3, the main arguments for a 'maximal' interpretation were: (1) the location of the quotation at the very beginning of the Gospel; (2) the frequent use of Isaiah elsewhere in Mark; (3) the reoccurrence of the 'on the way' theme in Mark 8–10; and (4) the familiarity of the Isaian new exodus motif in the first century. Two major obstacles lie in the path of arguing the same for the Isaiah quotation in Rom. 2.24. First, it does not come at the beginning of the book and indeed it is only when the reader reaches Romans 9–11 that he or she will discover the importance of Isaiah for Paul. Secondly, it is by no means obvious that Paul is giving the plain meaning of the verse and so it is more precarious to argue that it would immediately be connected with a well-known Isaian motif. For Berkley and Stanley, this is sufficient to dismiss the 'maximal' interpretation of Isa. 52.5 in Rom. 2.24.

For Hays and Wagner, the key evidence lies in Romans 9–11. Here, we not only find a sustained engagement with Scripture (on average, a quotation every three verses) but also a quotation from Isa. 52.7, demonstrating that Paul is certainly aware of the 'salvation' context of Isa. 52.5. If we began with chapters 9–11, as Wagner does in his book, Berkley would not be able to sustain his argument that quotations are not usually sites of exegesis for Paul but merely proof-texts. And in the two examples that Stanley discusses from these chapters (9.25-6; 10.19-21), he concludes that for the 'informed' audience, the quotations do indeed provide 'substantial support for the argument of Rom 9–11'.[40] The issue then is one of reading strategy. Should we evaluate the significance of the Isaiah quotation in Rom. 2.24 based *only* on what has gone before? Or should we allow the rest of the book to play a role in determining its meaning? Author-

---

[39] Stanley, *Arguing with Scripture*, p. 149.
[40] Stanley, *Arguing with Scripture*, p. 165.

centred studies will naturally choose the latter, since determining Paul's overall strategy is an important prerequisite for determining the function of any particular part. The fact that Paul quotes Isa. 52.5 in Rom. 2.24 and Isa. 52.7 in Rom. 10.15 must play some role in determining how Paul understood these texts. However, Hays believes this also has implications for the reader:

> The letter's rhetorical structure lures the reader into expecting Israel's final condemnation, but the later chapters undercut such an expectation, requiring the reader in subsequent encounters with the text to understand the Isaiah quotation more deeply in relation to its original prophetic context.[41]

The reader-centred scholar, however, will question Hays's confidence to state what a text will or will not achieve in its readers. Indeed, since Hays and Wagner are both putting forward innovative ways of reading Paul's quotations, it is evident that the text has not achieved these ends for the majority of its readers until their monographs were published. One detects a certain ambivalence here. On the one hand, Hays and Wagner can argue from Romans 9–11 and other places that Paul is a sophisticated interpreter of Scripture, thus adding credence to their particular proposals. And since Paul is clearly head and shoulders above most, if not all, of his readers in Rome, it would be foolhardy to limit our understanding of Paul to the capabilities of his first readers. On the other hand, both are reluctant to sever the connection between author and reader completely, for that would make Paul a poor communicator who seriously misjudged the abilities of his readers. Thus at the end of his exposition of Romans 9–11, Wagner can claim that Paul:

> taps into a broad and deep stream of thought that is characteristic of Isaiah's vision – a stream of thought, moreover, that is shared by numerous other prophetic texts and that is kept vigorously alive in later Jewish literature. Paul could probably assume that many of his listeners in Rome would be familiar with the broad outlines of this widely-diffused eschatological hope ...[42]

In a different way, Stanley is also reluctant to sever the connection between author and reader. Although his emphasis is on what his three types of first-century reader might have understood by Paul's words, he nevertheless uses this to make judgements about Paul's thinking and intentions. For example, he denies that Paul uses sophisticated arguments that require knowledge of the surrounding context because very few of his readers would have had such knowledge. Instead, by 'framing his quotations in such a way that their "meaning" could be determined from the context of his letter, Paul did his best to insure that his quotations would be under-

---

[41] Hays, *Echoes of Scripture*, p. 46.
[42] Wagner, *Heralds of the Good News*, p. 297.

stood in the manner in which he intended them'.[43] Thus although Stanley is more willing than Hays or Wagner to entertain the idea that Paul may have been a poor communicator who misjudged the capabilities of his recipients, his view of Paul is largely shaped by his understanding of the competence of his readers.

I would suggest that there is an element of special pleading in both positions. For Hays and Wagner, the capabilities of Paul's readers are surreptitiously increased by using such expressions as 'the broad outlines of this widely-diffused eschatological hope'. But as Stanley points out, such 'broad outlines' would hardly be sufficient for his readers to understand the 'numerous "misreadings" of Scripture that Wagner labels "shocking" (82), "tendentious" (185, 212), "stunning" (205), and "brazen" (211)'.[44] Although it is true that the LXX has made a judgemental interpretation of Isa. 52.5 more plausible, two points stand in the way of accepting Wagner's argument that 'in the context of 52.1-10, the words Paul quotes in Romans 2.24 stand as a word of judgment on Israel, laying the blame for their exile squarely on their shoulders'.[45] The first is the pathos used to describe Israel's plight. They were 'sold for nothing (*dōrean*)' (v. 3), lived as aliens in Egypt (v. 4a), forcibly taken by the Assyrians (v. 4b), and have now been 'taken away without cause (*dōrean*)' (v. 5). Indeed, it is this emphasis that has led some scholars to suggest that vv. 4-6 are an interpolation.[46]

The second point is that textually, this is an extremely difficult passage, as can be seen by the diversity of modern translations and interpretations. It is unclear from the Hebrew text whether the 'rulers' pertain to Israel or to the Babylonians, and correspondingly, whether they howl with anguish or with triumph. This is hardly made clearer by the LXX's change from a noun ('rulers') to a verb ('you marvel'), a change not followed by any of the early Greek versions.[47] Both points make it difficult to accept that the Christians of Rome would hear the theme of 'eschatological hope' as Rom. 2.24 is read out to them.

On the other hand, Stanley's reconstruction of even his 'informed' reader appears to be deliberately distant from Paul, almost closer to a modern historical critic than a first-century Christian. Such a reader apparently knows nothing about Jewish or Christian exegesis and one wonders how they arrived at their 'informed' status. If they are former members of a synagogue, they would be familiar with the Jewish exegetical techniques that Hays, Wagner and Berkeley often use to explain what Paul is doing. If they had no such background, they would presumably have been taught the Christian interpretation of texts from the beginning. Though we know very little about early catechetical instruction, we must assume that the contents of the New Testament bear *some* relationship to what was being taught in the churches. Stanley is right to remind

---

[43] Stanley, _Arguing with Scripture_, p. 176.

[44] See note 33 (Stanley, _Arguing with Scripture_, p. 56 n.46).

[45] Wagner, _Heralds of the Good News_, p. 177.

[46] So C. Westerman, _Isaiah 40–66_ (OTL; London: SCM, 1969), p. 248.

[47] Aquila and Symmachus have _exousiazontes_ ('those exercising authority'), while Theodotion has _archontes_ ('those exercising rule').

us that we should not assume an expertise in Scripture comparable to Paul but neither should we expect a reader who would be resistant to Paul's Christian interpretation of texts. Judging by the rest of the New Testament, they would be predisposed to find Christ and their community in the Scriptures, for they would have been taught this from the beginning of their instruction.

Berkley occupies an interesting position in this debate in that he is seeking to retrieve Paul's *hidden* exegetical activity in order to explain the train of thought in Rom. 2.17-29. There is thus a deliberate gap between author and reader because Paul has not made explicit in his text the manner in which he arrived at his conclusions. Such a position could thus allow Hays and Wagner to pursue their sophisticated under-standings of Paul, while allowing Stanley to pursue the task of determining what Paul's first readers would/could have made of the text. Paul would not be guilty of miscalcu-lating the abilities of his audience because he never intended them to understand his prior exegetical activity. It is enough that they follow the gist of his arguments and accept his conclusions.

Three challenges can be directed to this, however. First, if it is difficult to go behind Paul's explicit quotations to reconstruct his probable thinking, it is even more difficult to go behind allusions and echoes. By definition, the coincidence of vocabulary is much less with allusions and echoes and so more reliance is placed on other factors, such as common themes. But can Jer. 9.23-4 really be said to have the same theme as Rom. 2.17-4? Paul's accusation is that they boast in their relationship with God while breaking the law. Jer. 9.23-4 exhorts the Jews not to boast in wisdom or wealth but to boast in their relationship with God. It could well be an allusion in the traditional sense but it is difficult to see why it *must* be a site of exegetical activity.

This leads to the second point, which is that it is difficult to understand why Berkley downplays the role of Isa. 52.5 when Isa. 52.7 is quoted later in the letter. Indeed, it is difficult to see why he downplays the role of quotations generally, when Romans contains over sixty of them. They cannot all be summarizing proof-texts!

Thirdly, the issue of reader competence is both solved and exacerbated in Berkley's account of Paul's hidden exegesis. For example, in discussing Rom. 2.17 ('If you call yourself a Jew'), he maintains that the 'address *Ioudaios* now takes on a significance it would not have if the OT texts Paul is drawing from were not taken into consideration'.[48] But this is problematic since these texts are part of Paul's hidden exegesis and thus hidden from the reader. They could not, therefore, be expected to follow what Paul is doing here. The footnote reveals Berkeley's ambivalence at this point:

> This is not to assume that the original readers were aware of Paul's references to those texts. But for those who were aware they give a greater understanding of how this passage fits into the larger whole of the epistle.[49]

---

[48] Berkley, *From a Broken Covenant*, p. 119.
[49] Berkley, *From a Broken Covenant*, p. 119 n.30.

To my mind, this almost invisible footnote undermines his whole position. He has been arguing throughout that the key exegetical reference texts have been deliberately kept from view. To add a caveat at this point, that readers would gain so much more if they recognized the origin of these texts, suggests that Berkley has not done justice to Paul's explicit quotations, where such direction is given. Though Stanley is probably correct that few of the Christians in Rome would immediately identify Paul's quotation in Rom. 2.24, the explicit formula ('as it is written') could well act as a prompt to discover it (initially, perhaps, by asking the lector). If this is so, then Berkley's suggestion that Paul has deliberately hidden his key exegetical texts seems perverse. Why keep in the background something that would have greatly enhanced the understanding of his readers?

Conclusion

In conclusion, rather than starting with either an exclusively author-centred or exclusively reader-centred approach and then vaguely suggesting that the other would have led to much the same conclusions, it would be better to develop an approach that takes into account both author and reader perspectives from the outset. Studies of the rest of the Pauline corpus, though not *determining* the meaning of any particular passage in Romans, will offer some guidance by reconstructing the major contours of his thought. On the other hand, studies in the reception of Romans down the ages will show how real readers have interpreted the book in their cultural setting, offering some clues as to how it might have been understood by its original recipients. Though scholars differ as to whether they (primarily) locate the meaning of a text in a reconstruction of the author's intentions, in the dynamics of the text itself, or in its reception in a community of readers, this chapter has shown that a relationship between them is unavoidable. Scholars who focus on Paul's intention inevitably make assumptions about the reader, while scholars who focus on the reader inevitably speak about how the author (or the text) guides the reader. There is nothing to be gained and plenty to be lost by exclusively focusing on one or the other.

5

Evoking a hermeneutical principle for interpreting Romans?
Rom. 1.16-17

Introduction
~

As we saw in the last chapter, Paul makes extensive use of Isaiah in Romans and a case can be made that these are not isolated proof-texts but belong to an overall narrative framework. On the other hand, it was noted that most of Paul's references come in Romans 9–11 (and 15), raising the question of whether a text appearing in Rom. 2.24 would be likely to evoke such a framework, at least on a first hearing of the letter. The quotation of Hab. 2.4 in Rom. 1.17 raises a different issue. Coming shortly after Paul's opening statement that 'the gospel of God' was 'promised beforehand through his prophets in the holy scriptures' (Rom. 1.2), it occupies a pivotal position in Romans (like Isa. 40.3 in Mk 1.3). After the introductory greetings (Rom. 1.1-15), Paul begins the main body of the letter with the following programmatic statement:

> For I am not ashamed of the gospel; it is the power of God for salvation to everyone who has faith, to the Jew first and also to the Greek. For in it the righteousness of God is revealed through faith for faith; as it is written, 'The one who is righteous will live by faith' (*ho de dikaios ek pisteōs zēsetai*).
> (Rom. 1.16-17)

There is considerable correspondence between the key terms of Paul's formulation (salvation, righteousness, faith) and the quotation from Habakkuk. The correspondence is closest with the noun 'faith', which occurs twice in Paul's formulation ('through faith for faith'), along with the corresponding verb ('to everyone who has faith'). It is noteworthy that the phrase translated 'through faith' (*ek pisteōs*) is a favourite of Paul's in Romans and Galatians,[1] precisely those letters where Hab. 2.4 is quoted. Hab. 2.4 is also the only verse in the LXX where the phrase is found. Either Paul was attracted to Hab. 2.4 because it contained one of his key phrases or Hab. 2.4 has been influential in Paul's formulation of the gospel message.

The noun 'righteousness' is paralleled by the adjective 'righteous', which presumably refers to one who possesses or exhibits righteousness. In Paul's formulation, it is the 'righteousness of God' that is revealed, but in Hab. 2.4 it is the righteousness of a person that is in mind. This could be seen as a major difference between Paul and Habakkuk and hence an argument that the text is not fundamental to Paul's thinking but merely a convenient proof-text. Such a view could also draw on the fact that Paul does not quote from any other verse of Habakkuk and according to NA[27], neither are there any allusions.[2] On the other hand, the importance of Hab. 2.4 for Paul can be shown by the fact that he cites it again in Gal. 3.11, where it also plays a pivotal role in his argument (see next chapter). Furthermore, many commentators and theologians have argued for a close relationship between the 'righteousness of God' and the 'righteousness of the individual' in Paul's thought and so the 'discrepancy' might not be as significant as it initially appears.

The noun 'salvation' does not occur in Hab. 2.4, though it is possible that Paul intends a correspondence with Habakkuk's verb 'to live'. Paul uses this verb frequently in Romans[3] and in contexts where it clearly means or implies 'salvation' (e.g. Rom. 8.13). Thus it could be argued that Paul has chosen the noun 'salvation' to correspond to Habakkuk's use of the verb 'to live'. On the other hand, one could equally argue that had this been Paul's intention, he could have used the noun 'life' and made the connection more obvious.[4] By using the word 'salvation' instead of Habakkuk's verb 'to live', a reader is more likely to experience dissonance with the Habakkuk quotation than conformity. Habakkuk says that the righteous person should live by faith but Paul has introduced the (Christian) concept of salvation.

Thus while it can be shown that there is a fair correspondence between the key themes of Paul's formulation of the gospel (salvation, righteousness, faith) and the text of Hab. 2.4 (to live, righteous, faith), there are also some significant differences. This becomes even more complicated when we consider the textual history of Hab. 2.4. The MT has a masculine third person suffix on the noun (*emunah*) and thus the text means, 'but the righteous person will live by *his* faith/fulness'. The Hebrew verb has connotations of 'firmness, steadfastness, fidelity'[5] and if one is to translate it by

---

[1] Rom. 1.17; 3.26, 30; 4.16; 5.1; 9.30, 32; 10.6; 14.23; Gal. 2.16; 3.7, 8, 9, 11, 12, 22, 24; 5.5.

[2] NA[27] records three quotations and ten allusions from Habakkuk in the New Testament but only the explicit quotation of Hab. 2.4 (Rom. 1.17; Gal. 3.11) is found in Paul.

[3] Rom. 6.2, 10, 11, 13; 7.1, 2, 3, 9; 8.12, 13; 9.26; 10.5; 12.1; 14.7, 8, 9, 11.

[4] As perhaps he does in Rom. 5.18 ('so one man's act of righteousness leads to justification and life for all'), 5.21 ('so grace might also exercise dominion through justification leading to eternal life') and 8.13 ('if by the Spirit you put to death the deeds of the body, you will live').

[5] BDB, '*emunah*'.

a single word, 'faithfulness' (so NJB) is preferable to 'faith'. As such, it is a human attribute, though in the context of Habakkuk, it clearly implies an object ('faithfulness to God'). The masculine suffix appears to be supported by the Qumran commentary (*1QpHab*), for although the lemma is missing from the bottom of column 7, the interpretation at the beginning of the next column applies it to 'those who observe the law in the house of Judah ... because of *their* suffering and because of *their* faith in the teacher of righteousness'.

Whether by accident or design, the majority of LXX manuscripts omit the third person pronoun 'his' and include a first person pronoun 'my'.[6] In manuscripts ℵ, B, Q, V and W*, the pronoun comes after *ek pisteōs* and should probably be rendered 'but the righteous one shall live by *my* faithfulness' (*ho de dikaios ek pisteōs mou zēsetai*). Dietrich-Alex Koch[7] thinks this is the oldest and original form of the LXX and is the easiest to understand. It would simply mean that the LXX translator mistook a final *wah* for a final *yod*. Manuscripts A and C are more difficult to explain, however, for they place the pronoun after *dikaios*, probably with the meaning, 'but *my* righteous one will live by faithfulness', though word order is not decisive in an inflected language like Greek. According to NA[27], this is the form quoted in Heb. 10.38.[8]

Paul quotes the text without first or third person pronouns (both here and in Gal. 3.11).[9] This could be because he wishes to rule out these interpretations and pave the way for his own. Thus Joseph A. Fitzmyer says that Paul 'not only drops the poss. pron. altogether, but understands *pistis* in his own sense of "faith," and "life" not as deliverance from invasion and death, but as a share in the risen life of Christ ... In this way Paul cites the prophet Habakkuk to support the theme of his letter.'[10] Rhetorically speaking, perhaps he does not wish his readers to raise such questions as 'who are God's righteous?' or 'to whom is God promising faithfulness?' at this point in the letter. On the other hand, it could be that he does not wish to limit his interpretation of the text to one or other of these interpretative options. Thus while Dunn agrees with Fitzmyer that omitting the pronouns allows Paul to give 'faith' a distinctive Christian meaning, he denies that Paul is trying to exclude all previous meanings: 'In the tradition of Jewish exegesis Paul would not necessarily want to narrow the meaning to *exclude* other meanings self-evident in the text forms used

[6] The exception is manuscript 763*. The reading in the Minor Prophets scroll found at Nahal Hever agrees with the Hebrew.

[7] D.-A. Koch, 'Der Text von Hab 2.4b in der Septuaginta und im Neuen Testament', *ZNW* 76 (1985), pp. 68–85.

[8] Supported by p[46]ℵ A H* 33. 1739 *pc* lat sa bo[ms]; Cl. A few manuscripts place the pronoun after *ek pisteōs* (D* *pc* µ sy) but the majority omit the pronoun altogether, probably influenced by the Pauline texts.

[9] NA[27] only lists C* as including 'my' in Rom. 1.17 and no manuscripts for Gal. 3.11.

[10] J. Fitzmyer, *Romans: A New Translation with Introduction and Commentary* (AB, 33; New York: Doubleday, 1992), p. 265.

elsewhere, so much as to extend and broaden the meaning to include the sense he was most concerned to bring out.'[11] This of course depends on whether his readers would have known or had access to more than one form of the text and would thus have spotted the discrepancy.

Despite being more succinct than the Greek or Hebrew traditions, Paul's quotation nevertheless contains ambiguities of its own. First, there is dispute as to whether the phrase 'through faith' should be taken with 'righteous', as in RSV ('He who through faith is righteous shall live') or with 'live', as in NRSV ('The one who is righteous will live by faith'). Some commentators think this can be decisively answered by a combination of grammar, style and content but since both options are supported by a significant number of scholars, it would appear that this is not the case. What Paul has written is ambiguous, whether intentionally or by accident.[12]

Secondly, it has generally been assumed that Paul took the adjective *ho dikaios* ('the righteous one') to refer to Christian believers but Anthony Hanson has suggested that Paul could have read the LXX text as a messianic prophecy.[13] Not only is 'The Righteous One' used as a messianic title in *1 Enoch* 38.2, but it is also applied to Jesus in Acts 3.14, 7.52 and 22.14, and possibly also in 1 Pet. 3.18 and 1 Jn 2.1, though the definite article is lacking in the last two references. Given this background, Hanson suggests that Paul could have taken the masculine pronoun in LXX Hab. 2.3 to refer to a person ('if *he* delays, wait for *him*'), rather than the vision, since unlike the Hebrew, the word 'vision' in Greek (*horasis*) is feminine rather than masculine. That being so, the most natural way of taking the participle *erchomenos* ('coming') in the next phrase is also about a person, rather than the vision. Hanson thus translates LXX Hab. 2.3-4:[14]

dioti eti horasis eis kairon kai	Because the vision still awaits its time, and
anatelei eis peras kai ouk eis kenon	will rise to its fulfilment and not be in vain;
ean husterēsē hupomeinon auton	If he delays, wait for him,
hoti erchomenos hēxei	because a Coming One[15] will arrive
kai ou mē chronisē	and will not linger,
ean hupsteilētai	if he draws back,
ouk eudokei hē psuchē mou en autō	my soul will have no pleasure in him;
ho de dikaios ek pisteōs mou zēsetai	but the Righteous One shall live by my faith

---

[11] Dunn, *Romans 1–8*, p. 45.

[12] Having named a list of scholars who support one or other of these readings, Dunn (*Romans 1–8*, p. 46) asks: 'how could Paul have expected his readers to opt one way or other without clearer guidance?'

[13] A.T. Hanson, *Studies in Paul's Technique and Theology* (London: SPCK, 1974), pp. 39–45.

[14] Hanson, *Studies in Paul's Technique and Theology*, p. 42.

[15] The quotation of Hab. 2.3-4 in Heb. 10.37 actually adds the definite article: 'The coming one will come and will not delay', though the author is not interested in exploiting the messianic potential of the text. See further R. Gheorghita, *The Role of the Septuagint in Hebrews* (WUNT, 2.160; Tübingen: Mohr Siebeck, 2003), pp. 180–224.

This suggestion has been taken up by Hays, who argues that Paul's initial statement that, the 'gospel of God' which was 'promised beforehand through his prophets' (Rom. 1.1\-2), is said to concern his 'Son ... Jesus Christ, our Lord' (Rom. 1.3-4). When we thus encounter Paul's first quotation from the prophets, we would naturally expect it to be about his Son, rather than those who believe in his Son. Hays defends this view by arguing that Paul consistently uses the term *pistis Iēsou* as a subjective genitive ('faith/fulness of Jesus') rather than an objective genitive ('faith in Jesus'), a view that now musters considerable support.[16] In confirmation, he notes that in Rom. 5.18-19, right-eousness and life flow to all because of the 'righteous deed' of Jesus. He acknowledges that the actual title 'Righteous one' is not used here and so

> None of these considerations is entirely compelling, but the strongly apocalyptic theological context of Romans 1 creates at least a presumption in favor of the messianic exegesis of Hab. 2.4 as the interpretation that would have been most readily at hand for Paul and that makes the best sense out of the letter's argument.[17]

The question for this chapter then is whether a six-word quotation from Hab. 2.4 can bear the theological weight that is being placed on it, especially when Paul shows no other interest in the book of Habakkuk. We will focus on three writers who each argue for the importance of Hab. 2.4 in Paul's thinking, but offer very different accounts of its function. We will begin with Dunn, who argues that the omission of both first and third person pronouns is not intended to limit the meaning of the quoted text but in keeping with contemporary Jewish exegesis, facilitates a maximal interpretation by evoking both the Greek and Hebrew traditions. We will then consider Hays's view that the quotation is intended to evoke the theodicy theme of Habakkuk, a significant factor in concluding that Romans is more about defending God's faithfulness than explaining how individuals can be saved. Thirdly, we will consider Francis Watson's argument in *Paul and the Hermeneutics of Faith*[18] that the anonymous formula that introduces the quotation ('as it is written') does not point specifically to the book of Habakkuk but is being used as a hermeneutical principle. Paul sees in the Habakkuk text a prophetic statement by which he will (controver-sially) interpret the law as divided against itself.

---

[16] In the second edition of Hays's 1983 work, he notes an impressive list of scholars who have now adopted the subjective genitive interpretation: B. Byrne, D. Campbell, C.B. Cousar, C.A. Davis, G.N. Davies, T.L. Donaldson, L. Gaston, B.R. Gaventa, M.D. Hooker, G. Howard, L.T. Johnson, L.E. Keck, B.W. Longenecker, R.N. Longenecker, J.L. Martyn, F.J. Matera, P.T. O'Brian, M.L. Soards, S.K. Stowers, B. Witherington, S.K. Williams, N.T. Wright. A critique by J.D.G. Dunn is included as an appendix. See R.B. Hays, *The Faith of Jesus Christ. The Narrative Substructure of Galatians 3:1-4:11* (2nd edn; Michigan: Eerdmans, 2002).

[17] R.B. Hays, '"The Righteous One" as Eschatological Deliverer: A Case Study in Paul's Apocalyptic Hermeneutics' in J. Marcus and M.L. Soards (eds), *Apocalyptic and the New Testament: Essays in Honor of J. Louis Martyn* (JSNTSup, 24; Sheffield: JSOT Press, 1988), p. 209.

[18] F. Watson, *Paul and the Hermeneutics of Faith* (London and New York: T&T Clark, 2004).

The Function of Hab. 2.4 in Rom. 1.17

&

Evoking the tradition history of Hab. 2.4

As one would expect in a commentary, Dunn explores the meaning of Rom. 1.16-
17a before he discusses the function of the quotation in Rom. 1.17b. He links 'not
ashamed' with various Psalms (35.26; 40.14-15; 69.19; 71.13; 119.6) and the Jesus
tradition preserved in Mk 8.38/Lk. 9.26. The 'power of God' is particularly understood in the light of 1 and 2 Corinthians; it is the transforming force of the gospel,
both to convert to a new way of life and to sustain it. This contrasts with the magical
connotations of the phrase found in many Jewish writings. Salvation is understood
in the light of Christian tradition as 'the end product of God's good purpose for
humankind',[19] citing Mark and Acts, as well as other Pauline letters. He points out
that the present tense 'to all who believe' is typical of Paul (examples from Romans,
1 and 2 Corinthians, Galatians, Philippians and 1 Thessalonians) but alerts the
reader that we should see v. 17 for the meaning of *pistis* ('faith').

As expected, there is a lengthy discussion of the phrase 'righteousness of God',
which begins with the advice that we must 'penetrate through Paul's Greek language
in order to understand it in the light of his Jewish background and training'.[20] Thus
'God is "righteous" when he fulfills the obligations he took upon himself to be
Israel's God, that is, to rescue Israel and punish Israel's enemies ... [it is] God's
activity in drawing into and sustaining within [a] covenant relationship'.[21] It is
therefore an error to view objective interpretations (God's gift of righteousness) and
subjective interpretations (God's righteous being or activity) as mutually exclusive.
Where Paul differs from his Jewish heritage is in the 'conviction that the covenantal
framework of God's righteousness has to be understood afresh in terms of faith – "to
all who believe, Jew first but also Gentile"'.[22]

After stating that Paul understands 'faith' (*pistis*) as both 'that which can be
trusted' and 'trust itself', Dunn offers seven reasons for taking the phrase 'from faith
to faith' (*ek pisteōs eis pistin*) as referring to its origin (*ek*) in God's *faithfulness* and
its goal (*eis*) in human *faith*, deliberately exploiting the dual meaning of the word.
He then notes that although the citation formula ('as it is written') is a well-known
legal expression, Paul uses it 'to document or prove an assertion just made'.[23] As for
the cited text, Dunn notes that Hab. 2.4 is known to us in four different traditions
(MT, LXX, Paul, Hebrews) and insists that Paul's omission of both first and third

[19] Dunn, *Romans 1–8*, p. 39.
[20] Dunn, *Romans 1–8*, p. 40.
[21] Dunn, *Romans 1–8*, p. 41.
[22] Dunn, *Romans 1–8*, p. 42.
[23] Dunn, *Romans 1–8*, p. 44.

person pronouns is not intended to limit the meaning of the text but rather to 'read *as much meaning* into the verse as possible – just what we would expect a Jewish exegete, especially a Pharisee, to do with a text of Scripture':[24]

> In short, Paul probably intends the Habakkuk quotation to be understood with a richness of meaning which can embrace within it the fuller understanding of the gospel for which Paul stands, in its continuity with the revelation to Israel. He who is maintained within or has been brought into the relationship with God which brings about salvation, by the outreach of God's faithfulness to his own faith, shall experience the fullness of life which God intended for humankind as he lives in the dependence of faith on the continuing faithfulness of God.[25]

Evoking the theodicy motif of Hab. 2.4

Hays begins by noting that all of Paul's key terms in Rom. 1.16-17 echo the language of the LXX. Thus before discussing the function of Hab. 2.4, he notes how such texts as Ps. 98:2-3, Isa. 51.4-5 and 52.10 promise a 'future universal manifestation of God's salvation and righteousness'[26] that extends to the Gentiles. This also explains Paul's otherwise perplexing reference to not being 'ashamed'. He is not referring to a natural human embarrassment when speaking about religion, as some commentators have suggested (he cites Cranfield). Rather, Paul is echoing the language of the lament psalms and texts such as Isa. 50.7-8: 'I know that I shall not be put to shame; he who vindicates me (*ho dikaiōsas me*) is near'.

It is from this background that the quotation of Hab. 2.4 must be understood. Hays notes that most commentators have assumed that Paul is using Hab. 2.4 as a proof-text for his doctrine of 'justification by faith', with almost complete disregard for its original setting. But against the background of the texts just mentioned, Hab. 2.4 is now seen as supremely relevant, for it is a *locus classicus* for the issue of theodicy. Facing the calamity of a Babylonian invasion, Habakkuk cries out, 'why do you look on the treacherous, and are silent when the wicked swallow those more righteous than they?' (Hab. 1.13). Demanding an answer from God, he positions himself on a rampart:

> I will stand at my watchpost, and station myself on the rampart; I will keep watch to see what he will say to me, and what he will answer concerning my complaint. Then the LORD answered me and said: Write the vision; make it plain on tablets, so that a runner may read it. For there is still a vision for the appointed time; it speaks of the end, and does not lie. If it seems to tarry, wait for it; it will surely come, it will not delay. Look at the proud! Their spirit is not right in them, but the righteous live by their faith. (Hab. 2.1-4)

[24] Dunn, *Romans 1–8*, p. 48.
[25] Dunn, *Romans 1–8*, p. 49.
[26] Hays, *Echoes of Scripture*, p. 37.

The answer given by the Hebrew text is for the righteous person to remain faithful to God, despite such difficult circumstances. There is a vision for the end and it is presumably a vision of salvation but it is not for the present. Therefore the righteous person must wait with patience, demonstrating faithfulness or loyalty to God's promises. The implication, of course, is that God will prove faithful and the LXX has made this more explicit by substituting the third person pronoun for a first person one ('The righteous one shall live by *my* faithfulness'). By omitting either pronoun, Paul has allowed an ambiguity which, according to Hays, serves his purposes very well:

> The ambiguity thus created allows the echoed oracle to serve simultaneously as a warrant for two different claims that Paul has made in his keynote formulation of the gospel: in the gospel *God's own righteousness* is revealed; and the gospel is the power of God for salvation *to everyone who believes*. Around these foci Paul plots the ellipse of his argument.[27]

Hays recognizes that there is a considerable difference between the context of Habakkuk and the context of Paul's argument in Romans. Habakkuk is concerned about the 'military domination of the Chaldeans … over an impotent Israel', whereas Paul's concern is the 'apparent usurpation of Israel's favored covenant status by congregations of uncircumcised Gentile Christians'.[28] In that sense, the echo is 'off-center' and thus metaphorical (a trope). But there is sufficient similarity to deny that Paul is 'circumventing the text's original referential sense'. Instead, Hays maintains that Paul 'draws on that sense – indeed, on at least two different traditional readings of it – as a source of symbolic resonance for his affirmation of the justice of God's ways in the present time'.[29]

Evoking a hermeneutical principle

Watson begins his careful study of *Paul and the Hermeneutics of Faith* by drawing attention to the key role that Hab. 2.4 plays in Rom. 1.17. He notes that Paul frequently contextualizes his quotations by naming either the speaker (Moses, David, Isaiah, Hosea) or the recipient (Abraham, Rebecca, Moses, Pharaoh, Elijah) and that some commentators have used this to suggest that the anonymous formula ('it is written') implies that Hab. 2.4 is simply a secondary proof-text. Watson agrees that the anonymous formula does not draw attention to the book of Habakkuk and indeed adds that its function in Romans does not require the reader to have even

---

[27] Hays, *Echoes of Scripture*, pp. 40–41.
[28] Hays, *Echoes of Scripture*, p. 40.
[29] Hays, *Echoes of Scripture*, p. 41. Oddly, the messianic interpretation of Hab. 2.4 does not figure in Hays's exposition in *Echoes of Scripture*.

heard of the prophet. What is important for Paul is the assertion that these words are from a body of authoritative writings and thus represent the truth of Scripture.[30]

However, Watson does not deduce from this that the words are of secondary importance to Paul, for there is an unusually close lexical correspondence between assertion and citation. Normally when Paul cites texts, there is a close semantic correspondence between assertion and Scripture text but not a close lexical correspondence, for that would lead to redundant repetition. He cites Rom. 3.9-10 as typical of Paul's method. Paul asserts that 'we have already charged that all, both Jews and Greeks, are under the power of sin' and then supports it ('as it is written') by the text, 'There is no one who is righteous, not even one'. Conceptually, the cited text is in close agreement with the assertion but there is virtually no lexical correspondence. It is immediately obvious that Rom. 1.16-17 is quite different.[31] The particular genitive expression (*ek pisteōs*) is unlikely to have been formulated by Paul and only later discovered in Hab. 2.4. In fact, the assertion of Rom. 1.17a is virtually a paraphrase of Hab. 2.4: '*The one who is righteous* (that is, with a *righteousness* of God, revealed in the gospel) *by faith* (since this righteousness is received *by faith* and is intended for faith) *will live*'.[32] He notes the irony that many scholars have searched for an interpretative background for understanding the 'righteousness of God' in Deutero-Isaiah, the Psalms and the Qumran *Hodayot* but have largely ignored Paul's explicit statement that it is rooted in the cited text. According to Watson, 'Paul's doctrine of righteousness by faith is an exercise in scriptural interpretation, and intends itself to be understood as such'.[33] It is the commentary genre that has misled many scholars into thinking that they can explicate the meaning of Rom. 1.16-17b before discussing the cited text in verse 1.17b.

The theme of 'righteousness by faith' will be picked up in Romans 4 when Paul discusses Abraham, who 'believed God and it was reckoned to him as righteousness' (Gen. 15.6). Before that, Paul pursues an argument designed to demonstrate that 'no human being will be justified in his sight by deeds prescribed by the law' (Rom. 3.20). The word translated 'justified' (*dikaiōthēsetai*) is of course cognate with 'righteous' (*dikaios*) and Watson suggests that the hugely debated genitive phrase *ex ergōn nomou* ('of works of law') has been constructed in contrast to *ek pisteōs*. Though several chapters separate the two texts in Romans, they are brought together in Gal. 3.11 ('Now it is evident that no one is justified before God by the law; for "The one who is righteous will live by faith"'). In Galatians the connection is simply asserted but in Romans, an argument is put forward that 'enables us to hear the law's true voice

---

[30] The anonymous formula occurs nine times in Romans (1.17; 2.24; 3.4; 9.13, 33; 10.15. 11.8, 26; 15.9).

[31] Watson cites Rom. 9.32-3 as another example, where the formulation, 'They have stumbled over the stumbling stone' has clearly been modelled on the citation, 'See, I am laying in Zion a stone that will make people stumble, a rock that will make them fall'.

[32] Watson, *Paul and the Hermeneutics of Faith*, p. 48.

[33] Watson, *Paul and the Hermeneutics of Faith*, p. 53.

not in the promise that those who observe it will live thereby but in the declaration that, "works of law" notwithstanding, "there is no one who is righteous, not even one".[34]

However, Paul's evidence for this statement does not come from the law itself but a catena of quotations drawn from the Psalms and Isaiah. In Rom. 3.10-18, Paul or someone before him has amassed a set of phrases that condemn the wicked, probably understood as Gentiles, in contrast to the righteous. By beginning the catena with the universal statement of Ps. 14.1 ('There is no one who is righteous, not even one'), these condemnations are subsumed into a universal condemnation, which Paul considers to be the verdict of the law (3.19).[35] According to Watson, Paul would have considered the Psalms and Isaiah as commentary on the law and 'insofar as the later writers are all saying the same thing as Moses, they too articulate the voice of the law'.[36] He concludes that the 'juxtaposition of Habakkuk 2.4 and the catena of Romans 3.10-18 sets up an antithetical hermeneutic in which the voice of the prophet and the voice of the law represent the positive and negative side of the total scriptural testimony to the Pauline gospel'.[37] It is a 'radical new reading of Jewish scripture',[38] which allows Paul to view the law as divided against itself. On the one hand, it promises life to those who obey its commandments (Lev. 18.5); on the other hand, it proclaims that such a project is ultimately doomed.

This 'radical new reading of Jewish scripture' is not, however, to be regarded as an *imposition* on the Habakkuk text.[39] Drawing on the language of speech-act theory, Watson claims that the perlocutionary effect of the Habakkuk text is to address readers such as Paul (and the Qumran commentator) who believe that they are interpreting ('so that its reader may run') in the days of fulfilment. It is not inviting readers to think themselves back into Habakkuk's time in order to discern what Habakkuk had in mind, for the intended meaning (perlocutionary effect) was hidden from him.[40] The text points forward to an interpreter who will 'penetrate the written words in order to lay bear the mysteries they conceal and preserve'[41] and it is clear that both Paul and the Qumran commentator consider themselves to be such readers: 'Paul and the pesherist draw on the semantic potential of the scriptural text itself – while not allowing themselves to be confined self-effacingly within its limits, as though they had nothing of their own to contribute'.[42] According to Watson, it is a grave weakness of the historical-critical approach that categorically denies the validity of this form of interpretation.

---

[34] Watson, *Paul and the Hermeneutics of Faith*, p. 57.

[35] In terms of their 'original context', only Isa. 59.7 could plausibly be understood as supporting Paul's view that these texts condemn Jews as well as Gentiles. See Moyise, 'The Catena of Rom 3:10-18', pp. 367–70.

[36] Watson, *Paul and the Hermeneutics of Faith*, p. 58.

[37] Watson, *Paul and the Hermeneutics of Faith*, p. 66.

[38] Watson, *Paul and the Hermeneutics of Faith*, p. 72.

[39] Whether it is an imposition on Lev. 18.5 will be discussed in the next chapter.

[40] He considers 'the attempt to restore the entire book to a *Sitz im Leben* within the obscurity of "pre-exilic" Judah can only be regarded as historically naïve and hermeneutically perverse' (Watson, *Paul and the Hermeneutics of Faith*, p. 158).

[41] Watson, *Paul and the Hermeneutics of Faith*, p. 115.

[42] Watson, *Paul and the Hermeneutics of Faith*, p. 163.

Watson thus gives an account of how Paul and the Qumran commentator each draw out the semantic potential of the text, sometimes in agreement and sometimes in opposition with one another. For example, both interpret the key word 'faith/fulness' in opposition to what they consider to be a false view of the law held by the majority. The Qumran commentator opposes a position which is stereotyped as that of the 'Wicked Priest', 'whereas Paul traces it back to the revered yet ambivalent figure of Moses himself, whose claim that "the one who does these things shall live" (Lev. 18.5) cannot be harmonized with the soteriology of Habakkuk 2.4'.[43] On the other hand, the Qumran commentator not only assumes that 'faithfulness' means 'faithfulness to the law', he also introduces the term 'law' into his interpretations, even when it is not present in his lemma.[44] In contrast, Paul's interpretation is more an argument from absence. Both Paul and the Qumran commentator agree that Hab. 2.4 speaks of the 'divinely ordained way to salvation with a clarity and brevity virtually unparalleled in the rest of scripture'[45] but Paul finds significance in the fact that such a statement makes no mention of the law.

That Hab. 2.4 can bear this exegetical weight is shown by Rom. 3.21-2, which Watson regards as a gloss on Rom. 1.17 and therefore as further comment on Hab. 2.4: '*But now apart from law,* the righteousness of God has been manifested, *attested by the law and the prophets,* the righteousness of God through faith *of Jesus Christ* for all who believe'. The italicized phrases demonstrate the progression in Paul's argument. First, the phrase, '*apart from law*' confirms the view that Paul sees in the 'by faith' of Habakkuk a corollary, 'and not by law'. This has been the thrust of Paul's argument in Romans 3.

Secondly, the undifferentiated 'it is written' (1.17; 2.24; 3.4,10) now gives way to '*the law and the prophets*'. This is a traditional formula (Mt. 5.17; Lk. 22.40; Jn 1.45; Acts 13.15) and is generally a way of speaking about the whole of Scripture. For Paul, however, it probably has a more complex meaning. On the one hand, it suggests that there is more than one voice in Scripture, a voice of 'law' and a voice of 'prophecy'. On the other hand, Paul has shown (or thinks he has shown) that the voice of the law can be heard in Isaiah and the Psalms and so the phrase 'law and prophets' not only points to different blocks of material but also to different voices within Scripture. Thus when the prophet is speaking as a prophet and not as a commentator on the law, he testifies directly to the 'righteousness by faith'. On the other hand, in Romans 4, Paul will cite Gen. 15.6 to show that the law can sometimes speak of the 'righteousness by faith'. Thus the testimony of the law and the prophets is both affirmation and negation.

Thirdly, not only is the meaning of 'faith' interpreted by the gloss, 'apart from law', it is now specifically associated with Jesus Christ. The genitive construction ('of

---

[43] Watson, *Paul and the Hermeneutics of Faith*, p. 125.

[44] 1QpHab i.10-11; v.11-12; vii.10-11; viii.2-3; xi.17–xii.5.

[45] Watson, *Paul and the Hermeneutics of Faith*, p. 124.

Jesus Christ') is ambiguous and Hays and others have taken it to mean 'through the faithfulness of Jesus Christ'. Watson denies this, claiming that there is insufficient evidence in Rom. 1.16-17 that Paul is interpreting Hab. 2.4 christologically. Indeed, what is notable about Rom. 1.16-17 is that Paul 'exercises the christological restraint appropriate to his scriptural text and does not simply impose his christological convictions on it'.[46] Of course 'faith' for Paul is 'entirely and exclusively bound up with God's saving action in Christ'[47] and he now makes this explicit. But he does not assume that Habakkuk speaks about Christ, for the true meaning of Habakkuk's words were hidden from him. Paul's gloss that 'faith' means 'faith of Jesus Christ' does not involve the claim that this is what Habakkuk had in mind but the claim that Habakkuk's text presupposes a reader who lives in the time of fulfilment and so can interpret what has previously remained mysterious. It is not the 'literal sense' as understood by modern historical criticism but is 'literal' in so far as responding to the text in a way that the text authorizes.[48]

Analysis

~

Despite the fact that Paul does not quote or allude to any other verse of Habakkuk in his extant writings, Dunn, Hays and Watson all agree that the six-word quotation (*ho de dikaios ek pisteōs zēsetai*) is hugely significant. They differ considerably, however, on what is evoked and how it functions. For Dunn, the omission of first or third person pronouns allows the text to evoke both the Hebrew (human faithfulness) and Greek (God's faithfulness) traditions. It is not entirely clear if Dunn thinks it is necessary for Paul's readers to know both traditions in order to appreciate this or simply that Paul's abbreviated Greek is ambiguous and thus open to both possibilities. Though he states that it is necessary to set Paul's words in the context of his 'Jewish background and training', he does not specifically refer to the context of the verse in Habakkuk. Rather, it is the rich background of 'righteousness' and 'covenant' that should be borne in mind when interpreting Paul's words. Paul wishes

---

[46] Watson, *Paul and the Hermeneutics of Faith*, p. 161.

[47] Watson, *Paul and the Hermeneutics of Faith*, p. 161.

[48] Watson's explanation of the ambiguous 'of Jesus Christ' is as follows: 'God justifies the one who is of the faith of Jesus, since the name "Jesus" denotes nothing other than the saving action that God accomplished in his death. If, however, God's action in Christ intends the faith that leads to justification, this faith is itself the recognition and acknowledgement of the divine saving action. In a two-way movement from Christ's death and back to it again, God's saving act in Christ seeks to elicit the answering faith that acknowledges it as what it truly is. Faith, then, is "faith of Jesus Christ" in the dual sense that Jesus Christ, the embodiment of God's saving action, is as such both the origin and the object of faith' (*Paul and the Hermeneutics of Faith*, pp. 75–6).

to assert continuity with Scripture, while also making the point that 'the covenantal framework of God's righteousness has to be understood afresh in terms of faith'.

Hays, on the other hand, thinks the quotation would specifically evoke the theodicy motif of Habakkuk, a *locus classicus* for this theme. This is important for Hays as it shows that Paul's main concern in Romans is not how individuals are saved but a defence of the faithfulness of God. In his published dissertation (1983) and his chapter in the Lou Martyn Festschrift (1988), he champions a christological inter-pretation of the text, taking *ho dikaios* as a reference to Jesus, 'the Righteous One'. However, in *Echoes of Scripture*, this is relegated to a single endnote[49] and does not figure in his interpretation. Hays acknowledges that the situations of Habakkuk and Paul are very different and so the relationship is 'off-centre' but it would be wrong to speak of 'circumventing the text's original referential sense'. Paul evokes the theodicy motif from Habakkuk and his abbreviated quotation allows him to make points about both God's righteousness and the appropriate human response, namely, faith. Hays thus agrees with Dunn that it is important to interpret Paul from within his Jewish background and that the abbreviated quotation is intended to evoke multiple themes/traditions. He differs from Dunn in his messianic interpretation of the text (though this does not figure in *Echoes*) and the importance of specifically evoking Habakkuk's theodicy motif.

What is striking about Watson's interpretation is the canonical framework in which it is set. Paul has wrestled with the text of Habakkuk and it was foundational for the formulation of his gospel message. But his use of the anonymous formula ('it is written') does not direct his readers to the pre-exilic prophet but focuses on the precise meaning of the quoted words in the context of the Book of the Twelve. Paul seeks to hear the 'voice' of Habakkuk as it has been transmitted 'by the unknown editors and scribes responsible for the canonical process'[50] rather than their meaning in Habakkuk's day. Drawing on speech-act theory, Watson rejects both the historical-critical view that meaning is to be equated with authorial intention and the poststruc-turalist view that meaning is determined by readers (or reading communities). Rather, meaning is embedded in texts and so one can speak of being addressed by a text or even being the sort of reader the text intends.[51]

This could be seen as a circular form of apologetic; the Habakkuk text intends a reader such as Paul and so Paul's reading is *ipso facto* the true meaning of the text. However, Watson's exposition of Paul's use of Habakkuk runs in parallel with his exposition of the Qumran commentator, who is also an 'intended' reader: 'At this unique point at the heart of the Book of the Twelve, the Qumran hermeneutic

---

[49] Hays, *Echoes of Scripture*, p. 203, n.21.

[50] Watson, *Paul and the Hermeneutics of Faith*, p. 157.

[51] 'Vanhoozer rightly argues that a text is irreducibly "a communicative act of a communicative agent, fixed in writing" (p. 225): only as such does the text intend its own reader' (Watson, *The Hermeneutics of Faith*, p. 145, n.32). The reference is to K. Vanhoozer, *Is there a Meaning in this Text? The Bible, the Reader, and the Morality of Literary Knowledge* (Grand Rapids: Zondervan, 1998).

shows itself to be identical to the hermeneutic prescribed and presupposed in the prophetic texts themselves.'[52] Watson demonstrates with great skill how the interpretations of Paul and the Qumran commentator are based on serious theological engagement with the text and have much more in common than is usually recognized. He thus concludes that they belong to a 'single intertextual field' and that a simple valid/invalid dichotomy is inappropriate. He particularly wishes to refute the judgement of Barton that

> there is little likelihood that Paul has reproduced the meaning Habakkuk had in mind; his interpretation of this prophet, however much it differs from that current at Qumran, is no less the product of his own *prior* convictions about theological truth.[53]

However, it may be that we should not force Barton's words into a valid/invalid framework, either. While Watson has helpfully shown that Paul and the Qumran commentator have more in common (as serious exegetes) than is often supposed, the emphasis on law in the latter is precisely what Paul is intending to eliminate. On this point, they have interpreted the same text in diametrically opposite ways, which can either be explained as: (1) the needs of the readers were different (i.e. they had different rhetorical purposes); or (2) they held different prior convictions. Though the first is undoubtedly true, it is difficult to imagine any circumstances where Paul would have interpreted the verse as applying to 'those who observe the law in the house of Judah'. It must therefore be due to their very different prior convictions.

On the other hand, there is no reason to assume that Paul's 'prior convictions' did not involve some interaction with the Habakkuk text. We have already noted that it is unlikely that Paul formulated his gospel ('the righteousness of God is revealed through faith for faith') and only later discovered that Hab. 2.4 is the only Scripture to use the phrase *ek pisteōs*. Given the importance of this text within 'The Twelve', it is quite plausible to suggest that Paul would have pondered its meaning prior to his Damascus road experience, even if his interpretation developed or changed after it. At any rate, Watson has convincingly established that it is not simply an imposition on the text.[54] Whether the same can be said for his quotation of Lev. 18.5 will be discussed in the next chapter.

---

[52] Watson, *Paul and the Hermeneutics of Faith*, p. 112.

[53] J. Barton, *Oracles of God: Perceptions of Ancient Prophecy in Israel after the Exile* (London: Darton, Longman & Todd, 1986), p. 245 (cited in Watson, *Paul and the Hermeneutics of Faith*, p. 128).

[54] It is strange that B. Schliesser (*Abraham's Faith in Romans 4* [WUNT, 2.224; Tübingen: Mohr Siebeck, 2007]) devotes some 500 pages to demonstrating that Paul's use of Gen. 15.6 in Romans 4 is genuinely sensitive to its original meaning (p. 429), while readily concluding that the omission of any pronoun in his quotation of Hab. 2.4 was because the original (Greek or Hebrew) did not mean what he wanted to convey (p. 249).

6

Evoking a false legal framework?
Gal. 3.10-14

Introduction

S o far, we have considered the case for understanding Old Testament quotations
as evoking whole frameworks of meaning, and the challenges to this from
narrative (Hatina) and reader-centred (Stanley) approaches. In Gal. 3.10-14, a
different issue emerges. By quoting Lev. 18.5 and Deut. 27.26, Paul evokes a
framework that is so basic to religious sensibilities that one can assume his Galatian
readers would have understood it, namely, that God rewards obedience and punishes
disobedience. In Lev. 18.1-4, God instructs Moses to tell the people that they must
not live by the laws of the Canaanites. Instead, they must live by God's laws: 'You shall
keep my statutes and my ordinances; by doing so (*poiēsete auta*) one shall live
(*zēsetai*)' (Lev. 18.5).[1] The verse is a promise that keeping God's laws will lead to life,
while following the Canaanite laws will lead to death. The point is reiterated at the
end of the chapter: 'But you shall keep my statutes and my ordinances and commit
none of these abominations' (Lev. 18.26), and leads into the command: 'you shall be
Holy, for I the Lord your God am holy' (Lev. 19.2) and 'you shall love your neighbour
as yourself' (Lev. 19.18). The verse itself and its surrounding context are crystal
clear; God requires obedience and this is the way to life.

Deut. 27.26 focuses on the negative. On the brink of the Promised Land, Moses
warns the people of the temptations that await them. The positive command is that

---

[1] The second half of the verse is awkward. Literally, the Hebrew reads: 'which a person shall do them, and
shall live by/in them', a parallelism that could suggest that the two clauses mean much the same thing: one should
do/live the commandments. However, the first 'them' might not be the object of 'shall do' but simply indicates
that the Hebrew connective is functioning as a relative pronoun and should be translated: 'which a person shall
do, and shall live by/in them'. The LXX resolves this by turning it into a participial clause: 'which a person doing
shall live by/in them'. We shall discuss the alternatives 'by/in them' later.

you should 'obey the LORD your God, observing his commandments and his statutes that I am commanding you today' (Deut. 27.10). There then follows a set of curses, to which the people are instructed to reply, 'Amen':

- Cursed be anyone who makes an idol or casts an image, anything abhorrent to the LORD, the work of an artisan, and sets it up in secret (v. 15)
- Cursed be anyone who dishonours father or mother (v. 16)
- Cursed be anyone who moves a neighbour's boundary marker (v. 17)
- Cursed be anyone who misleads a blind person on the road (v. 18)
- Cursed be anyone who deprives the alien, the orphan, and the widow of justice (v. 19)
- Cursed be anyone who lies with his father's wife, because he has violated his father's rights (v. 20)
- Cursed be anyone who lies with any animal (v. 21)
- Cursed be anyone who lies with his sister, whether the daughter of his father or the daughter of his mother (v. 22)
- Cursed be anyone who lies with his mother-in-law (v. 23)
- Cursed be anyone who strikes down a neighbour in secret (v. 24)
- Cursed be anyone who takes a bribe to shed innocent blood (v. 25)

Deut. 27.26 then offers a summary: 'Cursed be anyone who does not uphold the words of this law by observing them (*poiēsai autous*)'. There can be no doubt that the passage advocates strict adherence to God's law, with the threat of a curse for *anyone* who disobeys. Thus the two quotations insist that those who *do* the statutes and ordinances (*poiēsete auta*) will live, while those who do not *do* the words of the law (*poiēsai autous*) will be cursed. How then can Paul possibly think that these quotations support his case that Gentile Christians do not need to obey all of the law?

Gal. 3.10-14

~

For all who rely on the works of the law are under a curse; for it is written, '*Cursed is everyone who does not observe and obey all the things written in the book of the law.*' Now it is evident that no one is justified before God by the law; for '*The one who is righteous will live by faith.*' But the law does not rest on faith; on the contrary, '*Whoever does the works of the law will live by them.*' Christ redeemed us from the curse of the law by becoming a curse for us – for it is written, '*Cursed is everyone who hangs on a tree*'– in order that in Christ Jesus the blessing of Abraham might come to the Gentiles, so that we might receive the promise of the Spirit through faith. (Gal. 3.10-14)

Two observations are immediately apparent. The first is that the quotations are in the service of an eschatological argument that 'the blessing of Abraham might come to the Gentiles, so that *we* might receive the promise of the Spirit through faith'. Paul facilitates this by asserting that 'Christ redeemed *us* from the curse of the law by becoming a curse for *us*', and supports it by a (seemingly) obscure text about criminals left hanging on a tree (Deut. 21.23). Paul's use of the adjective *epikataratos* here instead of the LXX's verb *kekatēramenos* for 'cursed' is almost certainly intended as a link back to the 'cursed is everyone' (*epikataratos pas*) of Deut. 27.26, thus forming an inclusion.[2]

Secondly, he seeks to guide the reader towards the desired conclusion by offering interpretative comments before each of the quotations:

> For all who rely on the works of the law are under a curse ...
> Now it is evident that no one is justified before God by the law ...
> But the law does not rest on faith; on the contrary ...

Had Paul omitted the quotations of Deut. 27.26 and Lev. 18.5, the logic would have been relatively clear, albeit controversial. Those who are seeking to impose circumcision and food laws on Gentile Christians are under a curse, for it is evident that no one is justified before God by the law. If that were possible, then Christ died for nothing (Gal. 2.21). Since that is out of the question, it is evident that being 'of faith' (*ek pisteōs*) is what matters. Abraham was 'of faith' (3.6) and Gentile Christians are 'of faith' (3.9) but those seeking to impose circumcision are not 'of faith' for the law is not 'of faith'. This is the controversial statement. There is (seemingly) nothing in the Abraham story that suggests a dichotomy between being 'of faith' and being 'of law'. God says to Abraham, 'walk before me, and be blameless' (Gen. 17.1) and then tells him to submit to circumcision as a 'sign of the covenant between me and you' (Gen. 17.11). It is true that some texts place the emphasis on God's unconditional promise (Gen. 12.3) but other texts make it clear that the promise is dependent on Abraham's obedience (Gen. 22.18).[3]

Paul has set in motion an obedience framework (obey the law and live, disobey the law and be cursed) that is so basic to the religious life that it is difficult to see how he can prevent it from colliding with his law-free gospel. As Stanley remarks, readers 'with an extensive knowledge of Scripture would have found Paul's quotations

---

[2] That Paul is responsible for this change is suggested by the following: (1) Neither the Greek nor Hebrew use the same word for 'cursed' in the two texts; (2) Both the Greek and Hebrew say cursed 'by God', which Paul omits; (3) By omitting 'by God' and changing to *epikataratos*, both quotations now begin with *epikataratos pas* ('cursed is everyone'). Interestingly, the statement that this is supposed to be supporting ('Christ redeemed us from the curse') uses the simple form *kataras*. It was evidently more important to obtain lexical agreement with Deut. 27.26 than the statement it is supporting.

[3] Gen. 12.3: 'I will bless those who bless you, and him who curses you I will curse; and by you all the families of the earth shall bless themselves'.

Gen. 22.17b-18: 'And your descendants shall possess the gate of their enemies, and by your descendants shall all the nations of the earth bless themselves, *because* you have obeyed my voice'.

troubling, to say the least, and some of them might have been led by their examination of his quotations to reject Paul's arguments in favor of the view of his
"opponents".[4] Not surprisingly, numerous proposals have been suggested to 'solve'
this problem but for our purposes, we will discuss them under two headings: (1) those
that seek to uphold the truth of all of the quoted texts; and (2) those that see a fundamental antithesis between what the law says in Lev. 18.5/Deut. 27.26 and the message
of faith in Hab. 2.4 (and Gen. 15.6).

Upholding the truth of the quoted texts

No one keeps the law perfectly

If Lev. 18.5 and Deut. 27.26 evoke an 'obedience' framework that is fundamental to the
religious or moral life, the only way to reinterpret them would be to evoke an equally
fundamental principle or truth. For some scholars, that truth is the fact that no one can
keep the law perfectly. Andrew Das, for example, considers Paul's rhetorical argument as
an enthymeme and reconstructs the implied premise as: 'All who rely on the works of the
law do not observe and obey all the things written in the book of the law.'[5] According to
Das, this is the only logical conclusion from Paul's statement and proof-text and so the
argument runs like this: (1) Deut. 27.26 *rightly* threatens a curse on all who do not keep
the law; (2) it is self-evident that no one keeps the law *perfectly*; hence (3) everyone is under
a curse. On the other hand, (1) Lev. 18.5 *rightly* promises life to those who keep the law;
(2) it is evident that no one keeps the law *perfectly*; therefore (3) no one gains life by
keeping the law. The consequence is that if anyone is to gain life, it will have to come some
other way, and Gen. 15.6 and Hab. 2.4 agree that that way is 'by faith'.

That Paul believed that no one keeps the law perfectly can be supported by the scriptural catena in Rom. 3.10-18, as we saw in the last chapter. Paul begins with a line from
Ps. 14.1 (or possibly Eccl. 7.20)[6] that there is 'no one who is righteous, not even one' (Rom.
3.10) and concludes that 'no human being will be justified in his sight by deeds prescribed
by the law' (Rom. 3.20). As Das says, 'If *Israel* had been unable to fulfill the law and thereby
avoid its curse, why would the Gentile Galatians want to rely on the law?'[7] Of course, this
does raise acutely the question as to why the law was given in the first place. If human
beings cannot keep it perfectly, then the curse becomes inevitable and the promise of life

---

[4] Stanley, *Arguing with Scripture*, p. 129.

[5] A.A. Das, *Paul, the Law and the Covenant* (Peabody: Hendrickson, 2001), p. 146.

[6] Lexically, Rom. 3.10 (*ouk estin dikaios oude heis*) is much closer to the LXX of Eccl. 7.20 (*hoti
anthrōpos ouk estin dikaios*) but since Rom. 3.11-12 is undoubtedly based on Ps. 14.2-3, most scholars think
Rom. 3.10 is Paul's paraphrase of Ps. 14.1 (*ouk estin poiōn chrēstotēta ouk estin heōs henos*).

[7] Das, *Paul, the Law and the Covenant*, p. 154.

in Lev. 18.5 is but a cruel deception. However, this is not necessarily a fatal objection to this view, for Paul goes on to discuss this very issue:

> Is the law then opposed to the promises of God? Certainly not! For if a law had been given that could make alive (*zōopoiēsai*), then righteousness would indeed come through the law. But the scripture has imprisoned all things under the power of sin, so that what was promised through faith in Jesus Christ might be given to those who believe. (Gal. 3.21-2)

This refers to Paul's earlier statement that the law came much later than the promise given to Abraham (Gal. 3.15-18). In that respect, the law was never intended to replace the promise made to Abraham or offer an alternative path to righteousness. Nevertheless, Lev. 18.5 does promise life (*zēsetai*), while Paul says that a law has not been given that can 'make alive' (*zōopoiēsai*). If these are not to be seen as contradictory statements, one must presume that Paul took *zēsetai* to mean something like 'continuance in the covenant', while *zōopoiēsai* refers to a quality of life that is free from the curse of the law and is the fulfilment of the promises made to Abraham. In other words, it is life in the Spirit (Gal. 3.5, 14).

There are, however, major problems with this view, both external and internal. The external problems have been most forcefully argued by Ed Sanders.[8] According to his analysis of first-century Jewish literature, no form of Judaism (for which we have evidence) insisted that perfect obedience was necessary to maintain the covenant. After all, much of the law is concerned with the means of atonement for when transgressions occur. The point of the covenant is not to reward perfection but to maintain fellowship. Indeed, Paul himself can be cited as first-century evidence for such a view when he describes his life as a Jew in the words, 'as to righteousness under the law, blameless' (Phil. 3.6). Paul is not implying that he was perfect but that he was zealous in his obedience of the law and (presumably) made atonement for transgressions when they occurred. In that sense, he could describe his life as 'righteous'. Thus if the logic of Gal. 3.10-14 requires the reader to assume the 'missing premise' that maintenance of the covenant is dependent on *perfect* obedience, then Paul's argument is weak from two perspectives: (1) he has grossly misrepresented his ancestral religion, for no form of Judaism unequivocally insists on this;[9] and (2) he has grossly misjudged the abilities of his readers, for they would not be able to supply what is crucial for understanding his argument.

---

[8] E.P. Sanders, *Paul and Palestinian Judaism* (London: SCM, 1977).

[9] I use the word 'unequivocally' deliberately. Das has shown that the documents cited by Sanders demonstrate a 'tension in Judaism between God's will that the law be perfectly obeyed and God's mercy granted to an elect people who often fell short of that demand' (*Paul, the Law and the Covenant*, p. 69). He rightly uses this to challenge Sanders's one-sided emphasis on 'election and mercy' but the fact that both themes are present in the documents (in varying proportions) implies that they do not 'unequivocally' teach that perfect obedience is a necessary requirement and so could hardly be assumed by Paul as an unexpressed premise.

There are also internal problems with respect to the situation Paul is addressing in Galatia. As Paul testifies in Gal. 2.15, Jewish belief held that Gentiles were 'sinners' by definition, because they did not live under the law. On the 'missing premise' view, the Gentiles would automatically fall under the law's curse because they were not even *trying* to keep it. But Paul says that Christ has redeemed 'us' from the curse of the law (Gal. 3.13). There is debate as to whether the 'us' here includes Gentiles or whether Paul is talking about 'us Jews' or even 'us missionaries'. If it is the former, then God has redeemed the Gentiles from the curse that came upon them for not even *trying* to keep the law. Is Paul now wishing to assert that the curse will in some way be *reactivated* if they wish to show their gratitude to God by at least *trying* to keep it?

On the other hand, if the 'us' of Gal. 3.13 means 'us Jews' or 'us missionaries', then although this would offer a rationale for why Gentile Christians should not take up the law, it is problematic for why the Gentiles need redemption in the first place. If Christ came to redeem the Jews from the unfortunate consequences of living under the law (having inevitably fallen under its curse), then they need to learn what the Gentiles have always known – that the law is best avoided. But if this is Paul's position, his case is not helped by quoting texts which strongly evoke the obedience framework. He would have done much better by quoting something like Ps. 40.6 ('Sacrifice and offering you do not desire'), as the author of Hebrews did (Heb. 10.5).

No one keeps the law for the right reasons

The weaknesses of the so-called 'missing premise' view has led some to a position that we might call the 'missing qualifier' view. This takes a number of forms. The most popular (in Protestant circles) has been to accuse Judaism and Paul's Jewish Christian opponents of 'legalism', that is, the attempt to gain merit through obedience to the law. Paul does not have a problem with Christians using the Scriptures as a guide to God's will, as 1 Cor. 9.8-12 makes clear. His problem, on this view, is with those who think that obedience to law will earn them salvation. This is the meaning of Paul's peculiar phrase, *ex ergōn nomou* ('of works of law'). The 'missing qualifier' is that Paul is not attacking those who obey the law as a faith-response to what God has done in Christ. For the sake of his missionary work, Paul is happy to live 'as one under the law' in order to win 'those under the law' (1 Cor. 9.20). Rather, he is attacking those who obey the law as a means of earning or perhaps completing their salvation and that is why he uses the technical term, *ex ergōn nomou*.[10] Two texts that are often quoted to support this view are Gal. 2.15-16 and Rom. 10.3:

---

[10] As R. Bultmann puts it, 'The reason, then, that man shall not, must not, be "rightwised" by works of the Law is that he must not be allowed to imagine that he is able to procure his salvation by his own strength; for he can find his salvation only when he understands himself in his dependence upon God the Creator', *Theology of the New Testament*, (London: SCM Press, 1952), 1, p. 264.

We ourselves are Jews by birth and not Gentile sinners; yet we know that a person is justified not by the works of the law but through faith in Jesus Christ. And we have come to believe in Christ Jesus, so that we might be justified by faith in Christ, and not by doing the works of the law, because no one will be justified by the works of the law. (Gal. 2.15-16)

For, being ignorant of the righteousness that comes from God, and seeking to establish their own, they have not submitted to God's righteousness. (Rom. 10.3)

The significance of these two passages is that as well as stating that 'justification' cannot come from 'works of law', they appear to imply that this is what the Jews believed and were ardently seeking. The problem then is not with God's law in itself but the attempt to use it to establish one's own righteousness.

However, such a wholesale accusation against the Jews has been successfully repudiated by Sanders. Law was undoubtedly important in all forms of Judaism for maintaining the covenant and even for increasing one's reward in the world to come (as it was for Jesus,[11] though no one accuses him of 'legalism') but it was not what Sanders calls an 'entry requirement'. Jewish self-understanding did not revolve around 'entry requirements' because the covenant was rooted in election and grace. If anything, the temptation was not so much to 'legalism' but 'exclusivisism', the desire to maintain their privileged status. Once again, Sanders concludes that if the argument depends on the 'missing qualifier' that Paul is not attacking the law but a 'legalistic' distortion of it, then he has grossly misrepresented his ancestral religion.

Dunn does not think that Paul has grossly misrepresented his ancestral religion and argues that the phrase *ex ergōn nomou* focuses on those aspects of the law that exclude Gentiles. Because Jewish Christians are maintaining these 'boundary markers', the Gentiles are being excluded from the promised blessing. And since this is against God's revealed will in Christ (as promised beforehand to Abraham), they are breaking the fundamental spirit of the law, namely, that it is an expression of God's will. In this way, Dunn can maintain that the law is obsolete in its 'boundary marking' functions but is still relevant as a guide to Christian living. According to Dunn, Paul's concludes that

the effects of the *curse* have been abolished for Gentiles, that the restrictiveness of a law which marked off Jew from Gentile as such had been overcome, not that the *law* has been abolished, rendered null and void, or without further relevance to Christians.[12]

---

[11] According to Matthew, Jesus frequently promises rewards in heaven (5.12, 19; 6.4, 6, 18, 20).

[12] J.D.G. Dunn, *The Epistle to the Galatains* (BNTC; London: A. & C. Black, 1993), p. 179. Emphasis original.

Law is now redundant as a guide to living
Both Sanders and Dunn have made significant contributions to understanding
Paul's argument by seeking to root it in the social conflicts that provoked Paul's
response, rather than abstract debates about 'doing' and 'believing'.[13] However,
according to Wakefield, this still does not resolve the problem of Paul's quotations:

> Whether Paul wants to say that the real problem with the law is reliance on "doing" (vs.
> "believing"), or that it is a legalistic or nationalistic distortion or attitude, Dt 27:26 does
> not help him, because it does *not* pronounce a curse on those who do the law, or who
> legalistically misunderstand it, or who nationalistically misuse it, but rather on those who
> *fail to do* the law.[14]

Wakefield argues that the quotations in Gal. 3.6-14 should be seen as a deliberate chiasm on Paul's part:

> Faith: "Abraham had faith … it was reckoned to him as righteousness" (Gen 15:6)
>   Blessing: "Through you the nations will be blessed" (Gen 12:3)
>   Curse: "Cursed be anyone …" (Dt 27:26)
>   Life: "The righteous will live by faith" (Hab 2:4)
>   Life: "The one who does these things will live in them" (Lev 18:5)
>   Curse: "Cursed be anyone … (Dt 21:23)
>   [Blessing: "… the blessing of Abraham …" (allusion to Gen 12:3)]
> [Faith: "… in order that we might receive the promise of the Spirit through faith"][15]

According to Wakefield, this makes it very unlikely that the crux of the chiasm
('Life') contains a contradiction. Both texts would have been understood by first-
century Judaism as complementary and Paul's rhetorical strategy shows that he
agreed. Wakefield offers two suggestions for how this could be possible. First, he
suggests a change in punctuation of Gal. 3.11. As punctuated in NA[27], *dēlon* is
followed by a comma, thus making Hab. 2.4 the supporting text for the assertion that
'no one is justified by God by the law'. However, if the comma is placed before the
dēlon, the main and subordinate clauses are reversed: '*Because* no one is justified
before God by the law, *it is clear that* "The righteous will live by faith."'[16] Wakefield
considers this as a point of agreement between Paul and his opponents, not the crux
of their disagreement:

---

[13] Dunn sees confirmation of his view in the discovery of the Qumran document 4QMMT (*DJD*
10,1994) where the corresponding Hebrew phrase (which gives the document its title) is found. Dunn
notes that it is the sect's adherence to these 'works of law' that caused it to separate from the rest of Israel.

[14] A.H. Wakefield, *Where to Live. The Hermeneutical Significance of Paul's Citations from Scripture in
Galatians 3.1-14* (Atlanta: SBL, 2003), p. 72. Emphasis original.

[15] Wakefield, *Where to Live*, p. 136. He acknowledges that the last two items are less explicit than the rest.

[16] Wakefield, *Where to Live*, p. 162.

That the law has no power to bring about salvation is, however, the point on which Paul and his opponents agree (Gal 2.16). The issue on which they disagree, and the issue that has diverted the Galatians from the gospel of faith, is whether the law has the power to effect righteousness in the daily life of the believer. Can or should the believer make use of the law in order to behave righteously?[17]

Wakefield argues that in their Old Testament contexts, neither Deut. 27.26 nor Lev. 18.5 is soteriological. They are not talking about how to 'gain life' but 'how to live life'. The main difficulty that scholars have had with Paul's juxtaposition of Deut. 27.26/Lev. 18.5 and Hab. 2.4 is that they have assumed a soteriological meaning, that is, that they offer competing ways of obtaining (eternal) life. But if that is not the case, then much of the dissonance disappears. Lev. 18.5 is quoted to make the point that the law is a closed system. It is not a false promise of (eternal) life by a cruel God that knows it could never be realized. It is a simple statement that the law is a complete way of life. That is why the Galatians should not adopt it, for a new way of living has been revealed in Christ:

> Paul rejects the law so vehemently, not because it perpetuates a sociological barrier between Jews and Gentiles, but rather because it is part of the old age. One cannot live by the law, even in the sense – or perhaps, especially in the sense – of using it to regulate behavior, because to do so is to return to the old age. This old age is the age of the flesh, the age of sin (and therefore the age into which God gave the law as a response to sin), the age of the elemental powers, the age under a curse – in short, it is the present evil age from which Christ has rescued us.[18]

Regarding the quoted texts as antithetical

Resolving scriptural antinomies

According to Nils Astrup Dahl, the rabbis recognized that Scripture does not always speak with one voice and so much exegetical debate was concerned with resolving scriptural antinomies. Paul would have been aware of the rabbinic principle that, 'Two scriptural passages which correspond to one another yet conflict with one another, should be upheld in their place until a third passage comes and decides between them.'[19] In Gal. 3.10-12, Hab. 2.4 and Lev. 18.5 are placed in stark juxtaposition.

---

[17] Wakefield, *Where to Live*, p. 194.
[18] Wakefield, *Where to Live*, p. 184.
[19] N.A. Dahl, *Studies in Paul. Theology of the Early Christian Mission* (Minneapolis: Augsburg Fortress, 1977), p. 162.

However, in what follows (Gal. 3.13-18), Paul shows that Hab. 2.4 is the primary passage because it coheres with the promises given to Abraham. Abraham 'believed God, and it was reckoned to him as righteousness' (Gen. 15.6), just as the later prophet declared that 'the one who is righteous will live by faith' (Hab. 2.4). But Paul does more than assert the primacy of Hab. 2.4. He shows in Gal. 3.19-26 that Lev. 18.5 can be reinterpreted to cohere with Hab. 2.4 if it is given a restricted temporal meaning. It was God's plan for his people to remain in the law (that is, remain in the covenant) until such time as a new covenant is instigated. Thus Paul resolves the antinomy by discerning the primary passage (Hab. 2.4) and then reinterpreting the secondary passage (Lev. 18.5) in the light of it.

Challenging the voice of the law

Though agreeing with Dahl that Paul juxtaposes Lev. 18.5 and Hab. 2.4, Lou Martyn denies that Paul is trying to find a positive function for Lev. 18.5 prior to Christ.[20] Rather, Paul is using a well-known form of argumentation which Martyn calls 'Textual Contradiction'. He traces the logic as follows:

1. On the basis of the truth of the gospel I make a fundamental assertion: Before God no one is being rectified by the Law.
2. I then undergird that assertion with a quotation from scripture: 'The one who is rectified by faith will live.'
3. In light of the way in which the Teachers quote – and will continue to quote – from the Law, I must add a second assertion: The Law does not have its origin in faith.
4. Finally, given that second assertion, I cite a text from the Law that does not have its origin in faith – I think it is one of the Teacher's favorite texts – 'The one who does the commandments will live by them.'[21]

Deut. 27.26 is in part quoted as a true witness to the nature of the law, for it identifies itself as a 'cursing law'. It is false, however, when it seeks to draw a distinction between the consequences of this for 'observers' and 'non-observers' of the law. The law is, as it were, out of control, cursing anyone and everyone, be they Jew or Gentile. Lev. 18.5 is then brought into this same orbit. It does not represent the voice of God but the voice of the law and so Gal. 3.11-12 is a sort of hermeneutical version of 'discerning the spirits'. Scripture contains both promise, the voice of God, and law, which brings a curse. Paul's hermeneutics are about learning to distinguish between them.

Watson reaches a similar conclusion but denies that this is a christological imposition on the text, or that Paul is reinterpreting Deut. 26.27 and Lev. 18.5 because these are the texts being used by his opponents. As we have seen, Deut. 27.26

---

[20] J.L. Martyn, *Galatians: A New Translation with Introduction and Commentary* (AB, 33A; New York: Doubleday, 1997), p. 331, n.139.

[21] Martyn, *Galatians*, p. 331.

is the last of twelve curses that summarize the warnings to Israel. However, the speech continues into Deuteronomy 28, where it appears to be assumed that the curses will in fact come upon Israel:

> All these curses shall come upon you, pursuing and overtaking you until you are destroyed, because you did not obey the LORD your God, by observing the command-ments and the decrees that he commanded you. (Deut. 28.45)

Modern scholars, of course, recognize here a case of prophecy after the event. The editors of the Deuteronomic history are writing in the light of the exile. Thus while they preserve the conditional nature of the threats, they know for a fact that they were realized and this has affected their editing of the material. Indeed, Deuteronomy 30 looks beyond the exile and offers (hopes for?) a fresh start:

> When all these things have happened to you ... if you call them to mind among all the nations where the LORD your God has driven you, and return to the LORD your God, and you and your children obey him with all your heart and with all your soul, just as I am commanding you today, then the LORD your God will restore your fortunes and have compassion on you, gathering you again from all the peoples among whom the LORD your God has scattered you. Even if you are exiled to the ends of the world, from there the LORD your God will gather you ... Moreover, the LORD your God will circumcise your heart and the heart of your descendants, so that you will love the LORD your God with all your heart and with all your soul, in order that you may live. (Deut. 30.1-6)

At first sight, this looks like the sort of promise that Paul could happily correlate with his gospel, for it appears to focus on God's action ('circumcise your heart') as the source of life ('that you may live') by enabling love for God. However, as Watson points out, if we continue reading, the conditional language is soon in evidence again ('*when* you obey the LORD your God by observing his commandments and decrees that are written in this book of the law' – 30.10). Thus Deuteronomy 27–30 begins with a conditional offer of blessing or curse, then asserts that the curse is inevitable, and finishes by re-instigating the conditional offer. According to Watson, it is this dynamic that Paul has grasped. His quotation of Deut. 27.26 not only evokes the inevitability of the curse from Deuteronomy 28 (that is why Paul can universalize it), but it also evokes the position of Paul's opponents (*ex ergōn nomou*), 'who under-stand their law observance as the way out of a past determined by the curse into a future determined by the divine blessing'.[22] Thus the key to understanding Paul's use of Scripture is that he

---

[22] Watson, *Paul and the Hermeneutics of Faith*, p. 433.

practises a consecutive reading of his texts from Leviticus and Deuteronomy, in which the latter effectively cancels out the former. In doing so, he identifies a severe internal tension within the crucial closing chapters of Deuteronomy: the tension between conditional statements, which imply that the choice between blessing and curse, life and death is genuinely open, and statements of prophetic denunciation, in which the realization of the curse has become a certainty.[23]

As we saw in the last chapter, Watson thinks that Paul understood the 'of faith' of Hab. 2.4 to carry the corollary, 'not by law'. In Romans, Paul justifies this by the catena of Rom. 3.10-18 and concludes that '"no human being will be justified in his sight" by deeds prescribed by the law' (Rom. 3.20). Here in Galatians, he simply states that it is 'evident (*dēlon*) that no one is justified before God by the law; for "The one who is righteous will live by faith"'. If it is evident, then it follows that texts in Scripture that say otherwise are false in that they have been superseded. And this is what Paul goes on to assert: 'the law does not rest on faith' (*ho de nomos ouk estin ek pisteōs*). He then quotes one of the prime culprits, Lev. 18.5, which (falsely) promises that, 'Whoever does the works of the law will live by them.'[24]

Analysis

It is generally agreed that this is one of Paul's most difficult passages and one can understand Stanley's comment that any of Paul's readers who were familiar with the quoted texts would have been deeply troubled by Paul's use of them. We will focus on Paul's use of Lev. 18.5. It is clear that Paul does not think this text expresses God's will for the Gentile Christians at Galatia and so his hermeneutics may fairly be described as 'radical'. But how radical? There would appear to be three main options as to how Paul regarded this verse: (1) It truly promised covenant life but this is redundant now that 'eternal life'/'life in the Spirit' has been made available; (2) It truly promised 'eternal life'/'life in the world to come' for Jews, but this has been superseded now that God has opened the way for Gentiles to be included; (3) It falsely promised 'eternal life'/'life in the world to come' but this is the voice of law rather than the voice of God.

---

[23] Watson, *Paul and the Hermeneutics of Faith*, p. 429. He offers this in support of his previous sentence: 'A negative assessment of Paul's interpretation of Deuteronomy 27.26 is understandable, but it is not justified.'

[24] Watson acknowledges that both the Greek (*en autois*) and the Hebrew (*bahem*) could be translated as 'in them' with the meaning 'those who observe the commandments will find in them the necessary orientation for their lives' (p. 320). However, he thinks the instrumental meaning ('by them') is more likely in the light of the tradition history of the passage, citing Deut. 4.1; 8.1; Ezek. 18.5-9; 20.11,13 and Philo (*Congr.* 86–7). He also notes that the LXX did not preserve the parallelism of the Hebrew and that to understand it thus would be 'pure tautology' (p. 322).

From a hermeneutical point of view, (1) and (2) have much in common. They both assert that Lev. 18.5 was true in its day (it expressed God's will for his people) but the coming of Christ has now made it redundant. Whether we call this a 'christological', 'messianic' or 'apocalyptic' interpretation, Scripture is being interpreted (in this case, annulled) in the light of later revelation. Embarrassed by previous caricatures of Judaism as 'legalistic works-righteousness', many scholars go to great lengths to show that Lev. 18.5 does not intend to deny the primacy of grace and later writers (including Paul) did not interpret it in that way. Indeed, Sanders' designation of Judaism as 'covenantal nomism' ('exodus/grace' maintained by 'obligation/law') parallels Paul's gospel where 'redemption/grace' is maintained by 'obligation/law of Christ' (Gal. 6.2). The major difference is that the response called forth by the 'redemption in Christ' is no longer obedience to the Jewish law but obedience to the demands of love (Gal. 5.14) or the promptings of the Spirit (Gal. 5.18).[25]

For our purposes, we might regard (3) as similar to (1) and (2) in that a later text (Deuteronomy 28) is being used to reinterpret the earlier promise of Lev. 18.5. The experience of exile showed that what seemed like a genuine offer of life (Lev. 18.5) was in fact doomed to failure. But Paul would not have considered Deuteronomy 28 to come from the exilic period. He would have assumed that it came from the same author (Moses) as Lev. 18.5 and hence the Torah speaks with more than one voice. On the one hand, there are 'conditional statements, which imply that the choice between blessing and curse, life and death is genuinely open'; on the other hand, there is 'prophetic denunciation, in which the realization of the curse has become a certainty'.[26] Thus position (3) is both more and less radical than positions (1) and (2). It is more radical in that it regards Lev. 18.5 as a false promise of life (extending to life in the world to come). But it is less radical in that it sees this as part of a fundamental disjunction within Scripture itself, and is therefore not being imposed by Paul's 'freestanding doctrine of righteousness by faith'.[27]

Watson admits that the covenantal interpretation of Lev. 18.5 is a 'serious exegetical possibility' and though he himself finds such texts as Deut. 4.1 and Ezek. 20.11,13 as convincing evidence that this is not how later tradition understood it, it is arguable that these texts exhibit the same ambiguities. For example, Deut. 4.1 says, 'So now, Israel, give heed to the statutes and ordinances that I am teaching you to observe (*poiein*), so that you may live (*zēte*) to enter and occupy the land that the

---

[25] Those who oppose the so-called 'new perspective' would argue that the parallel is superficial for there is a qualitative difference between obeying law and obeying the promptings of the Spirit. The difference is summed up in Jeremiah's new covenant prophecy: 'But this is the covenant that I will make with the house of Israel after those days, says the LORD: I will put my law within them, and I will write it on their hearts; and I will be their God, and they shall be my people. No longer shall they teach one another, or say to each other, "Know the LORD," for they shall all know me, from the least of them to the greatest, says the LORD; for I will forgive their iniquity, and remember their sin no more' (Jer. 33.33-4).

[26] Watson, *Paul and the Hermeneutics of Faith*, p. 429.

[27] Watson, *Paul and the Hermeneutics of Faith*, p. 331.

LORD, the God of your ancestors, is giving you'. Clearly this can be read as a conditional statement that Israel will only 'live' and occupy the land if she 'does' (*poiein*) the commandments. On the other hand, one could equally argue that this takes place within a covenantal framework where the promised land is what 'the God of your ancestors, *is giving you*'. There is no question of Israel's obedience in any sense 'earning' or 'meriting' the promised blessings. It depends entirely on grace ('is giving you'), though it is possible to forfeit such blessings through disobedience. It is at least arguable that Paul says much the same thing in Gal. 5.4, where he threatens his opponents: 'You who want to be justified by the law have cut yourselves off from Christ; *you have fallen away from grace*.'

On what basis then should we choose between a non-disjunctive covenantal reading of Lev. 18.5, and one that sees it as a conditional promise of life that has been superseded by Deuteronomy 28? According to Watson, there is a very definite reason why so many scholars have opted for the covenantal explanation over the last twenty years:

> Since the work of Sanders, a veto has been imposed on the supposition that the commandments could have been understood as the way to life in Second Temple Judaism. It is assumed that such an understanding of human action is incompatible, first, with God's covenant with Israel; second, with the divine mercy and forgiveness; and third, with the role of the commandments as marking out the boundary between the elect people and the Gentiles.[28]

Such a veto is understandable in the light of the unfortunate influence of anti-Semitism on previous scholarship,[29] but Watson thinks it is incorrect, at least as an interpretation of Leviticus. For example, while Sanders is correct to point out that obedience to the law is not seen as 'earning' or 'meriting' the promised blessings, his use of 'maintaining' or 'staying in' the covenant is equally problematic. Where in Leviticus, Watson asks, is this 'maintenance' function articulated? What Leviticus makes clear is that covenant and obedience are inseparable, in the sense that one cannot have one without the other. While this does indeed refute the caricature of 'earning' the covenant blessings, it also implies that the promises are conditional on human obedience. Thus while texts such as Lev. 26.40-42 show that God is not unresponsive to confession and repentance, this does not amount to an absolute promise, come what may. For Watson, 'The covenant with the patriarchs and the exodus generation simply keeps open the conditional promise of blessing announced at Sinai (cf. 26.3-13), but it does not guarantee it.'[30]

---

[28] Watson, *Paul and the Hermeneutics of Faith*, p. 323.

[29] 'The more recent inclination to minimize disagreement and to highlight more conciliatory possibilities may be understood as a justified attempt to exorcize that particular ghost' (Watson, *Paul and the Hermeneutics of Faith*, p. 25).

[30] Watson, *Paul and the Hermeneutics of Faith*, p. 324.

Conclusion

Mention of a 'veto' operative among scholars highlights a point that we have encountered several times in our case studies; interpretation seeks to place what is often fragmentary and disjointed into some sort of order or pattern. This inevitably involves prioritizing certain types of evidence and relegating other types to the margins. One does not have to sign up to deconstruction to recognize the truth in Derrida's statement that a text 'always reserves a surprise for ... a critique which might think it had mastered its game, surveying all its threads at once, thus deceiving itself into wishing to look at the text without touching it, without putting its hand to the "object", without venturing to add to it'.[31] Sanders' insight that 'Judaism' was not a legalistic religion has for many scholars seemed like a secure foundation on which to build (the so-called 'new perspective' on Paul). But his missionary zeal to oppose 'Lutheran' interpretations in all their forms has led him to offer his own generalizations. Thus according to Sanders, all forms of Judaism and early Christianity that we know about can be described as 'covenantal nomism', where an act of grace is *followed* by covenant stipulations. But as Watson has shown, the relationship between 'grace' and 'stipulation' is much more complicated than this, leading some texts to sound a distinctly 'conditional' note. The theme of competing theological agendas is uppermost in our next study, the 'theory of prophecy' enunciated in 1 Pet. 1.10-12.

---

[31] J. Derrida, *Positions* (Chicago: Chicago University Press, 1972), p. 71.

7

~

Evoking a theory of prophecy?
1 Pet. 1.10-12

Introduction

~

One of the difficulties that we have faced in our case studies is that the New Testament authors are seldom explicit about what they are doing. They quote, allude and echo the Scriptures of Israel but do not articulate a theory of how those texts relate to 'the events that have been fulfilled among us' (Lk. 1.1). Paul comes closest when he states that 'whatever was written in former days was written for our instruction' (Rom. 15.4) and even provides an example: the command not to muzzle an ox while grazing (Deut. 25.4) 'was indeed written for our sake' (1 Cor. 9.10). It is unclear whether Paul thinks that 'Moses' knew that he was writing 'for our sake' or that this was a divine intention hidden from 'Moses' but now revealed to Paul. His rhetoric at this point ('Is it for oxen that God is concerned? Or does he not speak *entirely* for our sake?') suggests the latter, but the verse is too enigmatic to draw definite conclusions.

The closest the New Testament comes to articulating a theory of prophecy is found in 1 Pet. 1.10-12, though the passage is not without its difficulties:

> Concerning this salvation, the prophets who prophesied of the grace that was to be yours made careful search (*exezētēsan*) and inquiry (*exēraunēsan*), inquiring about the person or time (*tina ē poion kairon*) that the Spirit of Christ within them indicated (*edēlou*) when it testified in advance (*promartyromenon*) to the sufferings destined for Christ (*ta eis christon pathēmata*) and the subsequent glory (*doxas*). It was revealed to them that they were serving not themselves but you, in regard to the things that have now been announced to you through those who brought you good news by the Holy Spirit sent from heaven – things into which angels long to look! (1 Pet. 1.10-12)

There are a variety of 'activities' mentioned in this theory of prophecy. First, there is a searching/inquiring activity by the prophets, though nothing is said about what they searched. 1QS 5.11 offers a partial parallel: 'They have neither inquired nor sought after him concerning his laws that they might know the hidden things'. This might suggest that the terms refer to some sort of exegetical activity, a view that could be supported by the use of *eraunaō* in Jn 5.39 ('You search the scriptures because you think that in them you have eternal life') and the use of *dēloō* ('indicate') in Hebrews. It should be noted that the passage does not state whether their search was successful.

Secondly, there are two verbs (*dēloō*, *promartyromai*) indicating an activity of the 'Spirit of Christ'. The first occurs seven times in the New Testament, the two uses in Hebrews being particularly instructive. In Heb. 9.8, the laws of the sanctuary are being interpreted: 'By this the Holy Spirit indicates (*dēlountos*) that the way into the sanctuary has not yet been disclosed as long as the first tent is still standing.' In Heb. 12.27, a scriptural text (Hag. 2.6) is quoted and then said to indicate (*dēloi*) 'the removal of what is shaken'. Thus there is ample precedent for seeing *dēloō* as referring to some sort of hermeneutical/discernment activity. The other word is *promartyromai*, unattested before 709 CE[1] and probably originating with the author. It is unclear whether 'Spirit of Christ' is simply a Christian way of referring to the Spirit of God in the Old Testament or specifically refers to an activity of the Holy Spirit prior to Pentecost or even the pre-incarnate Christ, a view particularly associated with Anthony Hanson.[2] Though it might seem unlikely that testimony borne by the Spirit of Christ could be unsuccessful, it remains the case that the passage does not state whether the prophets were able to grasp the testimony; only that testimony was made 'within them' (*en autois*) or perhaps 'among them', if they are being viewed as a collective.[3]

Thirdly, there is the activity of revelation to the prophet and 'things in which angels long to look'. The 'revelation' appears to be limited to the insight that 'they were not serving themselves but you', unless the following phrase ('in regard to the things that have now been announced') is intended to add content to that. The 'longing' of the angels clearly aims to enhance the value of what has now been made known, though their identity (fallen? all?) and motivation (envy? reverence?) is as obscure as Christ preaching to the imprisoned spirits in 1 Pet. 3.19 (and possibly connected).

This 'theory' of prophecy has also been important in discussions about the relationship between the meaning intended by the prophets and the meaning given

---

[1] According to W.L. Schutter, *Hermeneutics and Composition in 1 Peter* (WUNT, 2. 30; Tübingen: Mohr-Siebeck, 1989), p. 102. It appears to be comparable to Paul's *proevangelizomai* in Gal. 3.8.

[2] A.T. Hanson, *The Living Utterances of God* (London: Darton, Longman & Todd, 1983), p. 141.

[3] It is notoriously difficult to decide between individual and collective interpretations of such phrases. It is undoubtedly collective when an argument breaks out 'among' the disciples (Lk. 9.46; 22.24); when a schism breaks out 'among' the Pharisees (Jn 9.16); when Jesus performs miracles 'among' them (Jn 15.24); when there was not a needy person 'among' them (Acts 4.34); and when Lot had to live 'among' the wicked (2 Pet. 2.8). It is undoubtedly individual when Jesus says that he will live 'in' them and they in him (Jn 17.23, 26); when disciples should walk 'in' the good works prepared by God (Eph. 2.10); when ignorance is 'in' them because of hardness of heart (Eph. 4.18); and when the Spirit breathes new life 'into' the dead witnesses (Rev. 11.11).

in the New Testament. Walter Kaiser thinks it 'decisively affirms that the prophets spoke knowingly on five rather precise topics: 1) the Messiah, 2) his sufferings, 3) his glory, 4) the sequence of events (for example, suffering was followed by the Messiah's glorification), and 5) that the salvation announced in those pre-Christian days was not limited to the prophet's audiences, but it also included the readers of Peter's day'.[4] He uses this to assert that the meaning intended by the prophets is identical to the meaning given by the New Testament authors, even if that is not always apparent. On the other hand, Philip Payne thinks 'it would be difficult to defend that every prophecy identified in the New Testament as being fulfilled by Jesus Christ, such as Psalm 16, 22 or 110, was understood in just that sense by its author or that each was on his part intended as a messianic prediction'.[5] He thinks that 1 Pet. 1.10-12 claims that the meaning intended by God (what the Spirit of Christ testified in advance) is identical to what the Holy Spirit has now revealed in the gospel, but the only thing that the prophets are specifically said to have understood is that they were not serving themselves. In other words, they spoke more than they knew.

The difficulty in deciding between these options is that the object of the prophets' enquiry (*tina ē poinon kairon*) and the content of the Spirit of Christ's testimony (*ta eis christon pathēmata*) are both ambiguous. The NRSV translation cited above has taken *tina* as an interrogative pronoun and *poion* as an interrogative adjective modifying *kairon* ('time'). In other words, the prophets were seeking to discern the 'who' as well as the 'when'. In support, one notes that this is the meaning of the other three occurrences of interrogative *tis* in 1 Peter (3.13; 4.17; 5.8) and is the more usual meaning in the New Testament (all but 20 of over 1000 occurrences). Of particular relevance is the question asked by the Ethiopian eunuch (Acts 8.34) while reading Isaiah 53: 'About whom (*peri tinos*), may I ask you, does the prophet say this, about himself or about someone else?' It could thus be argued that the dual inquiry (who and when) of the prophets reveals a comprehensive ignorance on their part, at least at the beginning of their searching.

On the other hand, the majority of commentators think that both *tina* and *poion* should be taken with *kairon*, so that it is only the time of the events that puzzled them. Had they referred to different objects (who *and* when) we would have expected the conjunction 'and' between them, rather than 'or'. It is a commonplace in apocalyptic literature to enquire about the 'when' (Dan. 9.2; *4 Ezra* 4.33–5.13; 1QpHab 7.1-8) and the double reference ('what time or what sort of time') would be similar to the question put by the disciples in Mk 13.4 ('Tell us, when will this be, and what will be the sign that all these things are about to be accomplished?'). On this view, it could be argued that the prophets understood the content of their prophecies but did not know the time of their fulfilment.

---

[4] W.C. Kaiser, Jr., 'The Single Intent of Scripture' in G.K. Beale (ed.), *The Right Doctrine from the Wrong Texts?* (Grand Rapids: Baker Books, 1994), p. 57.

[5] P.B. Payne, 'The Fallacy of Equating Meaning with the Human Author's Intention' in Beale (ed.), *Right Doctrine*, p. 77.

The second issue concerns the use of the prepositional phrase *eis christon* when referring to the 'sufferings' (*pathēmata*) and 'glories' (*doxas*). The question is whether this should be interpreted as if it were a genitive ('the sufferings/glories of Christ'), as in 1 Pet. 4.13 and 5.1, or whether the syntax is deliberate and intended to mean something else. The preposition *eis* can indicate purpose and so the phrase could mean 'sufferings for the benefit of Christ', that is, the sufferings of Christ's followers. This is the view of Selwyn ('the sufferings of the Christward road')[6] and is the reading adopted by the REB ('sufferings in Christ's cause'). Such a meaning would clearly be relevant to the recipients of the letter and arguably does more justice to the plurals ('sufferings'/ 'glories') than a reference to Christ's death and resurrection.

Another possibility is that the *eis christon* shoud be taken in a temporal sense, meaning 'sufferings until Christ'. A parallel would be Gal. 3.24, where the law is said to be 'our disciplinarian until Christ came (*eis christon*)'. The meaning in 1 Peter would then be the sum total of the sufferings of God's people, from the prophet's own time to the time of Christ. The difficulty of this is that it would seem to exclude or at least play down the actual sufferings of Christ ('until Christ'). There is also debate as to whether Gal. 3.24 should be taken in this temporal sense. The NIV takes it as an expression of purpose ('So the law was put in charge to *lead us* to Christ').

Karen Jobes argues for the traditional view on the basis that the prepositional phrase in 2 Cor. 1.11 and 11.3 'expresses the recipients of the implied verbal action'[7] and 1 Pet. 1.10 uses a similar prepositional phrase to speak of the 'grace that was to be yours' (*eis hymas*). Her explanation for why the genitive is not used has far-reaching consequences:

> He chooses a prepositional phrase with *eis* rather than the genitive because of the prophetic perspective of the immediate context. In other words, the prophets in view were speaking long before the sufferings occurred, but they knew that sufferings would come to the Messiah. In the parallel syntax of verse 10, those prophets also foresaw the grace that would come and, in Peter's opinion, had come *eis hymas*, "to you," the Christians to whom Peter writes. Just as the Messiah would be the recipient of sufferings, God's people, among whom the Christians of Asia Minor now find themselves remarkably included, will be the recipients of grace.[8]

One further issue is that if the 'sufferings' are those of Christ, are the 'glories' that follow (*meta tauta*) restricted to Christ or can they refer to the subsequent benefits for his followers? Two points are in favour of a wider interpretation. First, the 'prophecy theory' begins by asserting that the prophets prophesied concerning

---

[6] E.G. Selwyn, *The First Epistle of St. Peter* (London: Macmillan, 1947), p. 136.

[7] K.H. Jobes, *1 Peter* (BECNT; Grand Rapids: Baker Academic, 2005), p. 100.

[8] Jobes, *1 Peter*, p. 100.

'the grace that was to be yours'. This suggests that the content of their prophecies was not simply the death and resurrection of Christ but the resulting benefits. Secondly, the plural 'glories' is an unlikely way of referring to the resurrection, though it could perhaps refer to the subsequent ascension and exaltation.

In this chapter, we will look at two questions: (1) Does the 'prophecy theory' act as a hermeneutical key for interpreting the author's actual uses of Scripture? (2) Do the actual uses of Scripture in 1 Peter help to elucidate the meaning of the 'prophecy theory'? Since nearly half of the quotations[9] and significant allusions[10] in 1 Peter come from the book of Isaiah, we will make that our focus, beginning with the quotation of Isa. 40.6-8 in 1 Pet. 1.24-5.

Isaiah in 1 Peter[11]

1 Pet. 1.24-5 (Isa. 40.6-8)

Isa. 40.6-8	1 Pet. 1.23-5
A voice says, 'Cry out!' And I said, 'What shall I cry?'	You have been born anew, not of perishable but of imperishable seed, through the living and enduring word (*logos*) of God. For
All people are grass, their constancy is like the flower of the field. The grass withers, the flower fades, when the breath of the LORD blows upon it; surely the people are grass.	'All flesh is like grass and all its glory like the flower of grass.
The grass withers, the flower fades, but the word of our God will stand forever.	The grass withers, and the flower falls, but the word (*rhēma*) of the Lord endures forever.' That word (*rhēma*) is the good news that was announced to you.

On the surface, the author's point seems fairly straightforward. He associates the new birth of his addressees with imperishable seed, through the agency of the living and enduring word of God, identified as the good news that was preached to them. The

---

[9] 1.24-5/Isa 40.6-8; 2.6-8/Isa 28.16+8.14; 2.25/Isa 53.6; 4.14/Isa 11.2.

[10] 2.9/Isa. 43.20-21; 2.22-5/Isa. 53.4, 5, 7, 9, 12; 3.14-15/Isa. 8.12-13.

[11] This section draws on my chapter 'Isaiah in 1 Peter' in S. Moyise and M.J.J. Menken (eds), *Isaiah in the New Testament* (London and New York: T&T Clark, 2005), pp. 175–88.

quotation confirms the point that God's word is enduring, adding the encouraging 'forever', while evoking a common experience of things perishable ('grass') and equating this with the lot of 'the flesh'. The quoted words do not appear to say anything about the 'sufferings' and 'glories' of Christ or his people.

There are four major differences between the MT and the LXX text accepted by Rahlfs and Ziegler: (1) The people's 'constancy' has become their 'glory'; (2) it is compared with the flower of the 'grass' (as in the first clause) rather than the flower of the 'field'; (3) the clause about the breath of the Lord is omitted entirely;[12] and (4) the flower 'falls' rather than 'fades'. In the first of these, 1 Peter agrees with the LXX's 'glory' but agrees with the MT in using a pronoun ('its') rather than the LXX's 'person' (*anthrōpos*).[13] For the other three differences, 1 Peter sides with the LXX. Though these differences have little effect on the overall meaning of the quotation, they do raise the interesting question of whether the author thought the LXX text known to him reproduces the testimony of the 'Spirit of Christ' in his 'prophecy theory'.

There are two differences between 1 Peter and both the MT and LXX of Isa. 40.6-8. The first is the inclusion of 'like' (*hōs*) between 'flesh' and 'grass', transforming the metaphor into a simile. Since the author makes frequent use of *hōs* as a comparative (x27), this is most likely a stylistic change, perhaps influenced by its presence in the parallel clause ('*like* the flower of the field'). The second is more substantial, the replacement of 'our God' with 'Lord'. There are several possible explanations for this: (1) This was the reading of the LXX text used by 1 Peter (and now found in L[1] 46-233-456 Co Syp[a]). If this is the case, then our main uncial witnesses (ℵ, A, B) represent a text that has been conformed to the Hebrew. Ziegler and Rahlfs think it much more likely that the text of 1 Peter has influenced these other LXX manuscripts; (2) A stylistic change by 1 Peter, perhaps drawing on the previous verse of Isaiah (40.5), which speaks of the 'salvation of God' and then says, 'for the LORD has spoken'; (3) A deliberate theological change to show that it is 'the word of/concerning Jesus' that endures forever.

Elliott argues for a deliberate change, noting that the author generally uses *kyrios* for Jesus (1.3; 2.2; 3.15) and *theos* for God the father (1.2, 3, 5, 21, 23 etc.). Furthermore, the text is applied to the readers by means of a specific identification: 'That word is the good news that was announced to you'. Since Elliott takes the 'sufferings followed by glories' of 1 Pet. 1.10-12 to refer to Christ, he deduces that it is not Jesus' word (i.e. his preaching) that is in mind. The substitution of 'Lord' for

---

[12] It would appear that Isa. 40.7 fell out through haplography, as also witnessed by 1QIs[a].

[13] Following a suggestion by Kraft, Jobes thinks the majority reading of 1 Pet. 1.24 (*anthrōpou*) is not scribal conformity to the LXX but is original. She suggests that it was abbreviated to *anou*, which was corrupted to *autou* (the reading of Sinaiticus) and then *autēs* to agree with the feminine *sarx*. This is possible but *autēs* is well attested (p[72] ℵ[2] A B C). See K. Jobes, 'Septuagint Textual Tradition in 1 Peter' in W. Kraus and R.G. Wooden (eds), *Septuagint Research. Issues and Challenges in the Study of the Greek Jewish Scriptures* (Atlanta: SBL, 2006), p. 318.

'God' has resulted in a change of meaning. The subjective genitive ('God's word abides forever') has become an objective genitive ('the word *about* Christ endures forever').[14] The 'prophecy theory' is thus acting as a hermeneutical key, changing the meaning of the original text.

Schutter agrees but goes further. He looks forward to 1 Pet. 2.1-3 and speaks of the author's 'creative elaboration of the text's figurative dimensions'.[15] He takes 2.1 to be an elaboration of the moral connotations of 'flesh', 2.2 to refer back to the 'word of God' and 2.3 to consolidate the application of 'Lord' to Christ, by using the wordplay, 'the Lord is good' (*chrēstos*). He concludes that 'the image of an infant's irrepressible urge to grow has been adroitly juxtaposed with the quotation's imagery of transience'.[16] However, this seems somewhat fanciful. The mention of malice, guile, insincerity, envy and slander in 2.1 does not obviously look back to the transience of the 'flesh' mentioned in the quotation, and the reference to 'pure spiritual milk' (*logikon adolon gala*) in 2.2 is an unlikely way of referring back to the 'word' (*rhēma*) of the quotation.

Jobes focuses on the contextual similarity between the two writings. Both are writing to exiles facing persecution and tempted to doubt the veracity of God's promises: 'Peter identifies the word of God as understood by Isaiah with the word that has been preached to Peter's readers, the gospel of the Lord Jesus Christ.'[17] Based on her understanding of 1 Pet. 1.10-12, the 'promises were more than historical prophecies for the future of Israel; they were also, perhaps more importantly, eschatological revelations of God's final redemption of humankind'.[18] If it is difficult to see how the quoted words (Isa. 40.6-8) could possibly refer to the 'sufferings' and 'glories' of Christ (or his people), she notes that 1 Pet. 2.20-25 will allude to the suffering servant of Isaiah 53 and hence 'Isaiah's eschatology for Israel is 1 Peter's eschatology for the Christian church.'[19] This may be the case for 1 Pet. 2.20-25 (see below) but it is not clear that this is how the author understood Isa. 40.6-8. By equating it with the 'good news (*evangelisthen*) that was announced to you', he may have in mind only that aspect of the gospel which promises an answer to transience and death. Of course, he believes that that was made possible through the death and resurrection of Christ (1.3-5) but he does not necessarily think that Isa. 40.6-8 is referring to those things – unless the 'prophecy theory' demands it.

---

[14] J.H. Elliott, *1 Peter: A New Translation and Commentary* (AB, 37B; New York: Doubleday, 2000), p. 391. J.R. Michaels, *1 Peter* (WBC, 49; Dallas: Word Books, 1988) makes a case for the subjective genitive (Jesus' preaching) but in the end, says, 'To Peter, the message of Jesus and the message about Jesus are the same message, just as they are to Mark (1.1, 14-15) and to the author of Hebrews (2.3-4)' (p. 79).

[15] Schutter, *Hermeneutic*, p. 128.

[16] Schutter, *Hermeneutic*, p. 128.

[17] Jobes, *1 Peter*, p. 126.

[18] Jobes, *1 Peter*, p. 126.

[19] Jobes, *1 Peter*, p. 128.

1 Pet. 2.6-8 (Isa. 28.16/8.14)

Isa. 28.16

See, I am laying
(*embalō*) in Zion
a foundation stone,
a tested stone
(*polutelē eklekton*),
a precious (*entimon*)
cornerstone,
a sure foundation.
One who trusts will
not panic.

1 Pet. 2.6-8

'See, I am laying
(*tithēmi*) in Zion
a stone,
a cornerstone
chosen and precious
(*eklekton entimon*);

and whoever believes
in him will not be put
to shame.'

Rom. 9.33

'See, I am laying
(*tithēmi*) in Zion
a stone that will make
people stumble,
a rock that will make
them fall
(*petran skandalou*),

and whoever believes
in him will not be put
to shame.'

Isa. 8.14

He will become a
sanctuary, a stone
one strikes against;
for both houses of
Israel he will become
a rock one stumbles
over (*petras ptōmati*)
– a trap and a snare
for the inhabitants of
Jerusalem.

Ps. 118.22

The stone that the
builders rejected has
become the chief
cornerstone.

To you then who
believe, he is precious
(*timē*);
but for those who do
not believe,
'The stone that the
builders rejected has
become the very head
of the corner', and
'A stone that makes
them stumble, and a
rock that makes them
fall (*petra skandalou*).'

Mk 12.10

Have you not read
this scripture: 'The
stone that the
builders rejected has
become the corner-
stone; this was the
Lord's doing, and it is
amazing in our eyes'?

Lk. 20.17-18

What then does this
text mean: 'The stone
that the builders
rejected has become
the cornerstone'?
Everyone who falls
on that stone will be
broken to pieces; and
it will crush anyone
on whom it falls.

The occurrence of these 'stone' texts in the Gospels, Paul and 1 Peter (and use of the imagery in Eph. 2.20) has been pivotal in discussions of a possible testimony book,[20]

---

[20] J.R. Harris, *Testimonies* (2 vols; Cambridge: Cambridge University Press, 1916, 1920).

collection of proof texts[21] or early Christian hymns[22] as the source of some of the Old Testament quotations in the New Testament. The textual data and implications may be briefly summarized as follows:

1. The presence of 'and if anyone trusts in him' in the LXX of Isa. 8.14, without a basis in the Hebrew text, already suggests a link with Isa. 28.16 in the eyes of the LXX translators. It is possible that 1QS 8.4ff also offers evidence for a link between the Hebrew texts.[23]

2. The MT of Isa. 8.14 says that God 'will become a sanctuary, a stone one strikes against'. The LXX turns this into a contrast: For the one who trusts, God will be a sanctuary and *not* a stone that causes stumbling.[24] 1 Peter and Romans agree that the stone is *not* a cause of stumbling for those who believe (from Isa. 28.16) but insist that God has laid in Zion a stone that causes stumbling. In no sense does Isa. 8.14 (MT or LXX) speak of 'suffering followed by glory' for either the stone or those who put their trust in it/him.

3. Luke is witness to a development of the stone's destructive role. The stone that falls and crushes is probably an allusion to Dan. 2.34 but falling on the stone and being broken might well be an allusion to Isa. 8.15 ('they shall fall and be broken').

4. All the quotations of Ps. 118.22 in the New Testament agree exactly with the LXX, which is an accurate rendering of the Hebrew. The rejected stone that became the chief cornerstone approximates to a 'suffering followed by glory' motif.

5. 1 Peter and Romans agree with the LXX of Isa. 28.16 against MT by including an object 'upon it/him'[25] for the verb 'believe' and using a form of 'ashamed' instead of the somewhat obscure Hebrew 'haste/panic'. The verse does not speak about 'suffering followed by glory' for the stone, though it does offer a promise for those who put their trust in it/him.

6. 1 Peter agrees with Romans against the LXX in using *tithēmi* for 'I am laying', omitting mention of the foundations[26] and using *skandalon* instead of *ptōma* ('fall, misfortune, disaster'). This either points to literary dependence between 1 Peter and Romans or use of a common source.

7. 1 Peter differs from Paul in using the subjunctive form for 'not ashamed' instead of the future, quoting the two texts separately and including comment between them.

---

[21] Dodd, *According to the Scriptures* (1952).

[22] Selwyn, *The First Epistle of St. Peter* (1952).

[23] So Schutter, *Hermeneutic*, p. 132, drawing on the work of Joseph Ziegler and David Flusser. However, he denies Flusser's claim that 1 Pet. 2.4ff and 1QS 8.4ff go back to a common *Vorlage*.

[24] The negative is not found in Aquila, Theodotion or Symmachus.

[25] Interestingly, the object pronoun is also found in the Targum and thus may represent an early messianic interpretation, taking *auton* to mean 'him' rather than 'it'.

[26] If it is correct that the double omission of the foundations is because Isa. 8.14 requires a stone one can trip over rather than a buried foundation stone, it suggests the origin of this text-type lies in the combination of the passages.

8. Paul uses the quotations as part of his explanation for why Israel has stumbled and Gentiles are finding salvation. 1 Peter is more general, referring to the 'unbelieving neighbors and authorities in the Roman provinces who are engaged in the kind of social harassment of the Christian communities that has provoked this letter'.[27]

1 Peter first alludes to Isa. 28.16 and Ps. 118.22 in 2.4 by exhorting his readers to, 'Come to him, a living *stone*, though *rejected* by mortals yet *chosen and precious* in God's sight'. He then quotes Isa. 28.16 to make the positive point that for those who believe, the stone is *precious*, and Ps. 118.22 that '*the* stone that the builders *rejected* has become the very head of the corner'. The initial allusion plays an important literary role for: (1) Had the full text of Isa. 28.16 been quoted at the beginning, he could not have made the comparison, 'like living stones, let yourselves be built into a spiritual house', for a building is not comprised of numerous corner-stones; (2) It suggests a semantic shift in the meaning of *eklekton* and *entimon*. When applied to building stones, the meaning is something like 'selected' and 'well-hewn'. When applied to people, the meaning is more relational, as in the NRSV ('chosen and precious'). It may even suggest a connection with the servant of Isa. 42.1 ('Here is my servant, whom I uphold, my chosen, in whom my soul delights'); (3) It makes it clear that the 'upon it/him' in the quotation refers to Christ and not simply the (masculine) stone. From a rhetorical point of view, 'the preliminary allusion makes a space for the crowning quotation to fill, giving a sense of completion and appropriateness'.[28]

Isa. 28.16 is phrased negatively; those who believe will not be put to shame. However, the opposite of shame is 'honour' (*timē*), which although cognate with *entimon*, should probably bear this meaning here, rather than something like 'precious'. Thus in the exposition, 1 Peter is not so much repeating the christological point (NRSV: 'he is precious') but making an ecclesiological point for believers; they will receive honour. On the other hand, for those who do not believe, Ps. 118.22 and Isa. 8.14 are applicable. On their own, we might deduce that their purpose is to elucidate the role of Christ but 1 Peter adds a conclusion: 'They stumble because they disobey the word, as they were destined to do (*etethēsan*)'. This suggests that the main purpose of quoting Ps. 118.22 was 'primarily to evoke the builder's shame over their mistake and only secondarily to refer to Christ's exaltation'.[29] As is commonly recognized, the use of *etethēsan* ('destined, appointed') forms a link back to the initial *tithēmi* ('I place, appoint') of the quotation.

It is clear that we are dealing with some intricate exegesis that draws not only on several texts but also on certain prior relationships between those texts (and

[27] P.J. Achtemeier, *1 Peter: A Commentary on First Peter* (Hermeneia; Minneapolis: Fortress Press, 1996), p. 161. Elliott thinks these variations 'eliminate the possibility of mutual influence or literary dependency and instead represent diverse Christian usage of a traditional combination of "stone" texts applied to Jesus and employed to distinguish Christian believers from either the house of Israel or all nonbelievers' (*1 Peter*, p. 321).

[28] F.J.J. Rensburg and S.Moyise, 'Isaiah in 1 Peter 2.4-10. Applying Intertextuality to the Study of the OT in the NT', *Ekklesiastikos Pharos* 84 (2002), pp. 12–30.

[29] Schutter, *Hermeneutic*, p. 136.

particular textual forms). Schutter considers Isa. 28.16 to be the base text and describes what follows as 'midrashic exegesis'. Others find this term unhelpful, as if the meaning of Isa. 28.16 was a problem to be solved, rather than a means to an end. Jobes' attempt to relate the exposition to the 'prophecy theory' is revealing: 'Peter understood that the Spirit of Christ revealed to Isaiah both the sufferings of Christ and the glories that would follow as an encouragement to Peter's Christians readers (1.10-12), *regardless of whatever meaning they would have had to Isaiah's own generation.*'[30] This would appear to suggest that the author of 1 Peter can only apply his 'prophecy theory' by changing the meaning of the texts (unless one agrees with Payne that Isaiah did not know the true meaning of his words). That might be our eventual conclusion but is it not entirely clear that the author of 1 Peter understood Isa. 28.16 and 8.14 as predicting the 'sufferings' and 'glories' of Christ (or his people). Certainly he equates 'believing in the stone' with 'believing in Christ' but he does not elaborate that this means believing in Christ's death and resurrection. That is only present if it is imposed in order to conform to the 'prophecy theory'.

1 Pet. 2.9 (Isa. 43.20-21)

Isa. 43.20-21	1 Pet. 2.9
The wild animals will honour me, the jackals and the ostriches; for I give water in the wilderness, rivers in the desert, to give drink to my chosen people (*to genos mou to eklekton*), the people whom I formed for myself (*periepoiēsamēn*) so that they might declare my praise (*tas aretas mou diēgeisthai*).	But you are a chosen race (*genos eklekton*), a royal priesthood, a holy nation, God's own people (*laos eis peripoiēsin*), in order that you may (*hopōs*) proclaim the mighty acts (*tas aretas exangeilēte*) of him who called you out of darkness into his marvellous light.

There are three differences between the quotation and the LXX text of Isa. 43.20-21 favoured by Rahfls and Ziegler. First, instead of the first person verb *periepoiēsamēn* ('I formed'), 1 Peter uses the noun *peripoiēsis* ('possession'). In the rest of the New Testament, the noun is usually qualified by a further noun such as 'salvation' (1 Thess. 5.9) or 'glory' (2 Thess. 2.14). Secondly, 1 Peter speaks of proclaiming (*exangellō*) rather than recounting (*diēgeomai*) the praises/acts of God. The change is surprising since *exangellō* is not used elsewhere in the New Testament (except the shorter ending of Mark). Schutter[31] suggests the change was prompted by Isa. 42.12 ('Let

---

[30] Jobes, *1 Peter*, p. 151. Emphasis added.
[31] Schutter, *Hermeneutic*, p. 40.

them give glory to the LORD, and declare his praise in the coastlands') but since the LXX uses *anagellō* in this verse, it still does not explain why the author of 1 Peter chose *exangellō*.[32] Michaels is more convincing when he suggests the influence of Ps. 9.15, especially as this would also explain the third difference, the use of *hopōs* + subjunctive to express purpose rather than an infinitive.[33]

According to Best, the author 'advances his argument with a skilful selection of OT phrases (taken from the LXX) and all originally applied to Israel'.[34] The implication appears to be that the author views the Church as having replaced Israel as God's people but there is no hint of such a polemic in the letter and he never speaks of the Church as the 'new Israel'. Michaels suggests that the author is perhaps guilty of a certain 'naïveté', in that he seems to ignore the fact that there ever was an old Israel. Indeed, it is surprising that he refers to the dispersed collection of aliens (1 Pet. 1.1) as a 'race' (*genos*), a designation later taken up by the Fathers (e.g. Clement, *Stromateis* 6.5.41) to refer to the Church as 'the third race', though 1 Peter shows no interest in such categories.[35] Isa. 43.20-21 says nothing about 'suffering followed by glory' for a future figure, though it does promise rescue ('water in the wilderness') for God's people. Neither is there anything to suggest that the author of 1 Peter is interpreting it to mean this.

1 Pet. 2.22-5 (Isa. 53.4, 5, 6, 7, 9, 12)

Isa. 53.4, 5, 6, 7, 9, 12	*1 Pet. 2.22-5*
Surely he has borne our infirmities (*hamartias*)[1]…	'He committed no sin, and no deceit was found in his mouth.'[5]
upon him was the punishment that made us whole, and by his bruises (*mōlōps*) we are healed [2]…	When he was abused, he did not return abuse; when he suffered, he did not threaten;[4]
All we like sheep have gone astray[3]…	but he entrusted himself (*paredidou*)[6]
He was oppressed, and he was afflicted, yet he did not open his mouth[4]…	to the one who judges justly. He himself bore (*anēnenken*)
he had done no violence, and there was no deceit in his mouth[5]…	our sins (*hamartias*)[1,7]
he poured out (*paredothē*)[6] himself to death …	in his body on the cross, so that, free from sins, we might live for righteousness; by his wounds (*mōlōpi*) you have been healed.[2]
he bore (*anēnenken*) the sin (*hamartias*) of many[7]…	For you were going astray like sheep,[3] but now you have returned to the shepherd and guardian of your souls.

---

[32] As pointed out by Achtemeier, *1 Peter*, p. 166.

[33] Michaels, *1 Peter*, p. 110. However, his further comment that 'Peter has chosen an equivalent term, but one more specifically focused on worship' is denied by Achtemeier (*1 Peter*, p. 166) and Elliott (*1 Peter*, p. 439).

[34] E. Best, *1 Peter* (London: Marshall, Morgan & Scott, 1970), p. 107.

[35] Michaels, *1 Peter*, p. 107. The designation *genos eklekton* is only found in Isa. 43.20 and additions to Esther 8.12 in the LXX.

Debates about the use of Isaiah 53 in the Gospels are complicated by the lack of explicit parallels with the language of the LXX.[36] There is no such difficulty in 1 Peter, where a mixture of quotation(s) and allusions make it the most 'elaborate reorganisation or rewriting of Is. 53'[37] in the New Testament. Schutter thinks a definite pattern can be perceived, with quotations or allusions before 1 Pet. 2.24 coming from the second half of the passage (#5, 4, 6) and those coming after 1 Pet. 2.24 from the first half of the passage (#2, 3). The splice, as he calls it, comes in 1 Pet. 2.24, which combines the 'our sins' (*tas hamartias hēmōn*) of Isa. 53.4 with the 'bore' (*anēnenken*) of Isa. 53.12 (#1, 7). In the context of an exhortation to slaves (1 Pet. 2.18), 1 Peter's reworking of the material makes three points.

1. *Jesus' innocence and non-retaliation.* 'He committed no sin, and no deceit was found in his mouth'. With one exception (*hamartian* for *anomian*), this is in verbatim agreement with Isa. 53.9.[38] The statement of non-retaliation does not draw directly on Isa. 53.7 and may reflect Christian tradition. Best thinks the *paredidou* ('entrusted himself') points to the divine passive *paradothē* ('was handed over by God') in Isa. 53.12a, thus providing a transition from Christ as example to Christ as redeemer.[39]

2. *Jesus' accomplishment.* 'He himself bore our sins', a fusion of Isa. 53.4 and 53.12b; and 'by his wounds you have been healed', using the singular *mōlōps* (only occurrence in the New Testament) and the passive of *iaomai* (in the second person to apply to either his readers in general or slaves in particular). The first allusion is glossed 'in his body on the cross', ultimately an allusion to the 'tree' of Deut. 21.23, though probably drawn from Christian tradition (cf. Gal. 3.13). Whether this allusion to crucifixion ('the slave's death') and the use of *mōlōps* ('wound, bruise') is particularly aimed at slaves is difficult to determine. The author also uses the first person for 'our sins', and the result is that 'we might live'.

3. *The reader's predicament and salvation.* 'For you were going astray like sheep'. It is the presence of 'for' (*gar*) that leads Elliott to classify this as a marked quotation, though it may simply be an attempt to strengthen the link between the 'bruising' and 'going away like sheep'.[40] Michaels says, 'his insertion of a connecting *gar* links the metaphor of the straying sheep more closely to the metaphor of healing than was the case in Isaiah ... In effect, v25 defines what Peter means (and what he thinks Isaiah means) by healing.'[41] The author goes beyond what Isaiah 53 says by adding, 'so that, free from sin, we might

---

[36] As famously pointed out by M.D. Hooker, *Jesus the Servant* (London: SPCK, 1959).

[37] Schutter, *Hermeneutic*, p. 143.

[38] As Achtemeier (*1 Peter*, p. 200) points out, 1 Peter does not use any words from the *nom-* stem and most likely conforms it both to his own usage (2.22, 24; 3.18; 4.1, 8) and the more frequent word in Isaiah 53 (vv. 4, 5, 6, 10, 11, 12).

[39] Best, *1 Peter*, p. 121. Achtemeier (*1 Peter*, p. 200) disputes this since the next verse alludes to Isa. 53.12b to make a different point.

[40] As Elliott (*1 Peter*, p. 537) recognizes.

[41] Michaels, *1 Peter*, p. 150.

live for righteousness' and 'but now have returned to the shepherd and guardian of your souls'. The latter might have been suggested by the link between 'turning' and 'healing' found in Isa. 6.10[42] or perhaps the shepherd imagery of Ezekiel 34, which speaks of both going astray (34.4) and being returned (34.16).[43] It should be noted that the author does not necessarily think that these 'glosses' were in Isaiah's mind; they could simply be his additions based on additional revelation.

It is clear from this passage that the author believed that Isaiah spoke about the 'sufferings' of Christ but did he think that he also spoke of the 'glories' to follow? Isaiah 53 could have provided such material ('out of his anguish, he shall see light') but the author of 1 Peter does not allude to this. Instead, he focuses on the 'benefits' for God's people, drawing on the 'we are healed' from Isa. 53.5, and expanding with his own deductions ('free from sin'; 'returned to the shepherd'). If we take the outcome ('we are healed') as a statement of former predicament, it could be argued that the quoted passages present a 'suffering followed by glory' for God's people. However, the emphasis on Christ's sufferings is so strong, it would be more accurate to say that 'suffering followed by glory' is not predicated to either Christ or his people but put in a causal relationship (sufferings of Christ followed by glories for his people).

1 Peter 3.14-15 (Isa. 8.12,13)

Isa. 8.12-13	1 Pet. 3.14-15
Do not call conspiracy all that this people calls conspiracy,	But even if you do suffer for doing what is right, you are blessed.
and do not fear what it fears	Do not fear what they fear
(*ton de phobon autou ou mē phobēthēte*),	(*ton de phobon autōn mē phobēthēte*),
or be in dread	and do not be intimidated
(*oude mē tarachthēte*).	(*mēde tarachthēte*),
But the LORD of hosts,	but in your hearts
him you shall regard as holy	sanctify Christ as Lord
(*kyrion auton hagiasate*);	(*kyrion de ton christon hagiasate*).
let him be your fear,	
and let him be your dread.	

---

[42] L. Goppelt, *A Commentary on 1 Peter* (Grand Rapids: Eerdmans, 1982), p. 152. In favour is the link between Isa. 6.10 and Isa. 53.1 in Jn 12.38-40 and the fact that *epistrephō* does not occur in Isaiah 53 or again in 1 Peter. On the other hand, it is an extremely common word (c. 500 in LXX) and Michaels (*1 Peter*, p. 150) thinks it is just as likely that it was suggested by the metaphor of sheep going astray.

[43] So Elliott, *1 Peter*, p. 538. The metaphor of God's flock straying and returning might seem incongruous for a Gentile audience but it appears to apply to their previous alienation from God.

Though there is no introductory formula or explicit marker to indicate a quotation, several things point in that direction: (1) The abrupt and somewhat unusual phrase *ton de phobon* occurs in the LXX only at Isa. 8.12 and Prov. 1.29; (2) This is followed by the same two verbs (*phobēthēte* and *tarachthēte*) as in LXX Isa. 8.12;[44] (3) This is followed by a command to sanctify (Christ) the Lord (*kyrion ... hagiasate*), as in LXX Isa. 8.13; (4) The author has already quoted Isa. 8.14 in 1 Pet. 2.8. This confirms that he has LXX Isa. 8.12-13 in mind.[45] But for what purpose? In Isaiah, the prophet is being told not to share the fear or dread that has overtaken 'this people'. The genitive is therefore subjective ('Do not fear what they fear'). However, in 1 Peter, the 'they' must refer to the opponents mentioned in the previous verse, those who are causing the readers to suffer. It would thus be strange for the author to urge his readers not to fear what his opponents fear for that would be irrelevant. 1 Peter surely intends an objective genitive ('do not fear *them*'). Best comments:

> In Isaiah the prophet is told not to fear the king of Assyria as the Israelites do; here the meaning has been changed; when the words are isolated from their context they can be translated as in 1 Peter; the original meaning 'do not fear with their fear' would be impossible in the context of 1 Peter.[46]

Selwyn attempts a justification: '*phobos* can take either a subjective genitive (fear felt *by* someone) or an objective genitive (fear felt *of* someone); and, even if the former was the construction in Is. viii.12, St. Peter was fully entitled to use the latter construction here'.[47] But the question is not whether *phobos* can bear both meanings but the change in meaning from Isa. 8.14. Jobes notes that Isaiah and 1 Peter have a similar purpose ('The nature of the threatening adversaries is different, but the basis for the command not to fear remains the same'[48]) but acknowledges that 'the quote sits differently in 1 Peter, with an altered sense'.[49] It is clearly not espousing a 'suffering followed by glory' theme for either Christ or his people and it is generally acknowledged that the author of 1 Peter has changed the meaning of the original.

---

[44] Some New Testament manuscripts (p[72], B, L) omit *mēde tarachthēte* and one could argue that a later scribe has added them in order to conform the text more closely to the LXX. However, the words are well attested and probably slipped out because of the common ending with *phobothēte*.

[45] F.J.J. Rensburg and S. Moyise, 'Isaiah in 1 Peter 3.13-17. Applying Intertextuality to the Study of the OT in the NT', *Scriptura* 80 (2002), pp. 275–86.

[46] Best, *1 Peter*, p. 133.

[47] Selwyn, *1 Peter*, p. 192.

[48] Jobes, *1 Peter*, pp. 229–30.

[49] Jobes, *1 Peter*, p. 229. Michaels (*1 Peter*, pp. 186–7) thinks the answer lies in an ambiguity created by the singular pronoun (*autou*) in the LXX, which could refer to a specific person, namely the King of Assyria. However, 'do not fear the fear of him' would be a very cumbersome way of saying 'do not fear him'.

1 Pet. 4.14 (Isa. 11.2)

Isa. 11.2	1 Pet. 4.14
The spirit of the LORD shall rest on him,	If you are reviled for the name of Christ,
the spirit of wisdom and understanding,	you are blessed, because (*hoti*)
the spirit of counsel and might,	the spirit of glory,
the spirit of knowledge	which is the Spirit of God,
and the fear of the LORD.	is resting on you.

Isa. 11.2 is the only verse in the LXX where Spirit, God and the verb 'to rest' occur together and Elliott regards it as a quotation because of the marker *hoti*, though most see it as an allusion. 1 Peter does not include any of the qualifying genitives of Isa. 11.2 but adds 'glory', resulting in some 'uncharacteristically awkward prose'.[50] Furthermore, he applies the text to his readers rather than the 'branch' predicted by Isa. 11.1. The quoted text does not contain a 'suffering followed by glory' motif and indeed the application to 'God's people' is not strictly this, for the glory is present in the suffering rather than following it (though no doubt implying eschatological blessings). Based on the 'prophecy theory' of 1 Pet. 1.10-12, one might think the author has taken Isaiah 53 and 11 as predicting the 'sufferings' and 'glories' of a future figure that he now identifies as Christ. But not only does Isa. 11.2 not speak of 'glory',[51] 1 Peter applies it to Christians rather than Christ. For Schutter, this confirms that the author is operating with a *pesher*-like hermeneutic similar to those at Qumran. Isa. 8.12-13 does not espouse a 'suffering followed by glory' theme and the author of 1 Peter does not find one there.

Conclusion

The most striking conclusion is that despite the 'prophecy theory' of 1 Pet. 1.10-12, none of the cited passages articulate a 'suffering followed by glory' theme, either for a future figure or for God's people. Isaiah 53 could have provided it if the author had cited verse 11 ('out of his anguish, he shall see light') but he does not. The combination of Isaiah 53 and Isaiah 11 could have provided it but the author applies the former to Christ and the latter to God's people. Furthermore, unless the 'prophecy theory' is imposed on the material, it does not appear that the author of 1 Peter finds such a theme in the cited passages. He identifies the recipients of the various promises

---

[50] Achtemeier, *1 Peter*, p. 308. The complexity is indicated by the number of variant readings.

[51] Glory (*doxa*) does in fact occur in LXX Isa. 11.3 but in quite a different sense. 'He will not judge according to appearance (*doxa*)'.

with the Church but does not explicitly draw out a 'suffering followed by glory' theme. It would thus appear that 'sufferings' followed by 'glories' is a general indication of what the author of 1 Peter thought the prophets spoke about, but not a hermeneutical key for interpreting each and every verse.

Looked at from the other end, as it were, the author of 1 Peter thinks that Isaiah knew about the imperishable word of the gospel message (Isa. 40.6-8), the non-retaliatory character of Christ and his redemptive activity on behalf of the straying sheep (Isa. 53.4-12), the endowment of the Spirit on those suffering in Christ's name (Isa. 11.2), the requirement to 'reverence the Lord' rather than give in to fear (Isa. 8.12-13), the duty of the people of God to proclaim his mighty acts (Isa. 43.20-21) and the fact that the appointment of Christ will mean salvation for some and stumbling for others (Isa. 28.16/8.14). This illustrates the view that the prophets 'prophesied of the grace that was to be yours' (1.10) but 'suffering followed by glory' is too narrow to capture the actual uses of Isaiah in 1 Peter.

On a number of occasions, the meaning assigned by the author could not have been what was in the prophet's mind. Kaiser wishes to use the 'prophecy theory' to insist that it was, but we have just shown the limitations of imposing it (or a particular interpretation of it) on the material. As Jobes acknowledges, some of the interpretations offered by the author could not have been understood in this way in Isaiah's time. Indeed, the fact that the author is interpreting a Greek text rather than the 'words of Isaiah' shows the superficiality of Kaiser's view. The object of interpretation, namely, a particular Greek text, was never in the mind of the prophet but already represents an interpretation (though this may not have occurred to the author of 1 Peter).

Can we then agree with Payne that the author of 1 Peter has offered the meaning that God intended, even if that was (sometimes) kept from the prophet? It is worth breaking this down into a series of sub-questions: (1) Did the author of 1 Peter think that he was giving the divine meaning of the ancient texts? (2) Did the author of 1 Peter reflect on whether this differed from what Isaiah originally meant? (3) Can we accept a literary theory whereby the 'true' meaning of a text is only revealed in a (specific) later period? (4) Can we accept a theological framework whereby God endows the Scriptures with this quality of 'extra' meaning, which is not present in 'ordinary' texts?

The first is straightforward. The author of 1 Peter applies texts from Isaiah directly to Jesus and the Church. Isaiah was a prophet and the prophets spoke of 'the grace that was to be yours' (1.10). It is one of the factors that leads Schutter to the view that the author's hermeneutics resemble that of the Qumran persherist.[52] The

---

[52] 'Its eschatological outlook, conception of time-periodization, concern for the disclosure of heavenly knowledge through special intermediaries, elaborate pneumatology, and emphasis on Messianic salvation, for example, virtually necessitate an origin for its hermeneutic in sectarian Judaism with a decidedly apocalyptic orientation' (Schutter, *Hermeneutic*, p. 170).

second also appears straightforward, since the author seems oblivious of any change of meaning, simply assuming that Isaiah spoke about Christ and the Church. On the other hand, small adjustments to the wording, such as changing 'God' to 'Lord' in the citation of Isa. 40.8, and 'Lord' to 'Christ as Lord' in Isa. 8.13, could suggest that the author was aware that some sort of 'transfer' was taking place. He does not defend this and appears to assume that his readers/hearers will not find it questionable or problematic. But he is aware that adjustments need to be made to the texts in order for this to happen.

The third and fourth sub-questions are the subject of our final chapter and concern the question of legitimacy. Some scholars are quite happy to offer a descriptive study without passing judgement on whether the various appropriations of Scripture should be seen as 'valid' or 'true'. This is often the case in comparative studies, which conclude that changes of wording, reference and even sense are common characteristics of first-century Jewish interpretation. Other scholars, however, wish to go beyond the descriptive task and offer some sort of evaluation of the various appropriations of Scripture in the New Testament. This can take the form of a literary theory that does not confine textual meaning to either the original intention of an author or the likely understanding(s) of its original readers. Biblical interpretation is then a particular example of a general phenomenon that texts gain new meanings as they pass through time. The challenge is whether there are criteria that allow us to differentiate between valid 'developments' and later 'impositions' to the meaning of a text. If a particular biblical interpretation is 'valid' because all later interpretations are 'valid', then it is hardly worth stating.

Alternatively, scholars like Payne would wish to evoke a theological principle that the biblical texts have certain unique properties as 'Scripture' that sets them apart from other texts. In particular, they have a divine author and hence a divine meaning. On such theories, meaning is not determined by the application of ordinary philological and grammatical rules but is spiritually discerned (individually or in community). The challenge here is whether anything can be said about the relationship between the so-called divine meaning of a text and its philological and grammatical meaning(s). If not, then it faces the same difficulties as those literary theories that cannot distinguish between 'valid' and 'invalid' developments.

Finally, it is also important to ask whether a particular literary theory or theological framework is thought to 'emerge' from the ancient texts themselves or is accepted on other grounds and then imposed upon them. Though it might appear that the theories of Kaiser and Payne are being imposed on the texts, both authors claim that their theories are implied by the (ancient) texts themselves. In other words, the New Testament authors are simply doing what the texts instruct them to do. These issues will be the subject of our final chapter.

8

Evoking a powerful image
in order to replace it?
Rev. 5.5-6

Introduction

It is commonly agreed that the Lamb symbol 'is the most pervasive means of trans-mitting the christological message of the book of Revelation'.[1] The diminutive *arnion* occurs 29 times in the book, all but one of them (Rev. 13.11) referring to Christ.[2] However, the distribution is uneven and raises a number of questions. For example, the first occurrence is not until Rev. 5.6, where it is juxtaposed with the image of 'the Lion of the tribe of Judah, the Root of David'. Prior to this, Jesus has been introduced as a powerful 'Son of Man' figure who holds seven stars in his right hand, whose eyes are like a 'flame of fire', feet like 'burnished bronze' and out of his mouth comes a 'sharp two-edged sword' (Rev. 1.12-16). This visionary description then forms the basis of the titles given to the one who addresses the seven churches in Revelation 2–3.[3] What then is the significance of introducing the 'Lamb' image in Rev. 5.6 and why on this first occurrence is it juxtaposed with a 'Lion'? There are a further nine occurrences of 'Lamb' in Revelation 5–7 and seven in Revelation 21–2, but it is absent from major sections of the book (Rev. 1.1–5.5; 7.18–12.10; 15.4–17.13;

---

[1] T.B. Slater, *Christ and Community. A Socio-Historical Study of the Christology of Revelation* (JSNTSup, 178; Sheffield: Sheffield Academic Press, 1999), p. 162.

[2] R.H. Bauckham thinks the precise number of references to Christ as Lamb (28) is deliberate, being the number of perfection or completion (7) multiplied by the number of the world (4). See R.H. Bauckham, *The Climax of Prophecy. Studies on the Book of Revelation* (Edinburgh: T&T Clark, 1993), p. 34.

[3] Ephesus (seven stars); Smyrna (first and last); Pergamum (sharp two-edged sword); Thyatira (flaming eyes and feet); Sardis (seven spirits and seven stars); Philadelphia (key of David); Laodicea (faith and true witness). For a discussion of the relationship between the letters and the vision, see S. Moyise, *The Old Testament in the Book of Revelation* (JSNTSup, 115; Sheffield: Sheffield Academic Press, 1995), pp. 24–44.

17.5–19.6; 19.10–21.8). The concentration of references in the final chapters makes its absence from the early chapters somewhat surprising, and some scholars have used this to support the view that Revelation 1–3 is a later addition to the book.[4]

Though the 'Lamb' is the central christological image of the book, the roles and functions associated with it are diverse and complex. Thomas Slater offers the following summary:[5]

- The Lamb is worthy to open the scroll by virtue of its sacrificial death;
- The Lamb inaugurates the events that lead to victory and salvation for the people of God;
- The Lamb makes war on the enemies of God and defeats them;
- The Lamb holds the book of life with the names of the 'saved';
- The Lamb protects the community from harm;
- The Lamb shares divine honours with God.

In view of this diversity of role and function, it is difficult to decide whether the image would evoke particular Old Testament passages or sources or practices known to John or early Christian tradition. If we take our cue from the other five passages in the New Testament that apply 'Lamb' imagery to Christ, then sacrifice would appear to be the prominent theme. Unfortunately, none of these passages (Jn 1.29, 36; Acts 8.32; 1 Cor. 5.7; 1 Pet. 1.19) uses the same Greek word as John. In 1 Cor. 5.7, Paul refers to Jesus as 'our paschal lamb' (*pascha*) who 'has been sacrificed'. The other four passages all use *amnos*. Thus in Jn 1.29, 36, John the Baptist hails Jesus as the 'Lamb of God who takes away the sin of the world'. It is not entirely clear what background this would evoke. There is no such ambiguity with Acts 8.32, however, for the Ethiopian eunuch is pictured as reading from an Isaiah scroll and Isa. 53.7 is explicitly quoted: 'Like a sheep he was led to the slaughter, and like a lamb silent before its shearer, so he does not open his mouth.' The sacrificial imagery is also present in 1 Pet. 1.18–19, where the author reassures his readers with the words: 'You know that you were ransomed from the futile ways inherited from your ancestors, not with perishable things like silver and gold, but with the precious blood of Christ, like that of a lamb without defect or blemish'. Thus if priority is given to early Christian tradition, it would appear that John's extensive 'Lamb' christology would most likely evoke Passover and sacrificial traditions.

On the other hand, some scholars think that Jn 1.19, 36 is very different from the sacrificial background of the other New Testament passages and it is this that lies behind John's use in Revelation.[6] Thus Charles H. Dodd cites 1 *Enoch* 90 and *Test.*

---

[4] E.g., J.M. Ford, *Revelation: Introduction, Translation and Commentary* (AB, 38; New York: Doubleday, 1975), pp. 38–46

[5] Slater, *Christ and Community*, pp. 200–03 (my summary).

[6] This section draws on my article, 'Does the Lion Lie Down with the Lamb?' in S. Moyise (ed), *Studies in the Book of Revelation* (London: T&T Clark, 2001), pp. 181–94.

Joseph 19.8 for the background of Jn 1.29 and concludes that 'we have here a prototype of the militant seven-horned "Lamb" of the Apocalypse of John'.[7] Raymond Brown concludes his discussion of Jn 1.29 with the words, 'Thus we suggest that John the Baptist hailed Jesus as the lamb of Jewish apocalyptic expectation who was to be raised up by God to destroy evil in the world, a picture not too far from that of Rev xvii 14.'[8] This line of interpretation reaches its climax in the commentary of Josephine Massyngberde Ford, who argues that the book of Revelation derives (largely) from followers of John the Baptist. Jewish apocalyptic texts, she says, predicted a conquering Lamb who will appear in the last days and destroy evil, as *Test. Joseph* 19.8 makes clear:

> I saw that a virgin was born from Judah, wearing a linen stole; and from her was born a spotless lamb. At his left there was something like a lion, and all the wild animals rushed against him, but the lamb conquered them, and destroyed them, trampling them underfoot.[9]

Ford maintains that there is nothing in the book of Revelation which compels us to depart from this picture. In the chapter that follows Revelation 5, the destruction brought about by the opening of the seals leads people to seek death rather than face 'the wrath of the Lamb' (Rev. 6.16). The beast may do all sorts of despicable things to God's people but none compares with Rev. 14.10, where God's enemies 'drink the wine of God's wrath, poured unmixed into the cup of his anger, and they will be tormented with fire and sulphur in the presence of the holy angels *and in the presence of the Lamb*'. In Revelation 17, a confederacy of kings 'make war on the Lamb' but it is really no contest for he is 'Lord of lords and King of kings' and destroys them (Rev. 17.14). This title makes it virtually certain that the Lamb is to be identified with the figure on the white horse in Revelation 19, from whose mouth 'comes a sharp sword with which to strike down the nations, and he will rule them with a rod of iron; he will tread the wine press of the fury of the wrath of God the Almighty. On his robe and on his thigh he has a name inscribed, "King of kings and Lord of lords"' (Rev. 19.15-16). According to Ford, John's use of the title 'Lamb' is thoroughly consonant with the militant victorious Lamb from the apocalyptic tradition.[10]

---

[7] C. H. Dodd, *The Interpretation of the Fourth Gospel* (Cambridge: Cambridge University Press, 1968), p. 232.

[8] R. E. Brown, *The Gospel According to John* (AB, 29; New York: Doubleday, 1966), 1. p. 60.

[9] There has been much discussion about the integrity of this text and hence its relevance for understanding Revelation. See L.L. Johns, *Lamb Christology* (WUNT, 2.167; Tübingen: Mohr Siebeck, 2005).

[10] Ford, *Revelation*, p. 31. I am informed that she no longer holds the position that the book derives from followers of John the Baptist and this will be reflected in the revised version of her commentary.

Enter the Lion

As already noted, the first occurrence of 'Lamb' is in Rev. 5.6, where it is juxtaposed with the symbol of a 'Lion'. John weeps because no one was found worthy to open the scroll (5.4) but is then told by one of the elders:

> 'See, the Lion of the tribe of Judah, the Root of David, has conquered, so that he can open the scroll and its seven seals.' Then I saw between the throne and the four living creatures and among the elders a Lamb standing as if it had been slaughtered, having seven horns and seven eyes, which are the seven spirits of God sent out into all the earth. (Rev. 5.5-6)

'Lion' is a universal symbol for power and strength. It occurs over 150 times in the Old Testament, sometimes for the actual animal[11] but mostly as a metaphor for devouring enemies. Num. 23.24 is typical: 'Look, a people rising up like a lion! It does not lie down until it has eaten the prey and drunk the blood of the stair.' Thus when 1 Peter wishes to portray the activity of the devil against Christians, he says, 'Like a roaring lion your adversary the devil prowls around, looking for someone to devour' (1 Pet. 5.8). And when John wishes to portray the terrifying activity of the locusts ('their torture was like the torture of a scorpion when it stings someone'), he says their teeth were like lions' teeth (Rev. 9.8). The same image is used of the devouring beast, which has a mouth like that of a lion (Rev. 13.2). It is therefore surprising to find the image being applied to Christ in Rev. 5.5. Is the message of Revelation simply that Christ's power is more devastating than the beast's power and that John's readers/hearers would be well advised to join forces with the eventual victor? This is the view of Stephen Moore, who thinks that the message of Revelation is that,

> God's imperial splendor far exceeds that of the Roman emperor, just as the emperor's splendor far exceeds that of any of his 600 senators, and just as the senator's splendor far exceeds that of any provincial plebeian, and so on down the patriarchal line to the most subdued splendor of the feeblest father of the humblest household.[12]

God is occasionally likened to a lion in the Old Testament. For example, Job speaks of God stalking him like a lion and displaying his awesome power against him (Job 10.16). Isaiah records an oracle where God speaks of himself as a lion coming to do battle (Isa. 31.4) and Jeremiah has a similar oracle where God will deal with Babylon as a lion (Jer. 50.44). The most graphic reference is Hos. 5.14, where God will attack Ephraim and Judah as a lion: 'I myself will tear and go away; I will carry off, and no one shall rescue' (Hos. 5.14). Perhaps John's application of 'Lion' imagery

---

[11] Jdg 14.5; 1 Sam. 17.34; 1 Kgs 13.24

[12] S.D. Moore, 'The Beatific Vision as a Posing Exhibition. Revelation's Hypermasculine Deity', *JSNT* 60 (1995), p. 40.

to Christ is intended to evoke the image of God as Lion, just as other divine attributes are applied to Christ in Revelation.[13]

The particular phrase, 'Lion of the tribe of Judah', points to Gen. 49.9, a text that receives a messianic interpretation in the *targumim* (*Neofitti; Pseudo-Jonathan*), *midrashim* (*Tanhuma Gen.* 12.12; *Rabbah Gen.* 97) and at Qumran (1QSb 5.29). On his deathbed, Jacob tells each of his sons what will happen to them in the future. To Judah, he says:

> Judah, your brothers shall praise you; your hand shall be on the neck of your enemies; your father's sons shall bow down to you. Judah is a lion's whelp; from the prey, my son, you have gone up. He crouches down, he stretches out like a lion, like a lioness – who dares rouse him up? The scepter shall not depart from Judah, nor the ruler's staff from between his feet, until tribute comes to him; and the obedience of the peoples is his. Blinding his foal to the vine and his donkey's colt to the choice vine, he washes his garments in wine and his robe in the blood of grapes. (Gen. 49.8-11)

As a description of the messiah's activity, the text shares with Rev. 19.13-15 the twin themes of 'ruling the nations' and 'robes soaked in wine/blood':

> He is clothed in a *robe dipped in blood*, and his name is called The Word of God. And the armies of heaven, wearing fine linen, white and pure, were following him on white horses. From his mouth comes a sharp sword with which to *strike down the nations*, and he will rule them with a rod of iron; *he will tread the wine press* of the fury of the wrath of God the Almighty. (Rev. 19.13-15)

This is all too much for Harold Bloom, who regards the book of Revelation as 'barbaric', 'lurid and inhumane' and 'without goodness, kindness, or affection of any kind'.[14] Like D.H. Lawrence before him, evoking the 'devouring lion' is just another aspect of the book's glorification of vengeance and delight in the destruction of one's enemies.[15]

Enter the Lamb

Having introduced Christ as the 'Lion of the tribe of Judah', Rev. 5.6 goes on to say that what John in fact saw was a 'Lamb standing as if it had been slaughtered' (*hōs esphagmenon*). Many scholars think this is a deliberate contrast to the Lion imagery and represents the Christian idea of 'victory through self-sacrifice' as opposed to 'victory through conquest'. Indeed, George Caird thought that this was not only the key to understanding John's christology, but it was also the key to understanding the whole of the Old Testament, as if John were saying to us,

[13] E.g. 'First and last' (Rev. 1.17), 'King of kings' (Rev. 17.14).
[14] H. Bloom, *The Revelation of St John the Divine* (New York: Chelsea House, 1988), pp. 4–5.
[15] D.H. Lawrence, *Apocalypse and the Writings on Revelation* (Harmondsworth: Penguin Books, 1930).

'Wherever the Old Testament says "**Lion**", read "**Lamb**". Wherever the Old Testament speaks of the victory of the Messiah or the overthrow of the enemies of God, we are to remember that the gospel recognizes no other way of achieving these ends than the way of the Cross.[16]

This judgement is quoted in a number of other commentaries. For example, John Sweet says:

We may agree, then, with Caird that what John *hears*, the traditional OT expectation of military deliverance, is reinterpreted by what he *sees*, the historical fact of a sacrificial death, and that the resulting paradox is the key to all his use of the OT.[17]

In his own words, the 'Lion of Judah, the traditional messianic expectation, is reinterpreted by the slain Lamb: God's power and victory lie in self-sacrifice'.[18] Eugene Boring says, 'It is as though John had adopted the familiar synagogue practice of "perpetual Kethib/Qere," whereby a word or phrase that appears in the traditional text is read as another word or phrase.'[19] He then quotes Caird: 'Wherever the tradition says "lion", read "Lamb".' The implication for both Sweet and Boring is that the apocalyptic violence of chapters 6–19 needs to be reinterpreted in the light of the slain Lamb. More recently, Mark Bredin has attempted to show that the picture of Christ in Revelation is the same as the Jesus of the Gospels, namely, a revolutionary of peace. He agrees that the Lion is a 'militant Messianic title' but quotes Caird to the effect that 'Lamb redefines violent imagery in terms of self-suffering through which victory is gained.'[20] He even extends this to the 'wrath of the Lamb' passage in Rev. 6.17, stating:

The juxtaposition of 'Lamb' and 'wrath' may, at first sight, appear incomprehensible, as was the combination of Lion and Lamb in Revelation 5.5-6. John reinterprets 'wrath' by placing it alongside the most non-militaristic image, Lamb. Wrath no longer depicts a military, conquering God on the battlefield; God is not one who slays with a sword. Suffering love is the essence of wrath, and therefore suffering love is that which brings about God's judgement and kingdom.[21]

---

[16] G.B. Caird, *The Revelation of St John the Divine* (London: A. & C. Black, 1984), p. 75.

[17] J.P.M. Sweet, *Revelation* (London: SCM Press, 1990), p. 125.

[18] Sweet, *Revelation,* p. 125.

[19] M.E. Boring, *Revelation* (Louisville: Westminster John Knox, 1989), p. 110.

[20] M. Bredin, *Jesus, Revolutionary of Peace. A Nonviolent Christology in the Book of Revelation* (Carlisle: Paternoster Press, 2003), p. 192.

[21] Bredin, *Jesus,* p. 195. It should be noted that Bredin adds a footnote at this point to my work and agrees with my conclusion that John does not intend to replace Lion with Lamb but wishes to maintain the paradox. However, as will become apparent, I draw rather different conclusions from this.

Such a view has been defended on both historical and literary grounds. For example, Nelson Kraybill thinks that John is writing to Christians who are being coerced and persecuted by the Roman authorities. John's purpose is to oppose the imperial ideology of 'victory through conquest' with his Christian ideology of 'victory through self-sacrifice':

> John looks to a future when human pretensions to divinity will end and God himself will live among mortals ... Death and pain – inevitable by-products of a corrupt Empire – no longer will torment humanity in the New Jerusalem ... Far from destroying art, wealth and beauty, the holy city will be a lavish place that gives everyone equal access to resources of the earth. Roman imperial society, with its pyramid of power and economic elites, will be gone forever. In contrast to class-conscious and exclusive Rome, the New Jerusalem will have three gates on each side, welcoming people from all directions of the compass. The gates will never shut (21.25), and no privileged group will monopolize wealth. Hope for human society redeemed, in every political, economic and social dimension, undergirds the message of John's Apocalypse. Rome will fall, and something better for humanity will take its place.[22]

For Kraybill, this historical background makes it certain that John is not advocating his own version of 'might is right' for that would undermine the central tenet of the gospel ('victory through self-sacrifice'). Thus while 'the world follows a beast with all its power and violence, Christians follow a gentle and (seemingly) powerless lamb'.[23] For Kraybill, the juxtaposition of Lion and Lamb implies *replacement* rather than *reinforcement*.

Similarly, Joel Musvosci thinks it is essential to understand the calls for vengeance in the book of Revelation in the light of its covenantal background and the reality of persecution: 'In the context of the Ancient Near Eastern and Old Testament covenants, the persecution may be seen as an unjust war against a loyal vassal, and God must step in as protector of the covenant community.'[24] Though he does not commit himself to a particular date for the book, his survey of persecution in the apostolic period and under emperors Nero, Domitian and Trajan leads him to the conclusion that, 'For John, as well as for his community, trial and hardship were daily realities. It is in this context that Revelation must be read and interpreted.'[25] In other words, the call for vengeance is acceptable given the covenant background and the persecution being experienced by the readers.

James Resseguie adopts a narrative approach to Revelation, analysing the book in terms of point of view, setting, characters and plot. He notes that readers are always

---

[22] J.N. Kraybill, *Imperial Cult and Commerce in John's Apocalypse* (JSNTSup, 132; Sheffield: Sheffield Academic Press; 1996), pp. 222–3.

[23] Kraybill, *Imperial Cult*, p. 201.

[24] J.N. Musvosvi, *Vengeance in the Apocalypse* (Berrien Springs: Andrews University Press, 1993), p. 276.

[25] Musvosci, *Vengeance*, p. 176.

required to fill in a number of indeterminacies in order to make sense of a text and he lists five relationships that are crucial for an understanding of Revelation: (1) the three septets; (2) the letters and the rest of the book; (3) what John hears and what he sees; (4) the scrolls of Rev. 5 and 10; and (5) the measured temple and unmeasured courtyard in Rev. 11. He thinks the plot of Revelation is the U-shaped structure of comedy, where a 'stable condition, moves downward due to a series of threatening conditions and instabilities, and at the end moves upward to a new stable condition'.[26] Thus he considers Revelation 4-5 to describe a

> scene of perfect order and symmetry [which] establishes a primacy/recency effect that determines the way the reader reads the subsequent chapters. The overwhelming primacy effect is that order and coherence rules the universe. The cosmos is centered around the throne and the one who sits on the throne. In this dramatic scene there is an unsurpassable unity among all creatures, which binds them to the creator and redeemer in an endless display of worship and praise. The recency effect of gloom and doom found in the subsequent chapters can not overturn this ebullient and marvelous primacy experience of splendor.[27]

Point of view is established by attending to a number of contrasts, such as hearing and seeing, above and below, outer and inner, and centre and perimeter. The first is established as a principle in the seven letters with the command to *hear* what the Spirit says to the churches. In Rev. 9.13-21, John *sees* a vision of horses with lions' heads and *hears* their number, 200 million. Resseguie says: 'The number is the inner reality that says something about the nature of evil.'[28] In Revelation 12, John *sees* a heavenly battle between Michael and Satan but does not understand its meaning until he *hears* the heavenly voice. In Revelation 14, John *sees* the 144,000 and *hears* a multitude singing. In Revelation 15, John *sees* those who have conquered the beast and *hears* the song of Moses and the Lamb. In Revelation 21, John *sees* a new heaven and earth and *hears* that God will wipe away every tear and make his dwelling with humanity. This principle of reinterpretation allows Resseguie to conclude: 'John overturns conventional expectations that the Messiah will subjugate Israel's enemies by conquest and might, and replaces that expectation with a new definition of conquest and might – a slaughtered Lamb.'[29]

Lion and Lamb
It is not difficult to see how replacing the (seemingly) destructive 'Lion' imagery in Revelation with the (seemingly) gentle 'Lamb' imagery makes for a more conducive

---

[26] J.L. Resseguie, *Revelation Unsealed. A Narrative Critical Approach to John's Apocalypse* (Leiden: Brill, 1998), p. 166.

[27] Resseguie, *Revelation Unsealed*, pp. 175–6.

[28] Resseguie, *Revelation Unsealed*, p. 34.

[29] Resseguie, *Revelation Unsealed*, p. 134.

reading of the book. But does this really do justice to the dynamics of the narrative? It is true that the Lamb is sometimes associated with sacrificial and protective roles in Revelation (Rev. 7.17) but it is also associated with conquest, even violent conquest. This makes it difficult to accept that the Lion, with all its destructive connotations, has been evoked only to be replaced or silenced by a gentle Lamb. Indeed, if that were John's intention, one would expect the rest of the book to be full of sacrificial and pastoral imagery, not scenes of violent destruction. As Aune notes, while the 'irony of kingship through crucifixion' is prominent in Revelation 5, it is a 'marginal conception elsewhere in the book'.[30] Thus the difficulty for those wishing to argue for some sort of replacement is that the rest of the book contains far more 'Lion-like' characteristics than sacrificial ones.

This difficulty can be seen in Resseguie's work, for having established the principle that 'hearing interprets seeing', he deduces that Lamb reinterprets Lion. But according to the established principle, Rev. 5.5-6 should offer the opposite of this: John *sees* a Lamb but *hears* about a Lion, which ought to mean that 'Lion' reinterprets 'Lamb', not the other way around. Sensing this difficulty, he is forced to modify the principle in this particular instance:

> The Lion of the tribe of Judah interprets what John sees. Death on the cross (the Lamb) is not defeat but is the way to power and victory (the Lion). *In this instance, seeing also reinterprets the hearing.* The traditional expectation of messianic conquest by military deliverance (the Lion of Judah) is reinterpreted so that messianic conquest occurs through sacrificial death (the Lamb).[31]

Many scholars, therefore, have explored why John might have wished to designate Christ as both 'Lion' and 'Lamb'. One way of doing this is to consider Christ's victory in temporal sequence. Thus Frederick Murphy acknowledges that the 'central issue is whether the warlike traits of a lion are replaced by the meekness of the Lamb or whether the messiah retains warlike qualities?'[32] His conclusion is that neither is replaced: 'Christ won his victory over Satan and made possible the victory of Christians through his suffering and death. This is nonviolent. But he will also exercise force against the partisans of evil (chapter 19) and will punish them as they deserve.'[33] Thus Lion and Lamb represent the two aspects of Christ's victory, traditionally known as his first and second coming. The Lion image is not evoked in order to be replaced but to prepare for Christ's final victory, when he returns in glory to punish all evil-doers. Greg Beale also adopts a temporal explanation, stating that the juxtaposition of Lion and Lamb is

---

[30] D. Aune, *Revelation 1–5* (WBC, 52A; Dallas: Word Books, 1997), p. 352.

[31] Resseguie, *Revelation Unsealed*, p. 34. Emphasis added.

[32] F.J. Murphy, *Fallen is Babylon. The Revelation to John* (Harrisburg: Trinity Press International, 1998), p. 193.

[33] Murphy, *Fallen is Babylon*, p. 193.

solved reasonably well by the 'already and not yet' presupposition of John's eschatology. Christ's past defeat of the enemy as a 'lion' has begun in an ironic manner
through death and suffering as a 'lamb', but the future, consummate form of the enemy's
defeat will be more straightforward. Christ will judge decisively and openly both his
earthly and cosmic enemies, including Satan himself.[34]

David Barr offers a different historical and literary analysis of the book. He
agrees with a growing number of interpreters that the context of the book is not
'Roman persecution' but 'Roman seduction'. If it were obvious to the churches that
Rome was a persecuting enemy, John would hardly need to struggle to denounce
'Jezebel' for advocating collaboration (Rev. 2.20). The violent imagery is not to be
'explained' (or justified) by the depth of suffering; after all, Jesus taught his disciples
to love their enemies, not pray for (and delight in) their destruction. Nor is it
answered by positing a two-stage victory which concludes at Jesus' second coming,
for 'if violence is not acceptable now how can it be acceptable at the Parousia?'[35]
According to Barr, the vision of military victory in Revelation 19 is not describing a
future battle, for the scene does not occur on earth. Furthermore, it is unlikely to be
evoking the 'second coming' tradition, since the figure comes on a horse, not the
traditional 'clouds of heaven' (Rev. 1.7). Thus for Barr:

> John's divine warrior is not some evil twin of the savior Jesus who conquered by his own
> death. He is the same person, and the battle has already been won. We have all the
> paraphernalia of Holy War, but no war.[36]

Richard Bauckham considers the form of the book of Revelation to resemble
a Christian war scroll, where John makes 'lavish use of militaristic *language* in a non-
militaristic *sense*'.[37] It is John's literary vehicle for communicating his message but that
does not mean that his meaning is identical to previous uses of that literary genre:
'In the eschatological destruction of evil in Revelation there is no place for real
armed violence, but there is ample space of the imagery of armed violence.'[38] Thus
Lion is not evoked in order to be silenced, for that would destroy the literary form
of John's message. Rather, it is evoked in order to be reinterpreted:

> By reinterpreting the militant Messiah and his army John does not mean simply to set
> aside Israel's hopes for eschatological triumph: in the Lamb and his followers these hopes

---

[34] G.K. Beale, *John's Use of the Old Testament in Revelation* (JSNTSup, 166; Sheffield. Sheffield Academic
Press. 1998), p. 46.

[35] D.L. Barr, 'The Lamb Looks Like a Dragon' in D.L. Barr (ed.), *The Reality of Apocalypse. Rhetoric and
Politics in the Book of Revelation* (Atlanta: SBL, 2006), p. 220.

[36] Barr, 'The Lamb Looks Like a Dragon', p. 215.

[37] Bauckham, *The Climax of Prophecy*, p. 233.

[38] Bauckham, *The Climax of Prophecy*, p. 233.

are both fulfilled and transformed. The Lamb really does conquer, though not by force of arms, and his followers really do share his victory, though not by violence.[39]

Rather different is Ron Farmer's attempt to develop a 'process hermeneutic' in order to explain the tension between 'Lion' and 'Lamb'. He notes that 'if chapters 6-20 stood alone, it would be hard to see them as anything other than a cry for vengeance arising from anger, hatred, and envy'.[40] However, these chapters are bracketed by the vision of God the Creator and Redeemer (Revelation 4–5) and the One who makes all things new (Revelation 21–2). Farmer's argument for a 'process hermeneutic' is that the dominant theme of violence (or 'lure' in process language) cannot easily be reconciled with the 'undercurrent' of self-sacrifice:

> Although the dominant 'surface' imagery portrays God's power as coercive, all-controlling, and unilateral, the analysis revealed a strong 'undercurrent' working against the dominant imagery by means of basal lures suggesting that divine power be understood as persuasive, all-influencing, and relational … Whether John created this 'undercurrent' intentionally or inadvertently, these basal lures nevertheless stand in tension with the deterministic worldview implied by the 'surface' lures.[41]

Farmer thinks this can only be resolved by rejecting classical theism's view of an unchanging omnipotent God and looking to process theology.

Analysis
∽

The question that concerns us in this chapter is whether John has evoked the destructive Lion imagery in order to replace it. This is clearly not the case when it is applied to the locusts and the beast and so the debate focuses on the Lion/Lamb juxtaposition in Rev. 5.5-6. In this passage, both Lion and Lamb are mentioned for the first time and it has been argued that this is a deliberate strategy. John intends the reader to reinterpret the violent imagery that follows (Lion) by means of the slaughtered Lamb. The arguments are both historical and literary. The historical arguments have often depended on the assumption that John is writing to Christians who are being persecuted for refusing to take part in the imperial cult. Since this is imposed by force, John wishes to contrast a 'victory through sacrifice' ideology with a 'victory through conquest' one.

---

[39] Bauckham, *The Climax of Prophecy*, p. 230.

[40] R. Farmer, *Beyond the Impasse. The Promise of a Process Hermeneutic* (Macon: Mercer University Press, 1997), p. 156.

[41] R. Farmer, *Beyond the Impasse*, p. 160.

However, the assumption that Revelation derives from a context of severe persecution has been largely abandoned and replaced either by some form of 'local harassment' theory or precisely the opposite, a context of 'complacency' and 'collaboration'. On the 'local harassment' theory, John's enemies (including fellow Christians) are demonized by aligning their behaviour with the cosmic battle between good and evil. On the 'complacency' theory, the language is deliberately excessive in order to shock Christians out of their lukewarm spirituality (Rev. 3.16) and collaboration with Rome (Rev. 2.20). It aims to expose the seemingly benevolent 'state' as a devouring beast (Rev. 18.2). Both views require a hermeneutic that would show how seemingly benevolent forces are in fact demonic. It is not clear how they are helped by a hermeneutic that shows that Lion (oppressive violence) is replaced by Lamb (sacrificial service). Thus historical arguments can hardly be said to support a 'replacement' hermeneutic.

We have already discussed Resseguie's literary arguments and found them unconvincing. He successfully shows that John establishes a 'hearing interprets seeing' hermeneutic but inexplicably adds a caveat to it when discussing Rev. 5.5-6. By his own principle, John's meaning should be that the Lamb is really a Lion and is certainly not being replaced. In fact, when he first introduces this principle in his Introduction, he cites the example of John hearing the number of those sealed (Rev. 7.4) and then seeing a 'great multitude that no one could count' (Rev. 7.9). He criticizes scholars like Mounce, who see here two separate visions, for the 'two are not separate, but mutually interpret each other'.[42] However, he does not speak of 'mutual interpretation' when discussing the Lion and the Lamb.[43]

This raises a difficulty for the literary theory espoused by Resseguie, for while he acknowledges that readers have to 'appropriate' texts by filling in gaps, he insists that this 'is not a subjective task ... but rather the reader fills in the gaps, *the way the author imagines those gaps should be filled in*'.[44] In order to maintain this, texts would need to offer readers clear interpretative guidelines that are self-evident and stable. But this is undermined when Resseguie has to admit that his principle of hearing/seeing is in fact rather complicated:

> By alternating between seeing and hearing on the phraseological level, John shows that the appearance of an event (*what he sees*) has a second, deeper meaning (*what he*

---

[42] Resseguie, *Revelation Unsealed*, p. 8.

[43] Unlike C.R. Koester (*Revelation and the End of all Things* [Grand Rapids: Eerdmans, 2001], p. 78), who can accept that the promise of a powerful ruler is not 'rejected but fulfilled through the slaughtered yet living Lamb, who is not a hapless victim but a figure of royal strength'.

[44] Resseguie, *Revelation Unsealed*, p. 30. Emphasis original. He aligns himself here with the 'authorial reading' of Peter Rabinowitz, *Before Reading: Narrative Conventions and the Politics of Interpretation* (Ithaca: Cornell University Press, 1987).

hears); or that what is heard (a traditional expectation) is to be reinterpreted by what is seen (a new reality). What John sees is complemented – sometimes corrected – by what he hears.[45]

Applied to the Lion/Lamb juxtaposition, this suggests that the reader has at least four interpretative options:

- Slaughtered Lamb has a *second deeper meaning*, namely, a devouring Lion.
- Devouring Lion is *reinterpreted* by slaughtered Lamb.
- Slaughtered Lamb is *complemented* by devouring Lion.
- Slaughtered Lamb is *corrected* by devouring Lion.

In my 1995 monograph on *The Old Testament in the Book of Revelation*, I drew on the literary theorist Thomas Greene to explore the 'mutual influence' of the Lion/ Lamb juxtaposition. In his analysis of Renaissance poetry, Greene develops a typology of 'imitation' using the terms, 'reproductive', 'eclectic', 'heuristic' and 'dialectic'. I found his last two categories particularly instructive for John's use of the Lion/Lamb imagery. Heuristic imitation, he says, is when the new work sets about defining itself by rewriting or modernizing a past text:

> Heuristic imitations come to us advertising their derivation from the subtexts they carry with them, but having done that, they proceed to *distance themselves* from the subtexts and force us to recognize the poetic distance traversed.[46]

In effect, they act out their own derivation, thereby drawing attention to the 'poetic distance traversed'. They evoke only to absorb. By contrast, dialectical imitation is when a poem engages a precursor in such a way that neither is able to absorb or master the other: 'The text is the locus of a struggle between two rhetorical or semiotic systems that are vulnerable to one another and whose conflict cannot easily be resolved.'[47] This seemed to be a good description of the Lion/Lamb juxta-position in Revelation. Each of these images evokes associations and connotations from very different linguistic fields and these 'voices' continue to resonate throughout the book. Neither is silenced or replaced but exists in tension with the other. Thus what John offers in Rev. 5.5-6 is not heuristic imitation, where images are evoked only to be absorbed, but dialectical imitation, where the tension is maintained.

However, in the light of the work of Barr and Farmer, I now realize that this position needs to be more nuanced. Barr asserts that violence is 'subverted' by the

---

[45] Resseguie, *Revelation Unsealed*, p. 9.

[46] T.M. Greene, *The Light in Troy. Imitation and Discovery in Renaissance Poetry* (New Haven: Yale University Press, 1982), p. 40.

[47] Greene, *The Light in Troy*, p. 46.

Lamb and deduces that 'John teaches the reader how to read violence by repeatedly showing its inverted meaning: violence inflicted must always be read as violence endured.'[48] I still maintain that the various juxtapositions in Revelation are more ambiguous than that. For example, Barr points out that the weapon used to 'strike down the nations' in Rev. 19.15 is not a literal sword but one that issues from his mouth. This is correct and no doubt represents a considerable reinterpretation, perhaps even subversion, of the military imagery. But I would deny that it is an 'inversion'. Christ remains the subject who strikes and the nations remain the object that is struck. That they are struck by words of judgement rather than a literal sword is significant but it does not amount to 'inversion' and Barr seems to recognize this when he says, 'This subversion is not complete, however, and we are left with the question of what to do with this surplus of violence.'[49]

On the other hand, his position has prompted me to ask whether 'Lamb' (victory through sacrifice) has in any sense been subverted by 'Lion'? It has certainly been modified as it picks up connotations of strength and victory ('not a hapless victim but a figure of royal strength'[50]) but that is not the same as subverted. Those who died for their faith may need reassurance that their suffering was not in vain (Rev. 6.11) but the principle of 'victory through sacrifice' is not denied or subverted. I maintain that the 'surplus of violence' that Barr speaks about precludes any straight-forward 'replacement' hermeneutic ('Wherever the tradition says "Lion", read "Lamb"') but acknowledge that 'dialectical tension' can also be misleading if it is taken to imply 'equality of role'. It would seem that Lamb subverts Lion in a way that Lion does not subvert Lamb.

Farmer is interesting in that he not only considers the two types of material to be in tension, but also regards the 'violence' as dominant, at least in terms of quantity: 'if chapters 6-20 stood alone, it would be hard to see them as anything other than a cry for vengeance arising from anger, hatred, and envy'.[51] But Farmer counters this by using an evocative image of the sea, with its 'strong undercurrent' being more influential on the swimmer than the calmer 'surface' waters:

> Although the dominant 'surface' imagery portrays God's power as coercive, all-controlling, and unilateral, the analysis revealed a strong 'undercurrent' working against the dominant imagery by means of basal lures suggesting that divine power be under-stood as persuasive, all-influencing, and relational.[52]

From a purely semantic perspective, one might question whether 'strong' beats 'dominant' but his point is that the two types of material operate in different ways.

---

[48] Barr, 'The Lamb Looks Like a Dragon', p. 218.
[49] Barr, 'The Lamb Looks Like a Dragon', p. 218.
[50] Koester, *Revelation*, p. 78.
[51] R. Farmer, *Beyond the Impasse*, p. 156.
[52] R. Farmer, *Beyond the Impasse*, p. 160.

The violent imagery, though quantitatively in the majority, corresponds to the surface of the sea, but the 'relational' material (chs 4–5, 21–2) corresponds to the undercurrent, and thus has more influence on the swimmer/reader. One could of course challenge the validity of the analogy and ask whether the 'violence' in Revelation is only 'surface' deep, but I acknowledge his point; tension need not imply 'equality of role'. On the other hand, his view that 'anger, hatred and envy' characterize Revelation 6–19 concedes rather more than Barr would wish to. Even if it is 'surface' rather than 'undercurrent', it represents the bulk of the book and thus remains a significant influence on the reader. It is hard to see how this can be *replaced* by the undercurrent, even if it is significantly affected by it.

Conclusion

At one level, John's introduction of the 'Lion' imagery in Rev. 5.5 requires no explanation. He has already described Christ in a series of powerful images (flame of fire, burnished bronze, holding seven stars, first and last, two-edged sword) and 'Lion' simply adds to them. However, this is also the first occurrence of 'Lamb' and the rest of the book makes it clear that the combination of 'seeing' and 'hearing' have hermeneutical significance. If the 'Lamb' is intended to evoke the apocalyptic warrior of *Test. Joseph* 19.18, then this could be seen as reinforcing the picture of Christ as 'divine warrior'. However, 'Lamb' is also associated with pastoral (Rev. 7.17) and sacrificial (Rev. 5.6) imagery and most scholars regard *Test. Joseph* 19.18 as corrupt (and hence ineligible as evidence of a 'warrior Lamb' tradition). Thus it appears that Lion and Lamb have been deliberately juxtaposed in Rev. 5.5-6, but for what purpose?

One explanation is that they represent Christ's victory at his first (sacrificial Lamb) and second (conquering Lion) coming but as Barr notes, that would establish a morally dubious example for John's readers ('submit now but we'll destroy them in the end'). Another explanation is that John deliberately introduces the Lion in order to replace it but the sheer quantity of apocalyptic violence in Revelation 6–19 counts against this (even if it is 'surface' rather than 'undercurrent'). Indeed, whatever explanation is adopted, it must do justice to the ongoing tension between 'violence' and 'sacrifice' in the book. In Greene's terms, neither 'voice' is silenced by the other. On the other hand, this need not impose an 'equality of role' on the material and in particular, it would appear that 'Lamb subverts Lion' in a way that 'Lion does not subvert Lamb'. In short, it is probably correct that some attempt has been made by John to subvert images of power and violence but it is incomplete; there remains what Barr calls a 'surplus of violence', and this is neither silenced, neutralized nor otherwise replaced. The juxtaposition maintains rather than obliterates the tension.

9

Evoking the wrong texts?
Rev. 15.3-4

Introduction

It is commonly said that there are no quotations in the book of Revelation because Scripture is never introduced by an introductory formula. This is not strictly true for Rev. 15.3 introduces Scripture with the words, 'And they sing the song of Moses, the servant of God, and the song of the Lamb'. The designation 'song of Moses' could point to either Exodus 15 or Deuteronomy 32, both of which are called songs and are associated with Moses:

> Then Moses and the Israelites sang this song to the LORD:
> 'I will sing to the LORD, for he has triumphed gloriously;
> horse and rider he has thrown into the sea.
> The LORD is my strength and my might,
> and he has become my salvation;
> this is my God, and I will praise him,
> my father's God, and I will exalt him.
> The LORD is a warrior; the Lord is his name ...
> Who is like you, O LORD, among the gods?
> Who is like you, majestic in holiness, awesome in splendour, doing wonders?
> You stretched out your right hand, the earth swallowed them.
> In your steadfast love you led the people whom you redeemed;
> you guided them by your strength to your holy abode.'
> (Exod. 15.1-3, 11-13)

Then Moses recited the words of this song, to the very end, in the hearing of the whole assembly of Israel:

Give ear, O heavens, and I will speak;
let the earth hear the words of my mouth ...
For I will proclaim the name of the LORD; ascribe greatness to our God!
The Rock, his work is perfect, and all his ways are just.
A faithful God, without deceit, just and upright is he;
yet his degenerate children have dealt falsely with him,
a perverse and crooked generation ...
Praise, O heavens, his people, worship him, all you gods!
For he will avenge the blood of his children,
and take vengeance on his adversaries;
he will repay those who hate him, and cleanse the land for his people.
(Deut. 31.30; 32.1, 3-5, 43)

That both songs were to be remembered and sung regularly is immediately established by what follows. In Exod. 15.21, the women take up tambourines and begin dancing as Miriam sings the first line: 'Sing to the LORD, for he has triumphed gloriously; horse and rider he has thrown into the sea.' Isaiah 11–12 consciously draws a parallel between the exodus from Egypt and accompanying victory song, and the gathering of the remnant followed by the reciting of two short songs. The first offers praise for God's rescue (Isa. 12.1-2), the second (Isa. 12.3-6) exhorts the people to 'make known his deeds among the nations'.

In Deut. 32.45-6, Moses recites the words to Joshua and the people and then says, 'Take to heart all the words that I am giving in witness against you today'. Philo refers to it as the 'great song' and treats it at length in *De Virtute* 72–5. It is also mentioned by Josephus (along with Exodus 15) and was particularly popular at Qumran, where it appears to have circulated as an independent text (4QDeut^q). There are quotations from Deuteronomy 32 in Paul's Letter to the Romans (Rom. 10.19; 12.19; 15.10) and Hebrews (Heb. 1.6; 10.30) and a number of scholars have argued for its pivotal importance in those writings.[1]

The reason that Rev. 15.3-4 is not usually classified as a quotation is that the words that follow bear little resemblance to either Exodus 15 or Deuteronomy 32. The phrase, 'Just and true are your ways' could come from Deut. 32.4 ('his work is perfect, and all his ways are just ... just and upright is he') but the rest of the words come from various Psalms, Jeremiah and Amos. Aune calls it a 'pastiche of stereotypical hymnic phrases gathered primarily from the Psalms'[2] and Beale notes that the 'actual contents of the song itself come not from Exodus 15 but from passages throughout the OT extolling God's

---

[1] G. Waters, *The End of Deuteronomy in the Epistles of Paul* (WUNT, 2.221; Tübingen: Mohr Siebeck, 2006); D.M. Allen, 'Deuteronomic Re-presentation in a Word of Exhortation: An Assessment of the Paraenetic Function of Deuteronomy in the Letter to the Hebrews' (PhD Dissertation; University of Edinburgh, 2007). See also M.J.J. Menken and S. Moyise (eds), *Deuteronomy in the New Testament* (LNTS, 356; London and New York: T&T Clark, 2007).

[2] D. Aune, *Revelation 6–16* (WBC, 52A; Nashville: Thomas Nelson, 1998), p. 874.

character'.[3] As we shall see later, Richard Bauckham has a theory about how John's song is related to Exodus 15 but he agrees that it is a 'correct observation that none of the words of the song in Revelation 15:3-4 derive from Exodus 15:1-18'.[4]

Revelation is not the only New Testament writing to offer such 'misdirection'. As we have seen, Mk 1.2 introduces a quotation of Isaiah but the words that (immediately) follow are from Exod. 23.20/Mal. 3.1. Paul includes a catena of quotations from the Psalms and Isaiah in Rom. 3.10-18 and concludes, 'Now we know that whatever the law says, it speaks to those who are under the law' (Rom. 3.19). In addition, we could also mention Mt. 27.9, which quotes words from Zech. 11.13 ('And they took the thirty pieces of silver …') but ascribes them to Jeremiah.[5] Now while these could simply be mistakes, as some later copyists assumed, many scholars believe that a rationale can be offered for the 'misdirection'. For example, Joel Marcus thinks that Isaiah is mentioned in Mk 1.2 to evoke an Isaianic framework for understanding the book. It is the most important part of the composite quotation and the ascription draws attention to it. Francis Watson thinks that one of the roles of the Psalms and the Prophets is to act as commentary on the law, and when acting in this way, they can properly be described as the voice of the law. And Maarten Menken thinks that Mt. 27.9 is composite, combining a reference to the 'potter's field' of Jeremiah 32 with the 'wages' of Zech. 11.13.[6] Unlike Marcus's explanation of Mk 1.2, he thinks that the attribution to Jeremiah is because this is the less obvious part of the quotation, as Gundry had already suggested.[7] Our task in this chapter is to investigate the hermeneutical significance of pointing readers/hearers to the song of Moses in what appears to be an introductory formula, and then offering something completely different.

Identifying the sources[8]

∾

Psalm. 86.8-10
The closest linguistic parallel to Rev. 15.3-4 is Ps. 86.8-10. Designated a 'Prayer of David', the psalmist strengthens his faith by reminding himself of God's incomparable attributes. In vv. 8-10, a statement about God's uniqueness ('There is none like you among the gods') and incomparable deeds ('nor are there any works like yours')

[3] G.K. Beale, *The Book of Revelation* (NIGTC; Grand Rapids: Eerdmans, 1999), p. 794.

[4] Bauckham, *The Climax of Prophecy*, p. 297.

[5] Mt. 13.35 could be another example if 'Isaiah' is the correct reading, since the quotation is from Ps. 78.2.

[6] M.J.J. Menken, *Matthew's Bible. The Old Testament Text of the Evangelist* (Leuven: Leuven University Press/Peeters, 2004), pp. 179–99.

[7] R.H. Gundry, *Matthew. A Commentary on His Handbook for a Mixed Church under Persecution* (2nd edn; Grand Rapids: Eerdmans, 1994), p. 557.

[8] This section draws on S. Moyise, 'Singing the Song of Moses and the Lamb: John's Dialogical Use of Scripture', *AUSS* 42 (2004), pp. 347–60.

is followed by the promise that the nations will come (*hēxousin*), worship (*proskunē-sousin*), and glorify (*doxasousin*) his name. This universal hope is the message of Rev. 15.3-4, and represents verbatim agreement in 17 or 18 Greek words (though the phrases appear in the order vii, viii, i, v, vi, ix, ii, iii, iv – see below). The level of agreement in the central section (ii–vi) reinforces the view that the extolling of God's works ('Great and amazing are your deeds') and incomparability ('For you alone are holy') has Psalm 86 in mind, though the influence of other texts (see below) is also likely.

Ps. 86.8-10	Rev. 15.3-4
There is none like you among the gods,	Great (*megas*)[vii] and amazing (*thaumasta*)[viii]
O LORD, nor are there any works like yours (*ta erga sou*)[i].	are your deeds (*ta erga sou*)[i],
	Lord God the Almighty!
All the nations (*panta ta ethnē*)[ii]	Just and true are your ways,
you have made	King of the nations!
shall come and bow down	Lord (*kurie*)[v], who will not fear and glorify
(*hēxousin kai proskunēsousin*)[iii]	your name (*doxasei to onoma sou*)[vi]?
before you (*enōpion sou*),[iv] O LORD (*kurie*)[v],	For you alone (*monos*)[ix] are holy.
and shall glorify your name	All nations (*panta ta ethnē*)[ii]
(*doxasousin to onoma sou*)[vi].	will come and worship
For you are great (*megas*)[vii]	(*hēxousin kai proskunēsousin*)[iii]
and do wondrous (*thaumasia*)[viii] things;	before you (*enōpion sou*),[iv]
you alone (*monos*)[ix] are God.	for your judgements have been revealed.

Jer. 10.7

The second text that is regarded as definite by most commentators is Jer. 10.7, which combines the epithet, 'King of the nations', with the question, 'who would not fear you?' The text is absent from the LXX manuscripts that have come down to us, being part of a lacuna between Jer. 10.5 and 10.9. This could mean that John is dependent on a Hebrew source, that he knows an alternative Greek translation such as that preserved in Theodotion,[9] or he has derived it from a liturgical source, perhaps one where phrases from Ps. 86.8-10 had already been combined with Jer. 10.7. It is surely no coincidence that Jer. 10.6 ('There is none like you, O LORD; you are great, and your name is great in might') is very similar to Ps. 86.8. John or someone before him has most likely linked these texts through their common vocabulary and theme.

---

[9] R.H. Charles categorizes the allusion as deriving from the Hebrew text but showing influence from a Greek version other than the LXX. See R.H. Charles, *A Critical and Exegetical Commentary on the Revelation of St. John* (ICC; Edinburgh: T&T Clark, 1920), 1. p. lxxxi.

Ps. 86.8-10	Jer. 10.6-7	Rev. 15.3
There is none like you among the gods, O LORD, nor are there any works like yours. All the nations … O LORD, and shall glorify your name. For you are great and do wondrous things; you alone are God.	There is none like you, O LORD; you are great, and *your name* is great in might. *Who would not fear you, O King of the nations?* For that is your due; among all the wise ones of the nations and in all their kingdoms there is no one like you.	Great and amazing are your deeds, Lord God the Almighty! Just and true are your ways, *King of the nations! Lord, who will not fear* and glorify *your name?*

Deut. 32.4/Ps. 145.17

There are two main suggestions for the 'just and true are your ways' clause, both of which are interesting because they use the much less frequent *hosios* for 'holy' (rather than *hagios*[10]), which also occurs in John's song ('For you alone are holy'). Linguistically, Deut. 32.4 is the strongest candidate, as it contains the four terms, *alēthina* ('true'), *hodoi* ('ways'), *dikaios* ('just') and *hosios* ('holy'). On the other hand, Ps. 145.17 is closer to Rev. 15.3-4 contextually, extolling God and his mighty deeds (*erga*) in a hymn of praise:

Rev. 15.3b, 4b	Deut. 32.4	Ps. 145.17
Great and amazing are your deeds (*erga*) … Just (*dikaiai*) and true (*alēthinai*) are your ways (*hodoi*) … For you alone are holy (*hosios*).	The Rock, his work is perfect (*alēthina*), and all his ways (*hodoi*) are just (*kriseis*). A faithful God, without deceit, just (*dikaios*) and upright (*hosios*) is he;	The LORD is just (*dikaios*) in all his ways (*hodois*), and kind (*hosios*) in all his doings (*ergois*).

Tob. 12.22/Ps. 111.2/Ps. 139.14

The opening words of the song ('great and amazing') as a description of God's works has its closest parallel in Tob. 12.22 ('The great and amazing works of God'). If this is thought to be an unlikely source for John, then it may come from a combination of Ps. 111.2, where God's works are extolled as great (*megala*), and Ps. 139.14, where they are amazing (*thaumasia*). Since the 'core' of the song appears to be Ps. 86.8-10, it is possible that John was led from the *megas* and *thaumasia* of v.10 to one or more of these texts.

---

[10] *Hagios* is approximately ten times more frequent than *hosios* in the LXX and thirty times more in the New Testament.

Amos 3.13; 4.13; 5.8 etc.
The epithet, 'Lord God, the Almighty' (*kurie ho theos ho pantokratōr*) is a favourite of John's (Rev. 4.8; 11.17; 16.7; 19.6; 21.22) and ten of its thirteen occurrences in the LXX come from the book of Amos (3.13; 4.13; 5.8, 14, 15, 16, 27 etc.).[11] Now it is quite possible that this is John's own formulation, perhaps in opposition to imperial claims, but since he alludes to the book of Amos elsewhere, it is possible and perhaps even probable that he has been influenced by the prophet for this important designation of God.[12]

Ps. 98.2/Jer. 11.20
Finally, John's song ends with the statement that God's *dikaiōmata* have been revealed. There is debate as to whether this should be taken as the revelation of God's 'judgements' (so NRSV) or the revelation of God's 'acts of saving justice' (so NJB). If the former, then Jer. 11.20 ('But you, O LORD of hosts, who judge righteously') could be in mind, especially as he alludes to the second half of this verse ('who try the heart and the mind') in Rev. 2.23. If the latter, then the positive message of Ps. 98.2 ('The Lord has made known his victory; he has revealed his vindication in the sight of the nations') is perhaps more likely. Either way, this would appear to be a possible rather than a probable allusion, and it is not italicized in Nestle-Aland.

Summary
Though there is some doubt about this last example, we conclude that Aune's judgement that the song is a 'pastiche of stereotypical hymnic phrases gathered primarily from the Psalms' is essentially correct. Some may object to the word 'pastiche' on the grounds that it implies a somewhat random collection, whereas it is clear that some of these texts can be linked through common words or phrases. But if we choose a more neutral word such as 'collection' or 'amalgam', the point remains. There is some connection with Deut. 32.4 but the 'core' text is Ps. 86.8-10, which seems to have 'attracted' other texts by common vocabulary and themes. There does not appear to be any connection with Exodus 15, despite the parallel contexts (God's people celebrating victory beside a sea). Why then does John specifically direct his readers to the 'song of Moses', only to offer something completely different?

Explanations

The reference to the song of Moses is spurious
Responding to Wilhelm Bousset's suggestion that the saints sing two songs, first the 'song of Moses' and then the 'song of the Lamb', Charles suggests that the former is

---

[11] The other three are Hos. 12.6; Nah. 3.5; Zech. 10.13.
[12] Notably Amos 3.7 in Rev. 10.7; 11.18.

an interpolation. Not only does John's song bear no literary relationship to Exodus 15, but he also suggests that it is quite different in intent. Exodus 15 is a celebration of triumph over Israel's enemies, but John's song is a 'paean of thanksgiving, which the martyrs sing, when in the first perfect unclouded vision of God they wholly forget themselves and burst forth into praise'.[13] According to Charles, the reference to 'the song of Moses' began as a marginal note and was mistakenly included in the text during transmission. Thus understanding John's use of Scripture in this passage does not arise, for the reference to the 'song of Moses' is spurious.

The reference to the 'song of the Lamb' is the key

Caird accepts the reference to the 'song of Moses' as genuine but finds greater significance in the addition, 'and the song of the Lamb'. The parallel with Exodus 15 is that: 'Like the Israelites after the crossing of the Red sea (Exod. xv.1), the Conquerors sing the song of God's servant Moses, celebrating the triumph of God over the enemies of his people'.[14] But there the similarity ends, for this 'triumph has been won by no other weapons than the cross of Christ and the martyr testimony of his followers.'[15] Thus it is fitting that John composed a new song, a 'jubilant anthem of Christian optimism' constructed from a 'cento of quotations from many parts of the Old Testament'.[16] Caird sees no need to discuss any of the underlying texts and indeed makes no mention of them. John has composed a new song that reflects his Christian theology ('no other weapons than the cross of Christ'). We see here a parallel to his understanding of the Lion/Lamb juxtaposition in Revelation 5; the reference to the 'song of Moses' is introduced only to be replaced by the non-violent 'song of the Lamb'. He thinks this is clearly implied by the completely different content of the two songs.

John is interpreting Deuteronomy 32

Ford acknowledges that John's song has been influenced by a large number of texts but thinks that Deuteronomy 32 plays the key role. Thus in addition to the influence of Deut. 32.4 (recognized by most commentators), she claims that the previous verse of Deuteronomy ('For I will proclaim the name of the LORD; ascribe greatness to our God!') has influenced Rev. 15.4a ('Lord, who will not fear and glorify your name?'). She also notes that the theme of the fire of God's anger is found in Deut. 32.32, while some of the plagues that follow (hunger, burning heat, pestilence, wild beasts, vermin, the sword) are reflected in Deut. 32.23-7. She concludes that the 'song seems more influenced by Deut 32 than Exod 15, but this is understandable in the light of the stress on wrath and justice in the Deuteronomic writings.'[17]

---

[13] Charles, *Revelation*, II. p. 35.
[14] Caird, *Revelation*, p. 198.
[15] Caird, *Revelation*, p. 198.
[16] Caird, *Revelation*, p. 198.
[17] Ford, *Revelation*, p. 257.

John is interpreting Exodus 15 but the links are all invisible

Bauckham argues that John *is* thinking of the song of Moses in Exodus 15, but has been led by verbal association from Exod. 15.11 ('who is like you, O LORD, among the gods?') to three other texts, namely, Ps. 86.8-10, Ps. 98.1-2, and Jer. 10.7. From these three texts, by the 'skilful use of recognized exegetical methods', John has discerned the content of the song to be sung in the new age. This corresponds to the *fulfilment* of the song of Moses as recorded in Exodus 15.[18] The error of many commentators, Bauckham says, is that they move

> from the correct observation that none of the words of the song in Revelation 15:3-4 derive from Exodus 15:1-18, to the claim that therefore there is no literary connexion between the two passages. The literary connexion, as we shall see, is made, as it were, beneath the surface of the text by John's expert and subtle use of current Jewish exegetical method.[19]

Bauckham defends this proposal in three ways. First, he shows that there are precedents for it in Jewish literature. For example, in the Biblical Antiquities of Pseudo-Philo 32, the opening words reproduce Judg. 5.1, but the song that follows is not the song of Deborah as recorded in Judg. 5.2-31 but a fresh composition. Closer to Revelation 15, he notes that Isaiah 11 ends with the promise that there will be a highway for the remnant 'as there was for Israel when they came up from the land of Egypt' and then records two songs which reproduce the first verse of Psalm 105, a psalm that has links with Exodus 15. Bauckham says:

> Therefore, the new version of the Song at the Sea in Isaiah draws on Psalm 105 as well as Exodus 15. It should be noticed that the verbal links between Exodus 15 and Psalm 105 are not visible in the text of Isaiah 12: they occur in parts of the text of Exodus 15 and Psalm 105 which are not quoted in Isaiah 12. This is a kind of implicit *gezērâh šāwâ* which is not uncommon in Jewish and Jewish Christian literature.[20]

Secondly, Bauckham seeks to show how the themes of Exodus 15 have been taken up in the book of Revelation. He suggests that when John read Exodus 15, he would have found the following five themes: (1) 'God's mighty act of judgment on his enemies, which was also the deliverance of his people (Exod 15:1-10, 12)'; (2) 'God's mighty act of judgment demonstrated his incomparable superiority to the pagan gods ... (Exod 15:11)'; (3) 'God's mighty act of judgment filled the pagan nations with fear (Exod 15:14-16)'; (4) 'It brought his people into his temple (Exod 15:13, 17)'; and (5) 'The song concludes: "The Lord shall reign forever and ever" (Exod 15:18)'.[21] He then proceeds to show how these themes are all present in the book of Revelation.

---

[18] Bauckham, *The Climax of Prophecy*, p. 306.
[19] Bauckham, *The Climax of Prophecy*, p. 297.
[20] Bauckham, *The Climax of Prophecy*, p. 300.
[21] Bauckham, *The Climax of Prophecy*, p. 301.

Thirdly, Bauckham seeks to account for John's precise wording on the basis of the Hebrew text. For example, he explains the phrase 'you alone are holy' by asserting that John is still following Ps. 86.8-10, but found the phrase 'you alone are God' puzzling, since the psalm has already asserted that there is 'none like you among the gods' (v.8). Bauckham thus suggest that John changed *elohim* ('God') to *hosios* ('holy'). He seeks to support this by noting that: (1) the LXX also found the reference to God puzzling and changed it to *megas* ('great'); and (2) *hosios* is an appropriate translation since it 'characterizes God as the only true God', whereas the more frequent word for holy (*hagios*) 'refers to a quality that can be shared by God's creatures'.[22] Another example is the *dikaiōmata* in the final clause, which Bauckham explains on the basis of Ps. 98.1-2, suggesting that John would have understood the Hebrew consonants to mean 'righteous acts', whereas the MT has added the vowel points for the word 'righteousness'.

John is interpreting both Exodus 15 and Deuteronomy 32

Beale agrees with Bauckham that John is alluding to the song of Moses and is not merely offering a 'pastiche' from the Psalms. He acknowledges that the 'actual contents of the song itself come not from Exodus 15 but from passages throughout the OT extolling God's character'[23] but suggests that more attention needs to be given to Deuteronomy 32. He notes the following: (1) Deuteronomy 32 is specifically called a 'song' (31.30) and is applied to judgement and reward in the world to come in the Babylonian Talmud (*b. Taanith* 11a); (2) the opening words of the song, 'Great and amazing are your deeds', come from the LXX of Deut. 28.59-60, where Israel is threatened with a judgement like God's 'great and amazing plagues'. Beale calls this an allusion, whereas Ps. 111.2 is referred to as an echo; (3) the noun phrase, 'just and true are your ways' echoes Deut. 32.4, as most commentators recognize; (4) Labuschagne[24] has already shown that the use of the 'who is like?' formula in the Old Testament, including Jer. 10.7 and Ps. 86.8, is always a reflection on the Exodus.

This is an important conclusion for Beale, for he wishes to challenge Bauckham's view that John has replaced the 'judgement of the nations' theme from Exodus 15 with the 'salvation of the nations' theme from the three quoted texts. Despite the fact that the song, as we now find it in Rev. 15.3-4, claims that all of the nations will come and worship and glorify God, Beale suggests that we must read the song in the light of its Old Testament background (and the judgement context of Revelation 14–16):

> [T]he fact that the eulogy in Rev. 15:3-4 is sandwiched between major sections narrating judgment suggests that the emphasis is on God's righteous acts in judging the ungodly

---

[22] Bauckham, *The Climax of Prophecy*, p. 304.

[23] Beale, *The Book of Revelation*, p. 794.

[24] C.J. Labuschagne, *The Incomparability of Yahweh in the Old Testament* (Leiden: Brill, 1966).

nations. This emphasis is supported by the broad OT context of the song of Moses in Deuteronomy 32 and especially Exodus 15, which underscores the idea of judgment of Israel's enemies leading to Israel's redemption.[25]

Analysis

~

Interpolation theories are of course impossible to prove or disprove. There is no manuscript evidence that anyone ever knew a text without the reference to the 'song of Moses' and so unless one is predisposed to this type of explanation, there is little to commend it. As is often pointed out, whatever reasons are offered for why an author could not have written a particular word or phrase, these are also reasons for why a later redactor is unlikely to have done so. It simply transfers the problem to another stage in the transmission of the text. Furthermore, in the light of the previous chapter, the juxtaposition of Moses and Lamb could be seen as parallel to the juxtaposition of Lion and Lamb in Revelation 5. It is not, therefore, as anachronistic as Charles maintains.

Caird acknowledges the contextual parallel between the act of deliverance by the sea in Exodus and those who 'conquered the beast … standing beside the sea of glass with harps of God in their hands' (Rev. 15.2). But as with his treatment of the Lion/ Lamb juxtaposition in Revelation 5, his interest lies in the differences between them. John's purpose in referring to the 'song of Moses' is to draw a contrast between its violent imagery and the Christian imagery of the new song ('a jubilant anthem of Christian optimism'). He is not interested in tracing the scriptural texts that lie behind the song or looking for a rationale for its composition. It is not an exposition, interpretation or even deduction from Exodus 15 or Deuteronomy 32 but a Christian replacement.

As with his explanation of the Lion/Lamb juxtaposition, however, this does not ring true with the immediate context of Revelation 14–16. The vision is introduced by the words: 'Then I saw another portent in heaven, great and amazing: seven angels with seven plagues, which are the last, for with them the wrath of God is ended' (Rev. 15.1). What immediately follows the song is the description of the seven plagues, many of which are similar to the plagues that befell Egypt. The conclusion is that the people 'cursed God for the plague of hail, so fearful was that plague' (Rev. 16.21). The connections with the Egyptian plagues are so strong that it is impossible to think that John is trying to distance himself from the violent language of Moses' song. As Roloff says, John wanted to 'create a typological correspondence to the

---

[25] Beale, *The Book of Revelation*, p. 799.

exodus … [where] the glassy sea might be an image of the world from which those who overcome were rescued, while fire is the symbol of the wrathful judgment that will befall God's enemies in the world'.[26] A replacement hermeneutic does not do justice to the judgement language of the surrounding context.

Bauckham's view that John has discerned the new song for the age to come has much to commend it. As he notes, there are precedents for it in Pseudo-Philo and Isaiah 11–12 and it would not be unreasonable to speak of this new song as the 'fulfilment' of Moses' song. However, his particular proposal that John has arrived at this song by careful exegesis of Exodus 15 is unlikely for the following reasons. First, the arguments based on John using Hebrew texts are weak. We have already shown that John agrees with the LXX of Ps. 86.8-10 in 17 words. Why should we accept speculative proposals that John rendered *elohim* with *hosios*, when there is a perfectly good text (Deut. 32.4) which not only contains *hosios*, but also *alēthina* ('true'), *hodoi* ('ways') and *dikaios* ('just')?[27]

Secondly, Bauckham is surely guilty of special pleading when he asserts that scholars have mistakenly assumed that lack of visible links implies lack of literary connection. He himself dismisses the view that John has Deuteronomy 32 in mind because the links are 'too tenuous'. This is somewhat ironic given the fact that there are links with Deut. 32.4 and they are visible (*hosios, alēthina, hodoi, dikaios*). And even if they were not visible, Bauckham's position should imply that they cannot be dismissed simply because they are 'too tenuous'. The links might be of the 'invisible' type that he thinks scholars have neglected.

Thirdly, Bauckham makes the assumption that despite the lack of visible links, John's hearers/readers would have assumed that John is engaged in detailed exegesis of Hebrew texts. There is here an assumption about the biblical competence of John's readers; he is, after all, writing them a Greek letter (Rev. 1.4; 22.18-21). What is the evidence that Christians in a late-first-century church in Asia would have the Hebrew text at their fingertips? Furthermore, where in the book of Revelation does John indicate that he is about to engage in detailed scriptural exegesis? His claim to authority is not based on the use of authorized exegetical methods but on visionary experience. Bauckham would no doubt respond that the book is full of scriptural allusion and so it is reasonable to assume that his hearers/readers would have understood it. But that in itself does not support his particular proposal. Indeed, I would suggest that the nature of the book of Revelation strongly suggests that detailed scribal exegesis, of the sort that Bauckham proposes, is the least likely deduction from the evidence. I agree with Bauckham that John points to Exodus 15 and then constructs

---

[26] J. Roloff, *Revelation*, (Minneapolis: Fortress, 1993), p. 183, though R.R. Osborne, (*Revelation* [BECNT; Grand Rapids: Baker Academic, 2002], p. 562) thinks the sea of glass is more likely a reference to the heavenly sea of Rev. 4.6.

[27] Recent commentators have also challenged his explanation that *hagios* can refer to a shared holiness but *hosios* is unique to God. See Osborne, *Revelation*, p. 567.

a song that has no visible links with it, but disagree that his hearers/readers would have deduced from this that John is offering an 'invisible' exegesis of it.

Does the solution lie in John's use of Deuteronomy 32, either exclusively (Ford) or in combination with Exodus 15 (Beale)? The additional parallels that are cited have little to commend them. For example, Ford notes that the phrase in Rev 15.4 ('King of the nations! Lord, who will not fear you?) comes from Jer. 10.6-7, Ps. 86.9 and Mal. 1.6 but also wishes to add Deut. 32.3. However, if the words derive from these first three sources, it is hard to see what Deut. 32.3 ('For I will proclaim the name of the LORD; ascribe greatness to our God!) adds to this. Similarly, Beale's suggestion that the opening phrase of the song ('great and amazing are your deeds') comes from Deut. 28.59-60 ('great and amazing plagues') is unconvincing. Not only is it a long way from Deuteronomy 32 (87 verses), there seems little reason to accept that John has changed 'plagues' to 'deeds' when other sources are available that proclaim God's great and amazing deeds.

Ford and Beale are correct to point out that the judgement themes of Revelation 14–16 are contextually closer to Deuteronomy 32 than Exodus 15 but are strangely reluctant to acknowledge the universalism of John's actual song. Thus Ford claims that the 'who will not fear and glorify your name' clause shows that 'fear' rather than 'love' motivates the song. On the other hand, the promise that 'all nations will come and worship before you' is only said to contain '*an element* of hope for the conversion of the nations'.[28] Beale justifies calling Deut. 28.59-60 an allusion, while Ps. 111.2 is only an echo, because Deut. 28.59-60 shares the same judgement background as Revelation 14–16. But even if Beale were correct that John has Deut. 28.59-60 in mind, one would have to point out that what he has done with it is change 'plagues' to 'deeds', in line with the universal outlook of Psalm 86. Against Caird's replacement hermeneutic, it is right to point out the judgement background of Revelation 14–16, but there seems little reason to downplay the salvation theme of his actual song. Even if the translation of *dikaiōmata* in Rev. 15.4 is the revelation of God's 'judgements', the consequence is that, 'All nations will come and worship before you'. There is no simple 'judgement of the nations, rescue of the elect' theme in John's song.

Narrative critics are well aware that 'misdirection' can play a significant role in the unfolding of a story. For example, a murder mystery will often highlight the 'suspicious' behaviour of a number of suspects before unveiling the true culprit. The success of the novel will depend on whether these earlier signals are regarded as contrived or become understandable in the light of further information. Perhaps the most obvious example of this in Revelation are the frequent suggestions that the story is about to end.[29] Under the guiding urgency of Rev. 5.4 ('I began to weep bitterly because no one was found worthy to open the scroll'), the seals are duly opened in

---

[28] Ford, *Revelation*, p. 257 (emphasis added).

[29] D. Barr, 'Waiting for the End that Never Comes: The Narrative Logic of John's Story' in S.Moyise (ed.), *Studies in the Book of Revelation* (Edinburgh: T&T Clark, 2001), pp. 101–12.

Revelation 6: the first (v. 1); the second (v. 3); the third (v. 5); the fourth (v. 7); the fifth (v. 9); and the sixth (v. 12). The expectation is that undoing the seventh will complete the process but this does not come until Rev. 8.1, which then begins another sequence, the blowing of seven trumpets. The first four follow quickly (vv. 7, 8, 10, 12) but then the process is slowed down, with the fifth occupying 9.1-11 and frustratingly relabelled as the *first* woe. We are told that there are two woes still to come, presumably trumpets six and seven. The sixth trumpet sounds in Rev. 9.13 and we are told in Rev. 10.6-7 that 'There will be no more delay, but in the days when the seventh angel is to blow his trumpet, the mystery of God will be fulfilled'. The seventh trumpet is not sounded until Rev. 11.14 and it transpires that further angels will need to pour out seven bowls of wrath on the earth before it can be realized (Rev. 16.1). And there are still five chapters to come.

Can a literary approach illuminate the puzzle of the 'song of Moses' ascription? In Rev. 15.1-2, John points to Exodus 15 by referring to a sequence of plagues, the imagery of the sea and the mention of 'the song of Moses, the servant of God'. This raises certain expectations that are then dashed; the song that follows bears no visible links with Exodus 15, as Ford, Bauckham, and Beale acknowledge. But that does not mean that the associations from Exodus 15 are completely silenced. The pointers are sufficiently specific to maintain an almost subliminal presence that accompanies a reading of the text. But it is no more than that. It is certainly not loud enough to turn a universalist song into a judgement song. Nor is it loud enough to convince readers that John is offering an (invisible) exegesis of Exodus 15. It remains in the background, barely affecting the interpretation of Rev. 15.3-4, but ready to be 'reactivated' when John begins the plague sequence in Revelation 16, with its obvious parallels (and differences) to the Egyptian plagues:

Seven plagues of Revelation 16	Ten plagues of Exodus
1. Foul and painful sores	6. Boils
2. Sea to blood	1. Rivers to blood
3. Rivers to blood	1. Rivers to blood
4. Scorched by the sun	
5. Darkness	9. Darkness
6. Euphrates dried up. Fouls spirits like frogs	2. Frogs
7. Earthquakes, hailstones	7. Hail

The idea of 'activating' allusions comes from Ziva Ben-Porat. She defines allusion as a 'device for the simultaneous activation of two texts'.[30] The author places

---

[30] Z. Ben-Porat, 'The Poetics of Literary Allusion', *PTL: A Journal for Descriptive Poetics and Theory of Literature* 1 (1976), p. 107; quoted in M. Jauhiainen, *The Use of Zechariah in Revelation* (WUNT, 2.199; Tübingen: Mohr Siebeck, 2006), p. 29.

in the text a 'marker' or 'sign', inviting readers to 'activate' the text by seeking meaningful connections. By definition, it points to a dynamic process which is not easily captured by a single rhetorical or theological purpose: 'The simultaneous activation of the two texts thus connected results in the formation of intertextual patterns whose nature cannot be predetermined.'[31]

Conclusion

We have explored a number of explanations for the ascription 'song of Moses' which have one thing in common: they wish to describe the phenomenon by a single principle without remainder. Some offer useful insights: Bauckham is correct that the ascription points to Exodus 15; Beale is correct that we should not ignore Deuteronomy 32 or the judgement context of Revelation 14–16. But the literary phenomenon is not captured by terms such as 'exegesis' or 'interpretation'. Narrative theory offers insights into how readers may experience the text but as Ben-Porat points out, allusions are elusive. They do not 'pester' (pesher?) the reader into particular interpretations but allow 'space' for creative involvement. It is surely of some significance that the only quotation formula to be found in Revelation remains enigmatic.

---

[31] Ben-Porat, 'The Poetics of Literary Allusion', p. 108.

10

Literary and theological reflections

Introduction

Though we have sometimes been able to make judgements between 'more likely' and 'less likely' solutions to our various case studies, two questions have always been in the background: What sort of literary theory is being assumed and what sort of theological framework is in operation? The questions can go hand in hand or can be kept separate. For example, a literary theory that suggests that the meaning of a text is not confined to its originating moment but develops through interaction with new readers (e.g. reader-response theory) could explain how the New Testament authors were able to give new meanings to old texts. Biblical interpretation would then be a particular example of a general literary phenomenon. On the other hand, some would want to argue that this property of new or expanded meaning is a function of inspiration or canonicity and is not a property of all texts. The New Testament authors have been inspired to discern the meaning that *God* intended in the light of further revelation (death and resurrection of Christ, birth of the Church, biblical canon). It is not a property of texts in general.

This is assuming that our case studies have shown that, at least on some occasions, the New Testament authors assign meanings to texts that differ from the meanings in their original setting. Some theological positions regard this as impossible and either look for a literary theory that offers a broader understanding of 'original meaning' (e.g. speech-act theory), or attempt to show that such dissonance is illusory or even the product of 'sceptical' scholars. On the other hand, some hold to a literary theory where textual meaning is fixed, either by the intention of the author or embedded in the grammar and philology of the text, and so conclude that the New Testament authors took texts out of context and imbued them with new meaning. For some, this is judged acceptable by noting that other ancient writers (Philo, Josephus, Qumran) did the same thing. The New Testament authors were people of their time and their use of Scripture naturally reflects contemporary exegetical practices. It would be wrong to judge them by modern standards. Others think this is beside the point. We are twenty-first-century people applying twenty-first-century methods to analyse ancient texts. Pointing out the differences between then and now, including criteria for valid exegesis, is what responsible scholarship is all about.[1]

Another issue is the tendency of scholars to favour either 'harmonizing' or 'dissonant' solutions to both literary and theological questions. For example, some regard quotations as an alien presence in a text and hence bound to create dissonance. In their introductory book on intertextuality, Michael Worten and Judith Still state as a principle that 'every quotation distorts and redefines the "primary" utterance by relocating it within another linguistic and cultural context'.[2] On the other hand, narrative approaches assume that a work has an overall coherence and so quotations derive their meaning from that. Whatever they may have meant in previous contexts, their meaning in the new work is determined by their role or function in achieving this coherence. Clearly it is important to know whether a scholarly judgement is being made through adherence to one of these positions or because the evidence has compelled them to adopt it (i.e. that a different conclusion would be possible if the evidence were different).

The same issue is also present in theological discussions. Some frameworks assume continuity between the two Testaments, either because 'one divine mind stands behind it all',[3] or because the New Testament authors were Jews and naturally operated within a 'Jewish' framework. New Testament interpretations represent particular 'configurations' of the tradition but are not, in principle, different from those of Philo, Josephus and Qumran.[4] On the other hand, other theological traditions see a fundamental discontinuity between the two Testaments, summarizing one as 'law' and the other as 'grace'.[5] Even the use of 'Old' and 'New' to designate the two collections

---

[1] Much confusion has been caused by mingling 'emic' explanations (what they thought they were doing) and 'etic' explanations (what we think they were doing). For example, the New Testament authors appear to have assumed that the Greek text known to them was 'Scripture' as given by God. We now know that the relationship between that text and an underlying Hebrew text is extremely complex and this inevitably affects our analysis of what is going on. Both perspectives have some merit but they should not be confused.

[2] M. Worten and J. Still, 'Introduction', *Intertextuality: Theories and Practices* (Manchester: Manchester University Press, 1990), p. 11. As M. Sternberg says ('Proteus in Quotation-Land: Mimesis and the Forms of Reported Discourse', *Poetics Today* 3 [1982], p. 108): 'However accurate the wording of the quotation and however pure the quoter's motives, tearing a piece of discourse from its original habitat and recontextualing it within a new network of relations cannot but interfere with its effect.'

[3] G.K. Beale, 'Did Jesus and His Followers Preach the Right Doctrine from the Wrong Texts? An Examination of the Presuppositions of Jesus' and the Apostles' Exegetical Method' in Beale (ed.), *Right Doctrine*, p. 401.

[4] The work of E.P. Sanders has been particularly significant here, seeing 'covenantal nomism' as a common pattern behind the various configurations of Christianity and Judaism.

[5] Often referred to as 'Lutheran' by 'new perspective' scholars, though there is a certain irony here. One of the main thrusts of the 'new perspective' was to challenge the use of labels (e.g. 'legalistic') to describe

suggests such a relationship, which is why advocates of continuity often prefer more neutral terms, such as 'Hebrew Bible' and 'Christian Testament'.[6]

More positions could be mentioned but this is sufficient to confirm the postmodern insight that 'what one knows and sees depends upon where one stands or sits'.[7] Of course, it is always easier to see this in others than in oneself. Thus Hatina finds it incredible that Marcus and Watts appeal to contemporary exegesis to support their view that Mark is a contextually aware exegete, when this is not characteristic of Apocrypha, Pseudepigrapha or the Qumran writings. Stanley finds it incredible that Hays and Wagner construct sophisticated theories of Paul's use of Scripture when general levels of literacy make it unlikely that his readers would have understood them. And Watson finds it incredible that the 'new perspective' on Paul has effectively put a moratorium on finding any discontinuity in his writings, despite such explicit statements as Gal. 3.12 ('But the law does not rest on faith').

However, this need not mean that scholarship is doomed to failure. If it is true that 'what one knows and sees depends upon where one stands or sits', the implication is not that we cannot know or see anything but that what we know or see needs to be interpreted in the light of where we are standing or sitting. For example, two scholars might declare that a particular quotation is a 'misreading' of Scripture but the implications are different if one of the scholars agrees with Worten and Still that all quotations are out of context. Similarly, claims that a particular quotation represents an 'organic' development of the original meaning has different implications if one of the scholars believes in the divine authorship of both Testaments. In some cases, we may feel that such commitments undermine the conclusions being put forward: what is the value of saying a quotation is out of context if all quotations are out of context? On the other hand, it might be worth asking whether some quotations are more out of context than others. Paul's sustained use of the Abraham narrative in Romans 4 is clearly different from his 'muzzling the ox' quotation in 1 Cor. 9.9, despite recent attempts to show that the latter is not as 'arbitrary' as is often claimed.[8]

In this final chapter, we will explore some of the positions mentioned above in order to better understand the conclusions of scholars who subscribe to them. We will begin with what many would regard as the common-sense view of language, that meaning should be identified with authorial intention. This clearly has relevance to the study of explicit quotations, where an introductory formula suggests some form of intent. It is less applicable to allusions and echoes, which might be the product of unconscious borrowing or even trance-like visions (depending on how these terms are defined).

---

the complex phenomena of a religion. It is arguable that labelling any position that maintains *some* discontinuity as 'Lutheran' is guilty of the same thing.

[6] Though, as pointed out in Chapter 1, 'Hebrew Bible' is not a helpful term for our topic, when the Christian authors are primarily citing Greek texts.

[7] W. Bruegemann, *The Postmodern Imagination* (London: SCM, 1993), p. 8.

[8] See D. Instone Brewer, '1 Corinthians 9.9-11: A Literal Interpretation of "Do not Muzzle the Ox"', *NTS* 38 (1992), pp. 554–65.

Meaning as intention

It is not difficult to see how oral communication revolves around intention. Whether it is the inarticulate sounds of a baby or the flamboyant speech of a politician, communication takes place because we assume they are trying to tell us something. As Dan Sperber and Deirdre Wilson state: 'To communicate is to claim an individual's attention: hence to communicate is to imply that the information communicated is relevant.'[9] Of course, we are aware of many other forms of utterance where the intent is not necessarily directed to us. The baby might be absorbed with a favourite toy and the politician might be rehearsing in front of a mirror. But we are quite capable of making such distinctions. We can recognize the difference between a 'speech-act' that is addressing us and one that is not. Indeed, we can overhear a 'speech-act' addressed to someone else and still get some sense of what the speaker was trying to communicate, though the risks of *mis*-understanding are that much greater. Everyday communication is largely about discerning intent.[10]

Paul's letters naturally lend themselves to this sort of analysis. He has been made aware of certain problems or deficiencies in the churches and since he cannot address them in person, he writes to them. The sheer practicalities of obtaining the materials, employing a scribe (Rom. 16.22), arranging for delivery of the message (several days' journey) and having it read out (and probably explained) to the churches, all imply intent. Paul wishes to communicate certain things to the churches. The distinction between parable and allegory in Gospel studies has led some scholars to search for a single purpose for each letter but others are content to acknowledge a number of purposes. Indeed, it is common to recognize digressions in Paul's writings and more than one 'target' for some of his polemics. Nevertheless, critical study of Paul's letters over the last few centuries has assumed that each section of his writing was *intended* to make a particular contribution to the overall purpose or purposes of the letter.

It is not difficult to see how explicit quotations can be seen in the same way. During the course of an argument or exhortation, Paul introduces a number of quotations with formulae that imply intent. He is quoting because he thinks the texts somehow support, strengthen or illustrate what he is trying to say:

| Rom. 1.17 | For in it the righteousness of God is revealed through faith for faith; *as it is written*, 'The one who is righteous will live by faith.' |
| Rom. 2.23-4 | You that boast in the law, do you dishonour God by breaking the law? For, *as it is written*, 'The name of God is blasphemed among the Gentiles because of you.' |

---

[9] D. Sperber and D. Wilson, *Relevance: Communication and Cognition* (2nd edn; Oxford: Blackwell, 1995), p. vii.

[10] See J.L. Austin, *How to do Things with Words* (Oxford: Clarendon Press, 1962); J.R. Searle, *Speech Acts: An Essay in the Philosophy of Language* (Cambridge: Cambridge University Press, 1969).

Rom. 3.9-10   for we have already charged that all, both Jews and Greeks, are under the power of sin, *as it is written*: 'There is no one who is righteous, not even one … '

Of course, determining Paul's intent for each quotation is not straightforward. It depends on how one views the letter as a whole and since he is not here to tell us (an essential difference between oral and written communication), this has to be constructed by the reader. It will take the form of a hypothesis that seeks to do justice to what we know about Paul, what we know (if anything) about the intended readers, and the various themes, signals and codes in the letter. As we have seen in our case studies, scholars vary as to the weight which they assign to each of these factors. Historically-minded scholars place great emphasis on reconstructing the circumstances of the letter and this fills the introduction of most commentaries: author, date, place of writing, destination etc. Others place more weight on the letter itself, either because the historical reconstructions are inconclusive or because of an ideological commitment to narrative or structuralist approaches. However, it would wrong to overplay this diversity. Even with a complex letter like Romans, there are only half a dozen or so hypotheses that are reckoned by most scholars to be serious contenders. The focus on authorial intent has been productive and almost unanimously embraced in critical scholarship.

Should allusions be treated in the same way? The question is important for a number of reasons. First, the distribution of explicit quotations in the New Testament is extremely uneven. With the possible exception of the reference to the song of Moses in Rev. 15.2, the book of Revelation contains no explicit quotations. Romans, Galatians and Corinthians contain many but there are none in Thessalonians and Philippians. Indeed, the distribution in Romans is uneven, concentrated in chapters 3–4, 9–11 and 15. Should we conclude that there is no *intention* to evoke Scripture in the books and sections where introductory formulae are lacking? The answer depends on our understanding (and definition) of allusion.

Secondly, some allusions seem to function like quotations, even though they lack an introductory formula. This might be because they reproduce several words of a well-known text ('son of man coming on the clouds') or the syntax suggests a break in composition (often with *gar* = for or *hoti* = because). Some would call these 'unmarked quotations' because they seem to imply a level of intent, though not as explicit as those with an introductory formula. It is clearly much more difficult to say *why* they are present and the likely effect on the reader/hearer is less certain.

Thirdly, some books (e.g. Revelation) and sections of the New Testament (e.g. Mark 13) contain a high density of scriptural allusion but with no syntactical markers to indicate that what follows is anything other than the author's own words. For Jauhiainen, this calls for a specific theory of allusion rather than treating them like quasi-quotations. In his monograph on *The Use of Zechariah in Revelation*, he draws on Ziva Ben-Porat and her definition of 'literary allusion', as a device for the simultaneous activation of two texts. The activation is achieved through the manipulation of a special signal: a sign (simple or complex) in a given text is characterized by an additional larger 'referent.' This referent is always an independent text. The simultaneous activation of the two texts thus connected results in the formation of intertextual patterns whose nature cannot be predetermined.[11]

Since the author of Revelation has not made it clear how he wants a particular allusion to be taken, the reader must 'activate' the allusion by finding a connection that is helpful, satisfying or stimulating. It is of course possible that John had a precise connection in mind and we could try and determine, from a number of possibilities, which seems to be the most likely. But are we then doing justice to the literary form that we have before us? Allusions are by definition elusive. Essential information has been withheld, allowing the reader/hearer space to 'activate' the allusion. In that sense, it is closer to poetry than prose, operating more at the emotional rather than the cognitive level (which is not to deny some cognitive content).[12]

A different strategy has been to categorize allusions as 'conscious' or 'unconscious', sometimes labelling the latter as 'echoes'. Conscious allusions are those that the author requires the reader/hearer to notice because the intended meaning depends on it. This is not a problem if the text is well known and/or a sufficient amount of it is reproduced. It is behaving like an unmarked quotation. But if the allusion is slight or the text is not well known, then unless the author has seriously misjudged the abilities of his readers/hearers, one can only speak of 'intention' in the sense of 'author satisfaction' rather than 'communicative intent'. It makes no sense to say that an author *intended* a particular meaning when she or he has withheld the information that would make such a meaning possible for the readers.

Intention and the meaning of the source texts

Debates about the status of allusions and echoes only serve to demonstrate the usefulness of the concept of 'communicative intent' for marked and unmarked quotations. However, this raises a number of difficulties when we try and apply it to the quoted texts themselves. First, many of the quoted texts are not 'marked' as texts to be quoted or fulfilled in the future and so deriving their 'communicative intent' is more problematic. Despite the arguments of Wagner, there is little in Isaiah 52 that marks out verse 5 as a text whose 'communicative intent' is to speak of Gentiles blaspheming God because of hypocritical Jewish teachers. If textual meaning is located in the 'communicative intent' of the author, then Isa. 52.5 and Rom. 2.24 have different communicative intentions and hence different meanings.

---

[11] Jauhiainen, *The Use of Zechariah in Revelation*, p. 29 citing Ben-Porat, 'The Poetics of Literary Allusion', pp. 107–8. In fact, Jauhiainen takes this definition of allusion as the general case, with quotations as a particular form of 'literary allusion'.

[12] It should be remembered that the 'intentional fallacy' to which Wimsatt and Beardsley drew attention in their seminal essay, concerned the meaning of poetry.

Secondly, in many cases, we have no idea who wrote the Old Testament text, to whom it was written or why. Indeed, since much of the Old Testament is composite, the idea of 'authorial intention' is itself problematic. For example, should the meaning of Isa. 52.5 be equated with the prophet's thought processes when he was experiencing his visions? Should it be equated with the motivations that led to such experiences being written down, either by (Deutero-) Isaiah himself or by one of his disciples? Or should it be equated with the purpose or purposes of the unknown editors who are responsible for the final form (or one of the final forms) of the book? Not only is it difficult to see why any one of these is 'correct' to the exclusion of the others, it is almost impossible to see how we could gain access to them (the first two in particular).

It is for this reason that most scholars, consciously or unconsciously, operate with a different understanding of 'intention' when studying the two Testaments. The intention of an Old Testament passage is a construct based on its role or function in the immediate context. The immediate context might be the particular psalm, the minor prophet, the law code or a section of Isaiah deemed to come from a particular period (e.g. Isaiah 40–55). There is no fixed rule about this; it is as large as it needs to be in order to give a context for understanding a communicative act. This language draws on speech-act theory. John Austin[13] argued that an utterance embodies a 'threefold communicative act' that can be described as its *locution* (the act of using words to express something), its *illocution* (what one does in saying something, such as issuing a promise or warning) and its *perlocution* (what is brought about, such as convincing or deterring). In other words, the focus is not on what an author planned to do (they might have been incompetent) but what has in fact been done, as embodied in the text that has come down to us. The argument would then be that Isaiah 52 embodies a communicative act, even if we cannot put a name to who is responsible for it.

But what is the relationship between this 'communicative act' and that of the New Testament author who quotes it? Some would say that it still highlights the dissonance between them (Hatina, Stanley) but others would argue that the 'communicative act' of the New Testament author falls within the 'communicative act' of the Old Testament text. Greg Beale, for example, draws on Hirsch's idea of 'extended' or 'transhistorical' meaning to defend the validity of New Testament interpretations. He begins by citing the following illustration: Suppose a traffic regulation was framed in such a way that it prohibited wheeled vehicles from passing through a red light. In the future, a vehicle might be invented that does not have wheels but runs on compressed air and this might require a change in the wording of the law, such as omitting the word 'wheeled'. But it would be wrong to claim that this constitutes a change in meaning. The original 'communicative intent' of laws like this is to be applied to analogous situations, even if they cannot at the moment be envisaged. Beale concludes by glossing Hirsch:

---

[13] Austin, *How to do Things with Words*, pp. 94–147.

Authors using some genres will extend meaning to analogous and even unforeseeable situations so that their meaning is intended to have presently unknowable, future implications. In this respect, one can 'speak of open-ended authorial intentions' and 'extended meaning' in which an original meaning can tolerate some revision in cognitive content and yet not be essentially altered … Interpretation should go beyond the author's letter, but it must never exceed the author's spirit.[14]

Thus Beale challenges those who speak of John's misappropriation of Scripture in the book of Revelation by asking, 'can we say with confidence that John's interpretations do *not* fall in line with legitimate extensions and applications of the meaning of Old Testament texts?'[15] He then asserts, 'surely it is possible that someone like Isaiah, if he were living in the first century, might well think the extended application of his prophecies to Jesus would fall within the parameters of his understanding of what he wrote'.[16] However, behind these rhetorical questions lies a particular theological commitment to the unity of Scripture:

if we assume the legitimacy of an inspired canon, then we should seek to interpret any part of that canon within its overall canonical context (given that one divine mind stands behind it all and expresses its thoughts in logical fashion).[17]

Beale is not genuinely interested in asking whether the interpretations found in the book of Revelation are parallel to Hirsch's example of 'wheeled' and 'unwheeled' vehicles. His theological commitment is such that no amount of evidence would ever persuade him that a New Testament interpretation 'exceeds the author's spirit'. But if John's vision of a 'temple-less' New Jerusalem (Rev. 21.22) is a valid 'extension' of Ezekiel's detailed description of the New Temple (Ezekiel 40–48), it is hard to see why the Qumran interpretation is not equally a 'valid extension'. In other words, if all the different interpretations found in the book of Revelation, which Beale groups into seven categories,[18] can be incorporated within Hirsch's understanding of 'extended' or 'transhistorical' meaning, then we are dealing with a very broad theory indeed:

---

[14] G. K. Beale, 'Questions of Authorial Intent, Epistemology, and Presuppositions and Their Bearing on the Study of the Old Testament in the New: A Rejoinder to Steve Moyise', *Irish Biblical Studies* 21 (1999), p. 157; drawing on E.D. Hirsch, 'Transhistorical Intentions and the Persistence of Allegory', *New Literary History* 25 (1994), p. 558.

[15] Beale, 'Questions of Authorial Intent,' p. 170.

[16] Beale, 'Questions of Authorial Intent,' p. 170.

[17] G.K. Beale, 'Did Jesus and his Followers Preach the Right Doctrine from the Wrong Texts?', p. 401.

[18] Beale, *John's Use of the Old Testament in Revelation*, pp. 75–128.

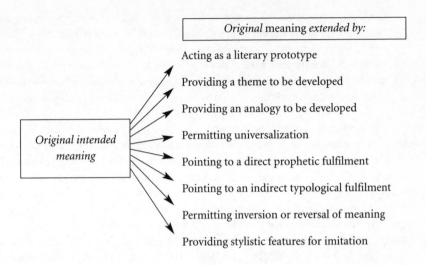

For example, it is hard to see how any of the nuanced interpretations of pre-millennialism, post-millennialism and a-millennialism would fall outside such a broad understanding of 'extended' meaning. But Beale makes such judgements on numerous occasions in his commentary. My conclusion is that it is his theological commitment to the unity of Scripture that is primarily dictating his judgements, not his allegiance to the literary theory of Hirsch.[19]

Vanhoozer also draws on Hirsch's notion of 'extended' or 'transhistorical' meaning, offering this illustration. When Joseph Priestly spoke of 'dephlogisticated air' in his *Observations on Different Kinds of Air* (1772), he was dependent on contemporary scientific understanding. We now know that what he was referring to as 'dephlogisticated air' is in fact oxygen, a pure element. Our understanding is thus quite different from his but it would be wrong to say that Priestly was not 'intending' to refer to oxygen. According to Vanhoozer: 'Priestly was *attending to* oxygen, though in a less explicit way than scientists today. The point is that an author's intended meaning can tolerate a small revision in mental content and still remain the same.'[20] However, it is surely doubtful that every interpretation of Scripture found in the New Testament can be explained as a 'small revision in mental content'. Indeed, Vanhoozer recognizes this:

---

[19] Though Thiselton sympathizes with Hirsch's concerns, he regards it as naïve in the light of Gadamer and Ricoeur. See A.C. Thiselton, *New Horizons in Hermeneutics* (London: HarperCollins, 1992), p. 13.

[20] K. Vanhoozer, *Is there a Meaning in this Text? The Bible, the Reader, and the Morality of Literary Knowledge* (Grand Rapids: Zondervan 1998), p. 262.

Could the author of Isaiah 53 have intended to predict, allude, or otherwise refer to Jesus' passion, an event that had not yet taken place at the time of composition? This particular text serves as a particularly sharp instance of what Christian readers say more generally about the Old Testament, namely, that it is, somehow, about Jesus Christ. Is it possible to hold to a view of meaning as past communicative action and still affirm that the Old Testament has a 'fuller meaning' than what its human authors could have intended? [21]

His answer is, Yes, but only if we are willing to entertain the idea of 'divine intention'. In other words, it is the canonical meaning that the words have (and were destined to have) when they take their appropriate place in the completed canon: 'The problem of the "fuller meaning" of Scripture and of determining the divine author's intent is precisely the problem of choosing the intentional context that best enables one maximally to describe the communicative action embodied in Scripture.'[22] Thus he argues that the unnamed servant of Isaiah 53 finds its 'intended' meaning in its application to Christ. He does not try and demonstrate that this is what the original meant or that this is how it would have been understood by (Deutero-) Isaiah's contemporaries. As prophecy, its 'speech-act' looks forward to a time when it can be interpreted in the light of the other biblical books. This is its true meaning, the meaning intended by the particular divine 'speech-act' that is now found in Isaiah's fifty-third chapter.

Unfortunately, Vanhoozer does not offer any examples where there is significant dissonance between old and new, and this is where Watson's study has the advantage. He agrees that the divine 'speech-act' of both Testaments is ultimately a unity but thinks it is a complex unity which can tolerate internal tensions. Thus he does not find it necessary to defend the veracity of every quoted text in the New Testament. Indeed, it is essential for his interpretation that the tensions in Paul's thought mirror the tensions found in the Old Testament itself. For Watson, the Old Testament does not speak with one voice, for

> the text that derives from the Sinai event is multiple and not singular in its origin (cf. Gal. 3.19-20). From one angelic voice we learn that the person who does these things will live by them; from another we learn that all who are of works of law are under a curse; a third instructs us to love our neighbour as ourselves; a fourth is concerned with the observance of sacred times and seasons (Gal. 4.9-10).[23]

Paul discerns the divine intention in the promise to Abraham (Gen. 15.6) and the assertion of Hab. 2.4, but not in Lev. 18.5 and the conditional promises of the law. Thus Watson can sometimes speak of Paul's interpretation of Scripture as 'radical',

---

[21] Vanhoozer, *Is there a Meaning in this Text?*, p. 264.
[22] Vanhoozer, *Is there a Meaning in this Text?* p. 265.
[23] Watson, *Paul and the Hermeneutics of Faith*, p.520.

not confining himself to the historical meaning of a text *as if he himself had nothing to contribute*.[24] On the other hand, he denies that this represents an imposition on the text for it is consistent with the intended 'speech-act' of the whole.

The role of readers in interpreting texts

What the theories discussed above have in common is that they wish to broaden the concept of 'authorial intention' to accommodate the sort of interpretations found in the New Testament. Reader-centred theories start at the other end. The reason why New Testament interpretations differ from the original is because they are interpreting in a different context. They *read* the text with different presuppositions and they *use* the text for different purposes. Thus, looked at in a different way, what our case studies have been trying to ascertain is how the New Testament authors *read* Scripture. Many will find the following 'reader-centred' diagram a more convincing explanation for what we find in the book of Revelation than the previous 'author-centred' one:

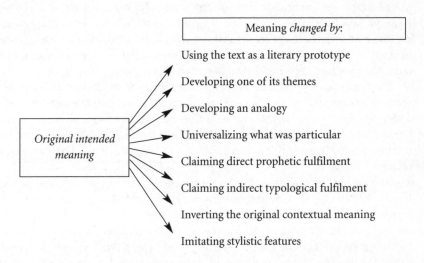

It is thus necessary to ask what sort of 'theory of reading' is being assumed by scholars as they seek to explain how the New Testament authors *read* Scripture. One theory that has had a significant impact on biblical studies is that of Wolfgang Iser.[25] Iser argues that reading is always a matter of 'completing' a text. A text inevitably contains 'gaps' or 'blanks', so that meaning is 'constructed' by readers when they

---

[24] Watson, *Paul and the Hermeneutics of Faith*, p. 163.
[25] W. Iser, *The Implied Reader: Patterns of Communication in Prose Fiction from Bunyan to Beckett* (Baltimore: Johns Hopkins University Press, 1974); *The Act of Reading* (Baltimore: Johns Hopkins University Press, 1978).

'actualize' it. A text has 'semantic potential' but it is only when a reader 'actualizes' it in a concrete situation that meaning emerges. This explains why the New Testament authors inevitably see the Church as the fulfilment of the ancient promises, while the Qumran writers look to their own community. Neither is doing anything intrinsically wrong by interpreting texts in the light of their own contexts, for the text is incomplete until it is actualized. And since both believe that their communities were specifically raised up by God in fulfilment of the ancient promises, both believe that this is how the text *authorizes* them to actualize it.

This also explains the different interpretations found in the New Testament itself. Most famously, James can quote Gen. 15.6 ('Abraham believed God, and it was reckoned to him as righteousness') to show that a 'person is justified by works and not by faith alone' (Jas 2.24). The debate that James is involved in ('What good is it … if you say you have faith but do not have works?') leads him to 'complete' the text in a different way from Paul in Romans 4 ('But to one who without works trusts him who justifies the ungodly, such faith is reckoned as righteousness'). This is an interesting example because author-centred approaches often claim that the wider context of the quotation explains (or justifies) the particular New Testament interpretation. But Paul and James both appeal to the text's wider narrative context and still produce different interpretations. On a reader-centred theory, they are 'completing' the text in different ways, resulting in their different interpretations.

Iser does not suggest that meaning comes 'solely' from readers, as if reading is only a reflection of one's own interests and commitments (the standard criticism of reader-centred approaches). A promise is a promise and a command is a command. A reader who does not understand the difference between a promise and a command or deliberately confuses them is not the sort of reader that the text 'implies'. As Thiselton notes, Iser 'does not question the "givenness" of stable constraints in textual meaning, but underlines their potential and indeterminate status independent of actualization by the reading process'.[26] There is clearly an overlap here with approaches that focus on the 'communicative intention' of a text (though not with those which focus on 'authorial intention'). The difference is that Iser's reader-response theory does not equate *the meaning* of a text with this 'idealized' or 'implied' reader, for this remains a hypothetical construct. Real readers do not share all the characteristics of the 'implied' reader, not through any particular wilfulness but simply because they are real readers and therefore inhabit specific contexts.

A criticism of Iser's theory is that it focuses too much on the individual reader, whereas real readers belong to communities where certain reading conventions operate. For example, if I receive a letter which begins, 'Dear Steve', belonging to a reading community that sees this as a conventional greeting is likely to be more influential on my interpretation than any personal circumstances. Indeed, my wife has spent many years telling me not to call her 'dear' (as in 'Shall we go, dear?') but would

---

[26] Thiselton, *New Horizons*, p. 517.

be most surprised not to find it in a personal letter. This 'conventional' element of reading has been particularly developed in studies of narrative and studies of rhetoric.

Narrative critics such as Chatman, Genette and Booth[27] argue that certain features of narrative, such as plot, characterization and point of view, fall into a relatively small number of conventional patterns. Being conventional, these patterns have predictable effects on readers who share such conventions. Thus on Hatina's view, the role of Mark's opening quotation to introduce the forerunner of Jesus is more significant than going outside of the text to ask what Exodus, Isaiah or Malachi might have had in mind. It is a reading convention to look for information that introduces the main characters of a story and sets in motion the plot. Hatina argues that since the composite quotation of Mk 1.2-3 fulfils these functions, readers are *not* prompted to look outside of the text for the meaning of the quotation.

As we noted earlier, letters also have their conventions and the study of rhetoric can be used to illuminate the role of quotations. Very little is found in the ancient handbooks about quotations, Aristotle (*Rhetorica*, 1.15; 2.21) and Quintilian (*Institutio oratoria*, 1.8; 2.7; 5.36-44) only mentioning them in passing. This is surprising since the 'fact' of quotation, particularly to Homer, was widespread and indeed offers a significant parallel to scriptural quotation in the New Testament. Stanley notes six parallels between the role of Homer in Hellenistic life and the role of Scripture in Jewish life. He says that both functioned as: (1) primordial texts, exercising formative influence on communal life and thought; (2) revelation, accessible only to those who are initiated into its traditions; (3) sources of knowledge, for both the human and divine order; (4) curricula, for the education of children; (5) authoritative texts, when used in argumentation. In addition, both were available in a relatively stable text-form.[28]

However, noting that little is to be gleaned from the handbooks about quotations as a rhetorical device, Stanley turns to modern theories ('etic' rather than 'emic') in order to analyse Paul's use of Scripture. He chooses four theorists that range from the *dramaturgical* (re-enactment) theory of Anna Wierzbicka[29] to the *parodic* (hijacking) theory of Gillian Lane-Mercer.[30] In between these extremes lie the *proteus* theory of Meir Sternberg and the *demonstration* theory of Herbert Clark and Richard Gerrig.[31] Both are concerned to show the inevitable change of meaning that results in *relocating* (Sternberg) the quoted words or drawing attention to a *selection* (Clark

---

[27] S. Chatman, *Story and Discourse: Narrative Structure in Fiction and Film* (Ithaca: Cornell University Press, 1978); G. Genette, *Narrative Discourse* (Ithaca: Cornell University Press, 1980); W.C. Booth, *The Rhetoric of Fiction* (2nd edn; Chicago: Chicago University Press, 1983).

[28] C.D. Stanley, 'Paul and Homer: Greco-Roman Citation Practice in the First Century CE', *NovT* 32 (1990), pp. 51–2.

[29] A. Wierzbicka, 'The Semantics of Direct and Indirect Discourse', *Papers in Linguistics* 7 (1974), pp. 267–307.

[30] G. Lane-Mercer, 'Quotation as a Discursive Strategy', *Kodikas* 14 (1991), pp. 199–214.

[31] H.H. Clark and R.R. Gerrig, 'Quotations as Demonstrations', *Language* 66 (1990), pp. 786–8.

and Gerrig) of them. Thus while it may be true that a reader of Paul's quotation of Gen. 15.6 might think of other aspects of the Abraham story (such as his passing his wife off as his sister), these would not be as 'loud' as the actual quoted words. There is thus a distorting effect in all quotations since the original does not draw attention to the particular selection of words in the way that the quoting author has done.

Intertextuality

According to theories of intertextuality, this description of how quotations 'work' is simply a subset of how all texts work. Drawing on the theories of Mikhail Bakhtin, Julia Kristeva suggests a dialogical relationship between 'texts', broadly understood as a system of codes or signs. Moving away from traditional notions of agency and influence, she suggests that such relationships are more like an 'intersection of textual surfaces rather than a point (a fixed meaning)'.[32] No text is an island and, contrary to structuralist theory, it cannot be understood in isolation. It can only be understood as part of a web or matrix of other texts, themselves only to be understood in the light of other texts (seen as traces). Each new text disturbs the fabric of existing texts as it jostles for a place in the canon of literature. Intertextuality suggests that the meaning of a text is not fixed but always open to revision as new texts come along and reposition it. It is not even necessary for the new text to quote the older text for this to happen; the very fact of its existence is enough. For example, I am not aware that J.K. Rowling ever quotes from J.R.R. Tolkien or C.S. Lewis but all who are familiar with Harry Potter will view *The Lord of the Rings* and *The Narnia Chronicles* in a different light.

It is easy to see how 'canonical' approaches can make use of such theories. As each new text is added to the authoritative collection, there is an inevitable repositioning or reconfiguring of what has gone before. This is true both within the Old Testament itself,[33] and when it is joined by later 'Christian' texts. The major dispute has been whether such 'repositionings' result in some sort of equilibrium (describable as biblical theology), or inevitably *'generate an infinite chain of semiotic effects'*.[34] The two are not as contradictory as one might think. To the human eye, a hair is an easily recognizable long thin line but under a microscope, its complexity makes it almost impossible to describe. It would be foolish to claim that one viewpoint automatically falsifies the other. Or to change the analogy, if one considers the number of variables that contribute to a performance of Beethoven's fifth symphony, it is clear that no two

---

[32] J. Kristeva, 'Word, Dialogue and Novel', in T. Moi (ed.), *The Kristeva Reader* (New York: Columbia University Press, 1986), p. 69. See S. Moyise, 'Intertextuality and the Study of the Old Testament in the New Testament', in Moyise (ed.), *The Old Testament in the New Testament* (JSNTSup, 189; Sheffield Academic Press, 2000), pp. 14–41.

[33] As demonstrated by M. Fishbane, *Biblical Interpretation in Ancient Israel* (Oxford: Clarendon Press, 1985).

[34] Thiselton, *New Horizons*, p. 506.

performances will ever be the same. But this capacity for 'infinite variety' should not be used to imply that some hearers would hear Beethoven's sixth symphony. It is possible to have 'infinite variety' while still being bound by certain parameters.[35]

Theories of intertextuality point to the complexity of textual interaction. An author may have a particular motive for citing Scripture but cannot control the effects (or figurations) that this may generate. As Richard Hays says:

> Despite all the careful hedges that we plant around texts, meaning has a way of leaping over, like sparks. Texts are not inert; they burn and throw fragments of flames on their rising heat. Often we succeed in containing the energy, but sometimes the sparks escape and kindle new blazes, reprises of the original fire.[36]

In part, this is the rationale for those who offer sophisticated explanations for the use of Scripture in the New Testament. Citing Scripture, whether by quotation, allusion or echo, sets in motion a number of interactions that are not easily captured by a single principle. Here is the obverse of Hatina's narrative claim. Mark's opening quotation points to at least three different sources, all of which are (probably) regarded as authoritative by author and reader alike. There is thus the potential to 'kindle new blazes' which are not entirely the product of over-active imaginations; the 'kindling' is embedded in the text itself. Even if studies of first-century literacy might make the 'activation' of some of the possible interactions seem unlikely, why should we limit our analysis of the *text* to what its first readers were able to accomplish (especially as we have no access to that anyway)?

On the other hand, the likely complexity of such interactions should lead to a degree of humility in putting forward specific 'solutions'. Definitive statements that the quotation of Mal. 3.1 ('See, I am sending my messenger') would bring with it the associations of Mal. 4.5 ('Lo, I will send you the prophet Elijah') are out of place, not because narrative theory says so, but because it is simply one of a number of possibilities. Intertextuality has sometimes been offered as 'the method' behind a particularly complex proposal but it does not, of course, add credence to any specific hypothesis. Indeed, the very complexity that it implies puts a question mark against the exclusive claim of any specific theory. There are always going to be other ways of looking at it, though (according to the author of the particular proposal) not as convincingly.

Hays notes that there are at least five different loci for identifying the meaning of one of Paul's citations: (1) Paul's intention; (2) the original reader's appropriation; (3) the text itself; (4) my reading of Paul; and (5) my reading of Paul within a community of readers.[37] He sees some benefit in each of these and is not prepared

---

[35] Those of a more mathematical frame of mind will know of iterative sequences that are infinite but bound. For example, the sequence 1/2, 3/4, 7/8, 15/16 etc. is infinite but will never exceed 1.

[36] Hays, *Echoes of Scripture*, p. 33.

[37] Hays, *Echoes of Scripture*, pp. 26–7.

to nominate any one of them as his principal focus. He intends to 'hold them all together in creative tension', noting that: 'Claims about intertextual meaning effects are strongest where it can credibly be demonstrated that they occur within the literary structure of the text and that they can plausibly be ascribed to the intention of the author and the competence of the original readers.'[38] The key word here is 'plausibly'. In the hands of those less sensitive to figuration than Hays, a piece of literary data (often capable of several interpretations) is used to deduce what Paul's intention *must* have been and what his readers *must* have understood. This level of certainty is rarely possible. At best, we can offer hypotheses that explain the literary data, offer a plausible intention or purpose for it, and show that it is not impossible for at least some of the readers to have understood it thus.

The main challenge of such an intertextual analysis is how to hold the different angles of view together 'in creative tension'. Negatively, we should be on our guard against 'premature closure'. In our search for the 'loudest' voice, we should not become deaf to the quieter voices that give the work its particular texture. Positively, Vernon Robbins has formulated an approach that will ensure such voices are not lost. He calls it 'socio-rhetorical criticism':

> [S]ocio-rhetorical criticism uses a strategy of reading and rereading a text from different angles to produce a 'revalued' or 'revisited' rhetorical interpretation ... The goal is to use the resources of other disciplines 'on their own terms' and to allow these resources to deconstruct and reconfigure the results of a particular focus and set of strategies in a particular discipline.[39]

Different approaches to textual meaning might be seen as a series of experiments, each of which illuminates some aspect of the 'specimen'. A scientist knows that the 'image' from an electron microscope is not a *picture* of the 'specimen' but a *representation* of how it looks when bombarded by electrons. Heating it up and monitoring its light emissions would offer a different *representation* of it. By having two or more representations, the scientist has a more complete *understanding* of the specimen, for they are both representing what is truly there, though only under certain conditions.

Conclusion

Evoking Scripture is a complex business. An author might have a specific purpose for a citation but loosing a text from its previous contextual moorings and forcing it to form new connections opens up new possibilities. Some of these might be anticipated

[38] Hays, *Echoes of Scripture*, p. 28.
[39] V. Robbins, *The Tapestry of Early Christian Discourse. Rhetoric, Society and Ideology* (London: Routledge, 1996), pp. 40–41.

by the author and an attempt made to use them to further his or her purposes. Others may remain hidden until readers from a different context and with different presuppositions 'configure' them in ways not envisaged by the original author. Some scholars would regard the latter as invalid, insisting that 'original intention' is the only valid goal of interpretation. But it is doubtful that this was a major concern for first-century interpreters or that it does justice to the claim that these texts constitute 'Scripture'. It is the conclusion of this study that this complexity is best served by combining a number of approaches rather than fastening on just one. Evoking Scripture 'opens up' rather than 'closes down' and our methods of study need to be sensitive to this. It is also why the subject retains its fascination.

Bibliography

Achtemeier, P.J., *1 Peter: A Commentary on First Peter* (Hermeneia; Minneapolis: Fortress Press, 1996).

Allen, D.M., 'Deuteronomic Re-presentation in a Word of Exhortation: An Assessment of the Paraenetic Function of Deuteronomy in the Letter to the Hebrews' (PhD Dissertation; University of Edinburgh, 2007).

Aune, D., *Revelation 1–5* (WBC, 52A; Dallas: Word Books, 1997).

—— *Revelation 6–16* (WBC, 52B; Nashville: Thomas Nelson, 1998).

Austin, J.L., *How to do Things with Words* (Oxford: Clarendon Press, 1962).

Barr, D.L., 'The Lamb Looks Like a Dragon' in D.L. Barr (ed.), *The Reality of Apocalypse. Rhetoric and Politics in the Book of Revelation* (Atlanta: SBL, 2006), pp. 205–20.

Barrett, C.K., *The Epistle to the Romans* (London: A. & C. Black, 1957).

Barton, J., *Oracles of God: Perceptions of Ancient Prophecy in Israel after the Exile* (London: Darton, Longman & Todd, 1986).

Bauckham, R.H., *The Climax of Prophecy. Studies on the Book of Revelation* (Edinburgh: T&T Clark, 1993).

Beale, G.K. (ed.), *The Right Doctrine from the Wrong Texts? Essays on the Use of the Old Testament in the New* (Grand Rapids: Baker Books, 1994).

—— 'Positive Answer to the Question Did Jesus and His Followers Preach the Right Doctrine from the Wrong Texts?' in Beale (ed.), *Right Doctrine from the Wrong Texts?*, pp. 387–404.

—— *John's Use of the Old Testament in Revelation* (JSNTSup, 166; Sheffield: Sheffield Academic Press, 1998).

—— *The Book of Revelation* (NIGTC; Grand Rapids: Eerdmans, 1999).

—— 'Questions of Authorial Intent, Epistemology, and Presuppositions and Their Bearing on the Study of the Old Testament in the New: A Rejoinder to Steve Moyise,' *Irish Biblical Studies* 21 (1999), pp. 151–80.

Ben-Porat, Z., 'The Poetics of Literary Allusion', *PTL: A Journal for Descriptive Poetics and Theory of Literature* 1 (1976), pp. 105–28.

Berkley, T.W., *From a Broken Covenant to Circumcision of the Heart. Pauline Intertextual Exegesis in Romans 2.17-29* (SBLDS, 175; Atlanta: SBL, 2000).

Best, E., *1 Peter* (London: Marshall, Morgan & Scott, 1970).

Black, C.C., *The Disciples According to Mark: Markan Redaction in Current Debate* (JSNTSup, 27; Sheffield: Sheffield Academic Press, 1989).

Black, M., *Romans* (London: Oliphants, 1973).

Bloom, H., *The Revelation of St John the Divine* (New York: Chelsea House, 1988).

Booth, W.C., *The Rhetoric of Fiction* (2nd edn; Chicago: Chicago University Press, 1983).

Boring, M.E., *Revelation* (Louisville: Westminster John Knox, 1989).

Bredin, M., *Jesus, Revolutionary of Peace. A Nonviolent Christology in the Book of Revelation* (Carlisle: Paternoster Press, 2003).

Brewer, D. Instone, *Techniques and Assumptions in Jewish Exegesis before 70 CE* (TSAJ, 30; Tübingen: Mohr Siebeck, 1992).

——— '1 Corinthians 9.9-11: A Literal Interpretation of "Do not Muzzle the Ox"', *NTS* 38 (1992), pp. 554–65.

Broadhead, E.K., 'Reconfiguring Jesus: The Son of Man in Markan Perspective' in T.R. Hatina (ed.), *Biblical Interpretation in Early Christian Gospels. Volume 1. The Gospel of Mark* (LNTS, 304; London & New York: T&T Clark, 2006).

Brown, R.E., *The Gospel According to John* (AB, 29; New York: Doubleday, Vol. 1, 1966).

Bruegemann, W., *The Postmodern Imagination* (London: SCM, 1993).

Bultmann, R., *Theology of the New Testament* (London: SCM Press, 1952).

Byrne, B., *Romans* (Collegeville: Liturgical Press, 1996).

Caird, G.B., *The Revelation of St John the Divine* (London: A. & C. Black, 1984).

Charles, R.H., *A Critical and Exegetical Commentary on the Revelation of St. John* (ICC; (Edinburgh: T&T Clark, 2 vols, 1920).

Chatman, S., *Story and Discourse: Narrative Structure in Fiction and Film* (Ithaca: Cornell University Press, 1978).

Chilton, B., *A Galilean Rabbi and His Bible: Jesus' Own Interpretation of Isaiah* (London: SPCK, 1984).

Clark, H.H. and Gerrig, R.R., 'Quotations as Demonstrations', *Language* 66 (1990), pp. 764–805.

Cranfield, C.E.B., *A Critical and Exegetical Commentary on the Epistle to the Romans* (ICC; Edinburgh: T&T Clark, 2 vols, 1975, 1979).

Crossley, J.G., *The Date of Mark's Gospel. Insight from the Law in Earliest Christianity* (JSNTSup, 266; London and New York: T&T Clark, 2004).

Culpepper, A., *Anatomy of the Fourth Gospel: A Study in Literary Design* (Philadelphia: Fortress Press, 1983).

Dahl, N.A., *Studies in Paul. Theology of the Early Christian Mission* (Minneapolis: Augsburg Fortress, 1977).

Das, A.A., *Paul, the Law and the Covenant* (Peabody: Hendrickson, 2001).

Davidson, H., *T.S. Eliot and Hermeneutics: Absence and Presence in the Waste Land* (Baton Rouge: Louisiana State University Press, 1985).

Derrida, J., *Positions* (Chicago: Chicago University Press, 1972).

Dodd, C.H., *According to the Scriptures. The Sub-structure of New Testament Theology* (London: Nisbet, 1952).

——— *The Epistle to the Romans* (London: Fontana Books, 1959).

——— *The Interpretation of the Fourth Gospel* (Cambridge: Cambridge University Press, 1968).

Dunn, J.D.G., *The Epistle to the Galatians* (BNTC; London: A. & C. Black, 1993).

——— *Romans 1–8* (WBC, 38A; Dallas: Word Books, 1988).

Elliott, J.H., *1 Peter: A New Translation and Commentary* (AB, 37B; New York: Doubleday, 2000).

Evans, C.A., *To See and Not Perceive: Isaiah 6.9-10 in Early Jewish and Christian Interpretation* (JSOTSup, 64; Sheffield: Sheffield Academic Press, 1989).

Farmer, R., *Beyond the Impasse. The Promise of a Process Hermeneutic* (Macon: Mercer University Press, 1997).

Fishbane, M., *Biblical Interpretation in Ancient Israel* (Oxford: Clarendon Press, 1985).

Fitzmyer, J., *Romans: A New Translation with Introduction and Commentary* (AB, 33; New York: Doubleday, 1992).

Ford, J.M., *Revelation: Introduction, Translation and Commentary* (AB, 38; New York: Doubleday, 1975).

France, R.T., *The Gospel of Mark* (NIGTC; Grand Rapids: Eerdmans/Carlisle: Paternoster, 2002).

Funk, R.W. *et al.*, *The Five Gospels. The Search for the Authentic Words of Jesus* (New York: Polebridge Press, 1993).

Gamble, H.Y., *Books and Readers in the Early Church. A History of Early Christian Texts* (New Haven: Yale University Press, 1995).

Gathercole, S.J., *Where is Boasting? Early Jewish Soteriology and Paul's Response in Romans 1–5* (Grand Rapids: Eerdmans, 2002).

Genette, G., *Narrative Discourse* (Ithaca: Cornell University Press, 1980).

Gheorghita, R., *The Role of the Septuagint in Hebrews* (WUNT, 2.160; Tübingen: Mohr Siebeck, 2003).

Goppelt, L., *A Commentary on 1 Peter* (Grand Rapids: Eerdmans, 1982).

Greene, T.M., *The Light in Troy: Imitation and Discovery in Renaissance Poetry* (New Haven: Yale University Press, 1982).

Guelich, R.A., '"The Beginning of the Gospel": Mark 1:1-15', *BR* 27 (1982), pp. 5–15.

Gundry, R.H., *Mark: A Commentary on his Apology for the Cross* (Grand Rapids: Eerdmans, 1993).

——— *Matthew: A Commentary on His Handbook for a Mixed Church under Persecution* (2nd edn; Grand Rapids: Eerdmans, 1994).

Hanson, A.T., *Studies in Paul's Technique and Theology* (London: SPCK, 1974).

——— *The Living Utterances of God* (London: Darton, Longman & Todd, 1983).

Harris, J.R., *Testimonies* (Cambridge: Cambridge University Press, 2 vols, 1916, 1920).

Harris, W., *Ancient Literacy* (Cambridge, MA: Harvard University Press, 1989).

Hatina, T., *In Search of a Context: The Function of Scripture in Mark's Narrative* (JSNTSup, 232; Sheffield: Sheffield Academic Press, 2002).

—— (ed.) *Biblical Interpretation in Early Christian Gospels. Volume 1. The Gospel of Mark* (LNTS, 304; London and New York: T&T Clark, 2006).

—— 'Embedded Scripture Texts and the Plurality of Meaning: The Announcement of the "Voice from Heaven" in Mark 1.11 as a Case Study' in Hatina (ed.), *Biblical Interpretation in Early Christian Gospels*, pp. 81–99.

Hays, R.B., '"The Righteous One" as Eschatological Deliverer: A Case Study in Paul's Apocalyptic Hermeneutics' in J. Marcus and M.L. Soards (eds), *Apocalyptic and the New Testament: Essays in Honor of J. Louis Martyn* (JSNTSup, 24; Sheffield: JSOT Press, 1988), pp. 191–215.

—— *Echoes of Scripture in the Letters of Paul* (New Haven: Yale University Press, 1989).

—— *The Faith of Jesus Christ. The Narrative Substructure of Galatians 3:1-4:11* (2nd edn; Michigan: Eerdmans, 2002).

Hengel, M., *Studies in the Gospel of Mark* (Philadelphia: Fortress Press, 1985).

Hirsch, E.D., 'Transhistorical Intentions and the Persistence of Allegory', *New Literary History* 25 (1994), pp. 549–67.

Hooker, M.D., *Jesus the Servant* (London: SPCK, 1959).

Iser, W., *The Implied Reader: Patterns of Communication in Prose Fiction from Bunyan to Beckett* (Baltimore: Johns Hopkins University Press, 1974).

—— *The Act of Reading* (Baltimore: Johns Hopkins University Press, 1978).

Jauhiainen, M., *The Use of Jechariah in Revelation* (WUNT, 2.199; Tübingen: Mohr Siebeck, 2006).

Jobes, K.H., *1 Peter* (BECNT; Grand Rapids: Baker Academic, 2005).

—— 'Septuagint Textual Tradition in 1 Peter' in W. Kraus and R.G. Wooden (eds), *Septuagint Research. Issues and Challenges in the Study of the Greek Jewish Scriptures* (Atlanta: SBL, 2006), pp. 311–33.

Johns, L.L., *Lamb Christology* (WUNT, 2.167; Tübingen: Mohr Siebeck, 2005).

Kaiser Jr., W.C., 'The Single Intent of Scripture' in Beale (ed), *The Right Doctrine from the Wrong Texts?*, pp. 55–69.

Koch, D.-A., 'Der Text von Hab 2.4b in der Septuaginta und im Neuen Testament', *ZNW* 76 (1985), pp. 68–85.

Koester, C.R., *Revelation and the End of all Things* (Grand Rapids: Eerdmans, 2001).

Kraus, W. and Wooden, R.G. (eds), *Septuagint Research. Issues and Challenges in the Study of the Greek Jewish Scriptures* (Atlanta: SBL, 2006).

Kraybill, J.N., *Imperial Cult and Commerce in John's Apocalypse* (JSNTSup, 132; Sheffield: Sheffield Academic Press, 1996).

Kristeva, J., 'Word, Dialogue and Novel', in T. Moi (ed.), *The Kristeva Reader* (New York: Columbia University Press, 1986), pp. 34–61.

Labuschagne, C.J., *The Incomparability of Yahweh in the Old Testament* (Leiden: Brill, 1966).

Lane-Mercer, G., 'Quotation as a Discursive Strategy', *Kodikas* 14 (1991), pp. 199–214.

Lawrence, D.H., *Apocalypse and the Writings on Revelation* (Harmondsworth: Penguin Books, 1930).

Loader, W.R.G., *Jesus' Attitude to the Law* (WUNT, 2.97; Tübingen: Mohr Siebeck, 1997).

Mann, J., *The Bible as Read and Preached in the Old Synagogue* (New York: KTAV, 1971).

Marcus, J., *The Way of the Lord. Christological Exegesis of the Old Testament in the Gospel of Mark* (Edinburgh: T&T Clark, 1992).

Martyn, J.L., *Galatians: A New Translation with Introduction and Commentary* (AB, 33A; New York: Doubleday, 1997).

Meier, J.P., *A Marginal Jew: Companions and Competitors Vol 3* (New York: Doubleday, 2001).

Menken, M.J.J., *Matthew's Bible. The Old Testament Text of the Evangelist* (Leuven: Leuven University Press/Peeters, 2004).

Menken, M.J.J. and Moyise, S. (eds), *Deuteronomy in the New Testament* (LNTS, 356; London & New York: T&T Clark, 2007).

Michaels, J.R., *1 Peter* (WBC, 49; Dallas: Word Books, 1988).

Moore, S.D., 'The Beatific Vision as a Posing Exhibition. Revelation's Hypermasculine Deity', *JSNT* 60 (1995), pp. 27–55.

Moyise, S., *The Old Testament in the Book of Revelation* (JSNTSup, 115; Sheffield: Sheffield Academic Press, 1995).

―――― 'The Catena of Rom. 3.10-18', *ExpT* 106 (1995), pp. 367–70.

―――― 'Does the Lion Lie Down with the Lamb?' in S. Moyise (ed), *Studies in the Book of Revelation* (London: T&T Clark, 2001), pp. 181–94.

―――― 'Singing the Song of Moses and the Lamb: John's Dialogical Use of Scripture', *AUSS* 42 (2004), pp. 347–60.

―――― 'Isaiah in 1 Peter' in S. Moyise and M.J.J. Menken (eds), *Isaiah in the New Testament* (London and New York: T&T Clark, 2005), pp. 175–88.

―――― 'The Wilderness Quotation in Mark 1:2-3' in R.S. Sugirtharajah (ed.), *Wilderness: Essays in Honour of Frances Young* (London and New York: T&T Clark, 2005), pp. 78–87.

―――― 'Deuteronomy in the Gospel of Mark' in M.J.J. Menken and S. Moyise (eds), *Deuteronomy in the New Testament*, pp. 27–41.

Murphy, F.J., *Fallen is Babylon. The Revelation to John* (Harrisburg: Trinity Press International, 1998).

Musvosvi, J.N., *Vengeance in the Apocalypse* (Berrien Springs: Andrews University Press, 1993).

Osborne, R.R., *Revelation* (BECNT; Grand Rapids: Baker Academic, 2002).

Payne, P.B., 'The Fallacy of Equating Meaning with the Human Author's Intention' in Beale (ed.), The *Right Doctrine from the Wrong Texts?*, pp. 70–81.

Perkins, L., 'Kingdom, Messianic Authority and the Re-constituting of God's People – Tracing the Function of Exodus Material in Mark's Narrative' in Hatina (ed.), *Biblical Interpretation in Early Christian Gospels Volume 1: The Gospel of Mark*, pp. 100–15.

Powery, E.B., *Jesus Reads Scripture. The Function of Jesus' Use of Scripture in the Synoptic Gospels* (Leiden: Brill, 2003).

Rabinowitz, P., *Before Reading: Narrative Conventions and the Politics of Interpretation* (Ithaca: Cornell University Press, 1987).

Rensburg, F.J.J. and Moyise, S., 'Isaiah in 1 Peter 3:13-17. Applying Intertextuality to the Study of the OT in the NT', *Scriptura* 80 (2002), pp. 275–86.

——— 'Isaiah in 1 Peter 2:4-10: Applying Intertextuality to the Study of the OT in the NT', *Ekklesiastikos Pharos* 84 (2002), pp. 12–30.

Resseguie, J.L., *Revelation Unsealed: A Narrative Critical Approach to John's Apocalypse* (Leiden: Brill, 1998).

Rhoads, D. and Michie, D., *Mark As Story: An Introduction to the Narrative of a Gospel* (Philadelphia: Fortress Press, 1982).

Robbins, V., *The Tapestry of Early Christian Discourse. Rhetoric, Society and Ideology* (London: Routledge, 1996).

Roloff, J., *Revelation*, (Minneapolis: Fortress, 1993).

Sanders, E.P., *Paul and Palestinian Judaism* (London: SCM, 1977).

——— *Jesus and Judaism* (London: SCM, 1985).

Schlier, H., *Der Römerbrief* (Freiberg: Herder, 1977).

Schliesser, B., *Abraham's Faith in Romans 4* (WUNT, 2.224; Tübingen: Mohr Siebeck, 2007).

Schneck, R., *Isaiah in the Gospel of Mark, I-VIII* (Berkeley: BIBAL Press, 1994).

Schüssler Fiorenza, E., *In Memory of Her: A Feminist Theological Reconstruction of Christian Origins* (rev. edn; London: SCM Press, 1994).

Schutter, W.L., *Hermeneutics and Composition in 1 Peter* (WUNT, 2.30; Tübingen: Mohr Siebeck, 1989).

Searle, J.R., *Speech Acts: An Essay in the Philosophy of Language* (Cambridge: Cambridge University Press, 1969).

Selwyn, E.G., *The First Epistle of St. Peter* (London: Macmillan, 1952).

Slater, T.B., *Christ and Community. A Socio-Historical Study of the Christology of Revelation* (JSNTSup, 178; Sheffield: Sheffield Academic Press, 1999).

Snodgrass, K.R., 'Streams of Tradition Emerging from Isaiah 40:1-5 and their Adaptation in the New Testament', *JSNT* 8 (1980), pp. 24–45.

Sperber, D. and Wilson, D., *Relevance: Communication and Cognition* (2nd edn; Oxford: Blackwell, 1995).

Stanley, C.D., 'Paul and Homer: Greco-Roman Citation Practice in the First Century CE', *NovT* 32 (1990), pp. 48–78.

———— *Arguing with Scripture. The Rhetoric of Quotations in the Letters of Paul* (New York and London: T&T Clark, 2004).

Sternberg, M., 'Proteus in Quotation-Land: Mimesis and the Forms of Reported Discourse', *Poetics Today* 3 (1982), p. 107–56.

Stowers, S.K., *A Rereading of Romans* (New Haven: Yale University Press, 1994).

Stuhlmacher, P., *Die paulinische Evangelium*, vol 1, *Vorgeschichte* (FRLANT, 95; Göttingen: Vandenhoeck & Ruprecht, 1968).

Svartik, J., *Mark and Mission: Mark 7.1-23 in its Narrative and Historical Contexts* (ConBNT, 32; Stockholm: Almqvist & Wiksell, 2000).

Sweet, J.P.M., *Revelation* (London: SCM Press, 1990).

Thiselton, A.C., *New Horizons in Hermeneutics* (London: HarperCollins, 1992).

Vanhoozer, K., *Is there a Meaning in this Text? The Bible, the Reader, and the Morality of Literary Knowledge* (Grand Rapids: Zondervan, 1998).

———— *First Theology: God, Scripture & Hermeneutics* (Downers Grove: Intervarsity/Leicester: Apollos, 2002).

Wagner, J.R., *Heralds of the Good News. Isaiah and Paul 'In Concert' in the Letter to the Romans* (Leiden: Brill, 2002).

Wakefield, A.H., *Where to Live. The Hermeneutical Significance of Paul's Citations from Scripture in Galatians 3.1-14* (Atlanta: SBL, 2003).

Waters, G., *The End of Deuteronomy in the Epistles of Paul* (WUNT, 2.221; Tübingen: Mohr Siebeck, 2006).

Watson, F., *Paul and the Hermeneutics of Faith* (London and New York: T&T Clark, 2004).

Watts, R.E., *Isaiah's New Exodus and Mark* (WUNT, 2.88; Tübingen: Mohr Siebeck, 1997).

Westerman, C., *Isaiah 40–66* (OTL; London: SCM, 1969).

Wierzbicka, A., 'The Semantics of Direct and Indirect Discourse', *Papers in Linguistics* 7 (1974), pp. 267–307.

Wimsatt, W.K. and Beardsley, M.C., 'The Intentional Fallacy' in *idem, The Verbal Icon. Studies in the Meaning of Poetry* (Lexington: University of Kentucky Press, 1954), pp. 1–18.

Worten, M and Still, J., 'Introduction' in *idem* (eds), *Intertextuality: Theories and Practices* (Manchester: Manchester University Press, 1990), pp. 1–44.

Index of Biblical Sources

Index of Modern Authors